The Spirit Within

A One in Four handbook to aid recovery from religious sexual abuse across all faiths

Christiane Sanderson

Text © Christiane Sanderson and One in Four
Title, design, layout and format © One in Four

Published by One in Four, 219 Bromley Road, Catford SE6 2PG · Telephone 020 8697 2112 · Email admin@oneinfour.org.uk
Printed and bound by Circle Services Group.
ISBN 978-0-9566541-1-3

Foreword

The survivors of religious sexual abuse are unlike any other sexual abuse victims. For Catholics the priest, as they are taught from their earliest years, takes the place of Christ. When a priest violates a devout and unquestioning believer, the shock penetrates to the depths of the soul. The victim experiences a unique kind of despondence because he or she feels betrayed by one who has been trusted even more than a parent, and even worse, abandoned by the God personified by the abusing cleric. Although the clergy of other Christian and non-Christian denominations may not always be held up to be joined in some mysterious way with God, they still are held in the highest respect and accorded a significant degree of unquestioning trust.

The utterly remarkable thing about the survivors is that many are able to rise above their spiritual devastation, emerging as strong and focused advocates for the Truth. Their experiences have taken us to a shocking yet deeper realisation of the dark side of organised religion. Many of the thousands who have had their bodies and their souls violated by members of the clerical elite have emerged from the depressive and defeating pit of victimhood to become survivors. Though used and often cast aside by the uncaring and callous official ministers of the church, these men and women have refused to stay beaten down and have risen to challenge the ecclesiastical institution and the secular societies that have stood silent and complicit.

We see the terrible consequences of the irrational power that clerics hold over countless believers... a power grounded in their self-styled exalted role as an essential intermediary, between the distant and often stern God and the helpless sheep-like lay folk. This power, which the victims are taught never to question, helps forge what psychologists have labeled the 'trauma bond'. This bond explains why victims are all too often powerless to stop a repeating clergy predator who abuses again and again, each time dragging his prey even deeper into the pit of despair.

This same bond is the reason why so many wait in fear for years or even decades before coming into the light to publicly name their abuse and the abuser. The survivors' stories reveal a pathetically inept and traitorous hierarchical superstructure that was so consumed by its own self-concept and controlled by its addiction to power that it was blinded to the horrendous rape and pillage going on in its very midst.

The reaction to the betrayal by church officials has been not only understandable anger but also a surprising and encouraging spiritual growth and development of not only the survivors but also an ever-increasing number of lay people and even a small number of clergy. They are coming forward, shedding the chains of clericalist oppression, and laying claim to their right to be true members of their faith.

The dysfunctional clerics who have inflicted the sexual violation assaulted the bodies of their victims. The religious leaders who have responded so callously and dishonestly have assaulted the souls, not only of the victims themselves but of all believers. The calling to account of the institutional churches over past quarter-century has revealed the courage of the survivors and a sorely-needed degree of spiritual maturity on the part of all. The devastating scandal of sexual abuse has been the unfortunate catalyst for a process of liberation from the spiritual devastation and religious slavery that has kept the membership of many faiths locked in a spiritual time warp from which they were not allowed to venture past late infancy.

The survivors are a unique group. They have suffered intensely. The leaders and the organisations they trusted without question have betrayed them. Now they are coming forward and pointing the way to a healthier and more authentic faith.

Father Thomas P Doyle JCD CADC

Acknowledgements

Dedication

To all those who have been affected by religious sexual abuse, and to James and Max who embody the spirit within.

Acknowledgements

I would like to thank Linda Dominguez, the Director of One in Four for her boundless energy, dedication and vision in supporting the work of One in Four and this book. My thanks also go to all the trustees, counsellors and staff at One in Four. It was a great pleasure to have Tom Doyle, Jeff Anderson and Anne Olivarius contribute to the book and I would like to thank them for their inspirational work.

Many others have contributed to this book, not least the survivors themselves, and I would like to thank them all for their courage. I would also like to thank all those survivor organisations such as SNAP, MACSAS, NAPAC and many others who work tirelessly on behalf of survivors of RSA. Their work not only supports survivors but also contributes to the safeguarding of future children across all faiths. For their inspiration I would like to thank Richard Sipe, Donald Cozzens, Derek Farrell, Graham Willmer, Barbara Blaine, Mike Coode, and Susie Hayward. A special thank you also goes got to the staff at St Martins in the Fields for helping to launch the book.

The book was brought to life by the impressive design and production of Nine Rogers and Steve Bucke and invaluable feedback from Elwyn Taylor. Inestimable thanks go to Michael, James and Max who were constant reminders of the power of the spirit within.

7

Introduction

'The Spirit is the true self.' *Cicero*

Religious sexual abuse (RSA), whether experienced in childhood or as an adult, traumatises not only individuals but whole communities. The impact radiates out from victims and survivors to families and partners, religious institutions, faith communities and society as a whole. The spiritual injury associated with RSA has the capacity to destroy faith in religious institutions and erode the belief in God or any higher power. It can also shatter spirituality and the spirit within, leading to a loss of meaning and purpose in life. This book offers survivors and all those affected by RSA an opportunity to heal and recover from the harm done and revive the spirit within.

This book is about compassion and healing

Its aim is not to be critical of any one denomination or faith, but to increase awareness and understanding and to revive the spirit of all who have been harmed by RSA. While it is primarily for survivors it is also for family, friends and partners. Indeed, it is intended for all those who have been affected by RSA, including devout believers and worshippers, non-offending clergy, religious institutions, faith leaders, and professionals. It is also for anyone working with victims and survivors, such as counsellors, child protection workers, safeguarding officers, advocacy workers, legal professionals, police officers, and those who work with perpetrators. In essence it is for anyone who is concerned about RSA and who seeks a better understanding of the harm done and how to move towards healing.

REMEMBER This book is about compassion and healing and provides a unique opportunity to increase understanding of religious sexual abuse so that all those affected can move towards recovery.

RSA knows no boundaries

It has been reported within and across all religious persuasions, including the Roman Catholic, Anglican, Protestant, Methodist, Episcopal, Jewish and Greek Orthodox, as well as in the context of the Islamic, Buddhist, and Hindu faiths. It is perpetrated against male and female children as well as adults, by both male and female abusers. The hidden nature of RSA makes it hard to know the precise number of victims and perpetrators and to what degree it occurs in any one faith. Many more are affected indirectly and must be viewed as secondary victims who also need to heal.

Opportunity for understanding and change

The Spirit Within aims to provide a unique opportunity for all religious institutions to ensure that they have a deeper understanding of how RSA affects victims and survivors, and how to protect and safeguard all those at risk, both children and vulnerable adults. The most powerful instrument of healing is listening. It is only through listening non-defensively and empathically that the truth can be heard. Listening more openly also allows for a deeper understanding of the many factors that contribute to RSA, both individual and institutional. This increased awareness and understanding will promote more effective responses and genuine acknowledgement of harm caused. This will allow for more open and transparent communication, and make it possible to work more collaboratively with psychologists and mental health and legal professionals, as well as helping survivors to move towards recovery and healing.

 REMEMBER The most powerful instrument of healing is listening.

While many religious institutions and faith organisations have responded to allegations of RSA and most now have safeguarding policies and procedures in place, there are still wounds that need to be healed. The better RSA is understood by religious institutions and faith communities the more healing and necessary changes can take place.

It is also a tool for survivors of RSA to understand their abuse experience, its impact and the range of long-term effects. While RSA impacts differently on each individual, there are many commonalities. The trauma of RSA impacts on psychological, emotional and physical well-being as well as on belief systems. The nature of RSA can shatter beliefs about the meaning and purpose of life, and belief in human goodness. This can feel like a spiritual death, as losing a deeply held faith is like losing both a sense of self and identity, and a sense of belongingness to the faith community or spiritual family.

Despite the erosion of faith and spirituality, it is possible to recover from RSA and reclaim the spirit within to reconnect with one's sense of self. In reviving the spirit within survivors will be able to heal the psychological and spiritual injury, enabling them to regain meaning in life and to live more purposefully. Connecting to their inner spirit will enable all those affected by RSA to find new, or renewed faith in self and others and reclaim their spirituality.

REMEMBER Despite the erosion of faith and spirituality, it is possible to recover from RSA and revive the spirit within to reconnect with one's sense of self.

Structure of the book

The book is divided into four parts. **Part One** focuses on understanding RSA by looking at what RSA is and the scale of the problem. It covers the nature and dynamics of RSA, and specifies those most at risk from and affected by RSA. It also throws light on the perpetrators. **Part two** aims to increase understanding of how RSA impacts on victims and survivors. Like childhood sexual abuse (CSA) and rape, RSA must be understood within the context of trauma and trauma reactions. Long term traumatic effects such as post-traumatic stress disorder, flashbacks, self-harm, shame, relationship and sexual difficulties, loss and grief, and the impact on spirituality and faith will all be examined to aid a deeper understanding of the harm done by RSA.

The focus in **part three** is on recovery from RSA, and will look at the process of healing. This entails rebuilding relationships, restoring spirituality and faith and triumphing over trauma. It also considers the how litigation can help survivors recover power, obtain validation and acknowledgement and help protect others from harm. **Part four** looks at how survivors can be supported in their healing by religious institutions and faith leaders and their communities. It will also highlight how families, partners and professionals can best support survivors to enable post-traumatic growth and reclaim the spirit within. Finally there is a list of resources, which includes helpful organisations, selected reading and related films that will enhance understanding and access to support.

Getting the most from this book

If you are a survivor, or are supporting one in whatever capacity, you will find it helpful to read *The Warrior Within: A One in Four Handbook to aid recovery from childhood sexual abuse and violence* by Christiane Sanderson. This companion volume contains many additional resources and helpful exercises to aid recovery and allow you to live a more fulfilling and meaningful life.

Readers who are familiar with *The Warrior Within* may want to skip the sections on understanding the impact of sexual abuse and focus on part one, three and four and those sections that promote understanding of the nature and dynamics of RSA and its impact on spirituality and faith.

Key to icons

 REMEMBER An important point that it will be useful to recall

 WARNING An alert to take care or be aware of danger

 READ Consult the relevant section in *The Warrior Within*

 **ONLINE** The One in Four website has a selection of relevant exercises and activities

Language

The language and terms associated with religion and faith are rich and varied and they all have specific meanings.

To keep the book user-friendly the term **clergy** is used to refer to those who hold office, or are appointed representatives of a particular religion or faith and who thereby occupy a position of power and authority. This will include those in a range of religious roles and institutional positions such as priests, bishops, cardinals, pastors, ministers, vicars, brothers, sisters, deacons, monks, rabbis, imams, and swamis. The term **faith community** or **laity** will refer to the communal body of religious worshippers within all faiths.

To avoid repetition, the term **religious institution** will be used to refer to the institutional structure and systemic organisation within each religion or faith. The term **God** will be used generically to define the deity or higher power within each of the faiths. To avoid cumbersome repetition a number of abbreviations will be used such as **RSA** for religious sexual abuse, **CSA** for childhood sexual abuse, **RC** for Roman Catholic and **CofE** for Church of England.

Given that the majority of RSA is committed by males, abusers will be referred to as **he**, unless specifically referring to RSA committed by females. The term **survivor** will refer to victims who have reached adulthood and are beginning to heal, while the term **victim** will refer to those who are still being abused and have not yet started the healing process. With regard to perpetrators of RSA the term **abuser** or **those who have abused** will be used. Although the majority of identified survivors of RSA are male, survivors will be referred to as **he or she**, when their sex is not dictated by the context.

It is important to note that much of the research, published data and media coverage of RSA have focused on the RC Church. As a result most of our knowledge about victims, offenders, and the institutional factors that contribute to RSA come from these sources, and from critics of the RC Church. Until specific research is conducted into other faiths it will not be possible to know: how prevalent RSA is in these contexts; the profiles of victims or perpetrators; or the range of contributory institutional factors. Consequently much of the information on the nature and dynamics of RSA used in this book is based on these RC data. This does not mean that the RC Church is being singled out, or that this data is representative of all faiths.

References in the text can be found in **Publications and references** on page 221.

REMEMBER This book does not replace the value of counselling or therapy but is an additional source of help or support. You can use it alongside other forms of healing or as a stepping stone to seeking such therapeutic assistance.

WARNING If you get upset or distressed at any point while reading this book, STOP. Do something pleasurable and when ready, resume reading.

WARNING If you are feeling suicidal contact a trusted friend, your GP, counsellor, support worker, or telephone Samaritans on 08457 90 90 90.

Part one
Understanding religious sexual abuse

1 What is religious sexual abuse?

Religious sexual abuse (RSA) is the sexual abuse of children and adults by those who hold office within any religious institution, church or faith. This includes all appointed representatives and faith leaders such as priests, bishops, monks, abbots, nuns, lay sisters or brothers, ministers, pastors, clerics, imams, rabbis and swamis. It also includes lay teachers, faith counsellors, religious health or child care professionals, pastoral workers, missionaries, lay youth workers and volunteers.

RSA occurs in a wide range of settings and places of worship including churches, mosques, temples and ashrams, as well as in faith schools, colleges, and universities, madrassas, faith run children's homes and youth clubs, missions, seminaries and convents. In Ireland, church-run industrial, and reformatory schools, including the Magdalene Laundries, have all been implicated in large scale physical and sexual abuse.

As RSA is denominationally blind it occurs across all religions and faiths throughout the world. There is considerable evidence of RSA in a diverse range of faiths and denominations including the Anglican Church, orthodox churches such as the Greek and Russian Orthodox, the Methodist, Pentecostal, Baptist, Episcopalian, and Presbyterian Churches, Seventh Day Adventists (Mormons), religious orders such as Christian Brothers, Jesuits, and Sisters of Mercy, as well as the Jewish, Muslim, Hindu and Buddhist faiths. Despite this, research and media attention has focused predominantly on sexual abuse by Roman Catholic priests in Canada, Ireland, the United States, Mexico, Belgium, France, Germany and the UK.

REMEMBER RSA is blind to both denomination and faith and occurs across all religions and faiths.

In the majority of reported cases the abusers are male although there is evidence of RSA by female ministers and nuns, which has remained largely hidden. Reported cases suggest that abusers exist across the hierarchy of religious institutions and range from priests through to bishops, cardinals, nuns and mothers superior, as well as clerics and senior faith leaders.

Definition of religious sexual abuse

RSA is the abuse of power and authority in which the abuser uses his or her religious authority and status to exert unquestioning obedience through fear of spiritual punishment in this life or in an afterlife. Abusers use their faith as an instrument of destruction and spiritual deception to define the victim's status with God. It is both a breach of trust and professional misconduct that results in significant emotional, psychological and spiritual harm.

Abusers do not abuse in isolation, and are consciously and unconsciously supported by institutional structures that thrive on silence and secrecy, and do not emphasise personal responsibility or accountability. This religious institutional abuse is most evident when religious institutions and faith leaders deny, minimise, silence or try to cover up the RSA perpetrated by their members. This secondary traumatisation increases the sense of betrayal and the abuse of authority and power which adds to survivors' psychological and spiritual injury.

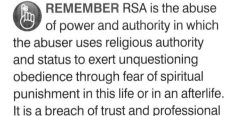 **REMEMBER** RSA is the abuse of power and authority in which the abuser uses religious authority and status to exert unquestioning obedience through fear of spiritual punishment in this life or in an afterlife. It is a breach of trust and professional misconduct.

The spectrum of religious sexual abuse

The spectrum of RSA ranges from non-contact behaviour, such as voyeurism and taking child abuse images, to inappropriate touching over or under clothing, kissing, forced masturbation, and oral and anal penetrative sex. It also includes the corruption of religious and spiritual beliefs as a means to entrap and groom the victim, and to ensure secrecy and silence. This spiritual abuse results in significant spiritual injury in which the victim and survivor is stripped of his or her spiritual identity and beliefs, and hindered in developing or practising their faith.

Underlying all RSA is a power differential which prevents the child or adult from exercising choice, or informed consent. This resembles the dynamics seen in CSA in the wider community, and especially in incestuous families (see **The nature and dynamics of religious sexual abuse** on page 32). In addition, RSA is rarely a one-off event and is often perpetrated over many months, or years, sometimes involving multiple abusers, including unresponsive faith leaders.

The scale of RSA

The hidden nature of RSA means it is hard to know precisely how many people have been affected. Estimates suggest that there are hundreds of thousands of direct victims who have experienced RSA, and equally many, if not more secondary victims who have been affected.[9] The '**ripple effect**' of RSA is such that it affects family, friends, partners and children, as well as faithful congregants and believers, and those in ministry who feel betrayed by the perpetrators and dismayed by faith leaders' responses to allegations of RSA.

Lack of research also makes it difficult to know precisely who is at risk of RSA and the range of perpetrators. The majority of research has been on RSA within the RC Church and much of our knowledge comes from this. Further data on the scale of RSA has come from a number of inquiries and commissions that have investigated historic allegations of sexual abuse, especially those in England, Ireland and Wales. Investigations and analyses in the United States have also provided valuable insight into the incidence of RSA.

To fully understand the scale of RSA across all faiths will require more research and investigation. Until such research is conducted our knowledge of the scale of the problem in other faiths, and perpetrator and victim profiles will be limited. For this reason, much of the information in this book is based on the available data which may not be representative across all faiths.

REMEMBER RSA remains largely hidden and reported data may be merely the tip of the iceberg.

The scale of the problem in England and Wales is particularly hard to assess as there has been no national inquiry and there is no coordinated data collection across all faiths due to the various ways in which cases are documented and reported (see **Appendix** on page 224 for more details on the commissions and reports on RSA in England, Ireland and the United States). In addition, as there are no standardised safeguarding procedures across faiths, there is considerable variation both across and within faiths in how these are implemented. It is clear that here are huge differences between individual dioceses, parishes or regions in how data is collected and recorded. The data that is available is limited as it only represents those victims and survivors that have come forward. Current investigations involving individual clergy, religious institutions and faith-run schools indicate that there are many more victims who have not yet come forward. For a more detailed exploration of the data see **Appendix** on page 224.

It is hoped that improved safeguarding policies and procedures, and data recording will make it easier to monitor the rate of current victims who are being sexually abused. However, these policies and procedures are only valid if they are properly implemented and reporting procedures are adhered to. This is crucial if religious institutions want to retain credibility and avoid criticisms of obstruction of implementing their own procedures, as was seen in the recent Cloyne report[12] – see **Appendix** on page 224.

Those affected by RSA

Primary victims

Given the hidden nature of RSA, it is hard to know precisely who are at risk. What is clear is that RSA is gender blind and that both males and females suffer RSA. Reported figures suggest that 80% of child victims are male and 20% female. This is reversed in the RSA of adults where females appear to be more at risk than males. However, the available data is likely to be skewed due to variation among gender in reporting rates (see **The nature and dynamics of religious sexual abuse** on page 32). The RSA of female children and adult females has been under-reported and may represent a silent majority that has not yet found a voice. In addition, the RSA of adult males has not been fully investigated and may be considerably higher than currently

reported (see **Religious sexual abuse of adults** on page 25).

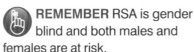 **REMEMBER** RSA is gender blind and both males and females are at risk.

It is likely that any data is merely the tip of the iceberg and that there are many more victims that remain hidden and still suffer in silence. Victims and survivors are often reluctant to disclose sexual abuse for fear of the consequence of such revelations, or because they feel too ashamed and fear stigmatisation. They may also wish to protect their family from the shame and hurt that such disclosures can generate. Many victims do not disclose until long after the abuse took place, having spent many years suffering in silence.

Secondary victims

RSA affects not only those who were subjected to sexual assault, it also impacts on the families of victims, partners of survivors and their children. Families of the perpetrators of RSA are also traumatised by the actions of a loved one. The '**ripple effect**' of RSA also affects faith communities and congregations in undermining their trust and faith in their ministers and religious institutions. In effect RSA affects all faiths and denominations in undermining trust in all faiths and religious institutions.

This has significant effects on religious institutions in reducing the number of faithful and regular worshippers, and a decrease in numbers of those seeking religious office as a vocation. RSA also impacts on non-offending clergy who are dismayed by the actions of their peers and the way allegations have been managed (see **Who is at risk and who has been affected?** on page 45). Ultimately RSA radiates outwards and affects all members of both religious and secular society.

REMEMBER RSA affects not just those who have been sexually assaulted but also families, partners, faith communities, religious institutions, non-offending clergy and the wider society.

Who are the abusers?

Abusers include both males and females although current reported data suggests that the majority of offenders are male. There is emerging evidence that females such as nuns and ministers also commit RSA. Sexual abuse by females is still considered by many to be not only inconceivable but also the ultimate taboo. As a result, victims and survivors RSA by females find it more

difficult to report such abuse for fear of not being believed (see **Who are the abusers?** on page 53).

Research, especially on male and female sexual abusers within the RC Church, has found that there are a number of individual factors associated with those who commit RSA, including the suppression and repression of sexuality, psychosexual immaturity as well as a history of CSA. In addition research suggests that some abusers have diagnosable psychological and personality disturbances and mental health problems such as alcoholism (see **Who are the abusers?** on page 53).

REMEMBER Factors associated with abusers include sexual suppression, psychosexual immaturity, and a history of CSA, as well as a range of psychological and personality disturbances.

A common feature of male and female abusers are narcissistic traits such as grandiosity, an inflated sense of self-importance and sense of entitlement, alongside an absence of empathy and denial of responsibility and shortcomings. Some abusers mask their narcissistic traits through altruistic (unselfish concern for others) and self-sacrificing behaviours which ensure that their duplicity goes undetected. When narcissism masquerades as altruism, abusers can adopt a 'double life' in which they feel that they are owed by others and society for the sacrifices they have made. This can lead to an inflated sense of entitlement in which sex, and in particular sexual abuse, becomes a modulator for anger, hostility and an insatiable need for power.[14]

These narcissistic traits essentially mirror some of the narcissism seen in clericalism (see **Church culture** right). Abusers do not abuse in isolation, and are to some degree supported by institutional structures that minimise personal responsibility, accountability or effective monitoring the behaviour of their members. As abusers are as diverse as their victims, each will have a unique profile and be influenced by a range of contributing factors, including the religious institutions to which they belong. While these factors do not excuse the abusive behaviour, they can help to understand what motivates abusers, and how their actions are conscious and unconsciously supported.

The role of religious institutions

As abusers do not abuse in isolation, it is important to understand what factors support, consciously or unconsciously

the sexual abuse of children and adults. While the responsibility for the abuse lies solely with the abuser, religious institutions need to be aware of systemic structures that support RSA. It is only with such awareness and understanding that healing and change can take place.

Church culture

Most of the analysis of systemic and institutional factors that contribute to RSA has focused on the RC Church, and while this is by no means representative of other faiths, it does provide some insight into how large religious institutions can, unwittingly or deliberately, contribute to RSA. It has been argued that the culture of the RC Church promotes a sense of superiority and elitism over the faithful through rigid religious doctrine and practice in which clergy are accorded special and privileged status. As God's intermediary on earth they have considerable power over the faithful, as only they can mediate spirituality and ensure spiritual security.

⚠️ **WARNING** Abusers do not abuse in isolation and are, to some degree, supported by institutional structures that thrive on silence and secrecy, and that minimise personal responsibility or accountability.

The assigning of power and authority is primarily based on the role of priest or minister and does not necessarily reflect individual personal qualities. Thus, clergy are given special privileges without necessarily possessing the personal qualities needed to manage such an elevated status. This leads to what Sipe[33] has called '**situational narcissism**', in which power and authority is not based on personal merit or achievement but the result of being associated with institutional authority.

Power can be extremely intoxicating and has the potential to corrupt not only individuals, but also institutions. Some individuals and institutions become so accustomed to power that it becomes part of their identity. In order to preserve this identity they become consumed, consciously or unconsciously, with the pursuit of power at all costs. When such power is unchecked, and the responsibility that comes with power is ignored, it can lead to the abuse of power and cultivate an authoritarian, rather than an authoritative, stance which distances clergy from laity.

Religious duress

The power and authority of the church and clergy exerts a potent conscious and unconscious influence on the faith community and secular society. This can lead to what has been referred to as 'religious duress'[1] in which the faithful, as well as seminarians and priests, are kept immature and dependent on faith leaders and religious institutions. By not engaging in open and honest communication about natural human instincts such as sexuality, laity and seminarians are kept naïve and ill-informed. This makes it harder for individuals to have freedom of choice and to challenge religious beliefs and doctrine.

Secrecy and silence

Lack of open communication promotes a culture of secrecy and silence which can support RSA. A fundamental principle in the RC Church is the bond of secrecy between clergy to protect the church from any scandal. This has allowed for considerable duplicity in religious doctrine and practice. This culture of secrecy and duplicity has been most exposed in relation to celibacy, sexual orientation and RSA. There is considerable evidence that many RC priests, especially in Africa and Latin America, have fathered children and live in open relationships.[14] Despite the widespread non-observance of celibacy among heterosexual clergy, the RC Church continues to deny the fact that celibacy is not practised.

To move towards healing, all religious institutions need to be aware of how RSA is supported by a culture of secrecy and silence. To minimise accusations of duplicity, or indeed hypocrisy, religious institutions need to become more transparent and review doctrine and practices that put children and adults at risk of abuse.

Celibacy

Celibacy is also not observed by large numbers of homosexual clergy. Reports suggest that there is a discreet and powerful network of active homosexual priests in seminaries and in the RC Church hierarchy.[15] To ensure that this remains hidden, all clergy are co-opted into silence and secrecy to avoid any scandal. The promotion and tolerance of a culture of secrecy and silence allows duplicity and deception to flourish, and provides a fertile environment for abusive behaviour. This is most evident in RSA where offending clergy have been protected by other priests and bishops in order to preserve the reputation of the church.

The duplicity in denying heterosexual and homosexual relationships and RSA allows many clergy to live a double life in which they preach abstinence and that sex outside of marriage is sinful, and yet engage in the very behaviour they condemn. This endemic culture of secrecy and deception has seriously undermined the credibility of the RC Church, leading to accusations of hypocrisy.[8,14] As a result survivors of RSA and many members of the faith community have become disillusioned with church culture in denying the duplicitous behaviour of many of its clergy, and how such tolerance allows abusers to lead double lives.

Ambition

The role of ambition in religious institutions is also largely ignored. Cozzens[14] has argued that ambition, like sex, is suppressed and repressed as it is incompatible with religious teaching. And yet the hierarchical nature of the RC Church fosters a culture in which ambition is necessary for advancement yet must remain hidden. This can lead to unhealthy strategies to obtain promotion, including keeping secrets and trading sexual favours in order to move up the hierarchy. The hidden nature of ambition, and the strategies used to obtain power, allow for sexual exploitation in which seminarians and junior priests are enticed into sexual relationships with promises of promotion or being assigned to prestigious diocese.

Clericalism

Clericalism has its roots in a church culture that ordains the church and clergy to be superior to the laity, secular society and even the state.[8] This attitude is reflected in the belief that canon law is above both civil and criminal law, and justifies not involving police and statutory agencies to investigate allegations of RSA. The danger of clericalism is that it allows religious institutions to adopt a haughty attitude to individuals, faith communities and the wider society, which stifles spiritual growth.

In essence, clericalism arises when religious institutions become absorbed in prioritising the needs and interests of the clergy above the faithful. This is further reinforced by institutional structures that promote a rigidly hierarchical and authoritarian style of leadership within its organisations, and over the faithful. This can lead to clerical narcissism which, like individual narcissism is characterised by grandiosity, an inflated sense of self importance, absence of empathy, defensive structures to protect a sense of entitlement and privilege, alongside denial, lack of responsibility and accountability.

If left unchecked, clericalism distorts fundamental faith principles and ultimately weakens the spiritual family and destroys the sense of community among the faithful. This is reflected in how religious institutions, especially RC bishops have treated those victims and survivors, and those who have expressed dismay at how allegations of RSA have been handled. In the eyes of survivors, faith leaders and bishops have not only consistently minimised their role in supporting RSA, but have also failed to treat individuals with the respect and courtesy that they deserve and receive in secular society. The lack of humility, and the demand for deference and obedience by faith leaders, blocks open communication and weakens any sense of common identity and humanity.

The danger of clericalism, and its pursuit for absolute power, is that it is vulnerable to corruption which diminishes the souls of the clergy as well as the faithful. In order to replenish the soul and to heal rifts between religious institutions and the faith community, faith leaders need to acknowledge the dysfunctional nature of clericalism and promote responsibility, accountability, non-defensive listening and open discussion, Only this will allow for the required changes to be made so that children and adults are protected from RSA, and that victims and survivors are no longer blamed for their abuse.

The role of faith communities

Faith communities are urged to (and frequently do) take their lead from religious institutions and therefore unwittingly support clericalism. This is facilitated by religious institutions who keep the faithful in a state of ignorance about human sexuality and denying any reported duplicitous behaviour of the clergy. In the face of such denial, and the absence of open and honest dialogue, the laity lacks the information to ask probing questions and is prevented from making informed choices in response to reports of RSA.

Lack of objective information and internalised religious duress means that some members of faith communities reinforce the reactions of religious institutions in how they respond to victims and survivors of RSA. All too often, victims and survivors have faced anger and hostility from their faith community and been stigmatised for bringing shame to the church and the community. This is especially the case in religions and faiths that devalue women, or see them as sexual temptresses. Faced with denial and rejection, victims feel abandoned by their spiritual family which adds to the spiritual injury and their traumatisation.

To move towards healing, faith communities must be given opportunities for open and honest discussion and debate about the nature and dynamics of RSA and how it impacts on victims, and how faith leaders respond to allegations. It is only though transparency and access to objective information that faith communities can respond effectively to those who have been harmed by RSA. Faith communities can play an important role in protecting future victims of RSA by voicing their concerns and asking for more open and honest communication to restore their faith.

REMEMBER Faith communities can play an important role in protecting future victims of RSA by voicing their concerns and asking for more open and honest communication.

The cost of religious sexual abuse

The cost of RSA is enormous in terms of damaged lives, spiritual injury, and death through suicide. This cost is not just to victims and survivors, but also to families of victims and abusers as well as the faithful who have suffered a diminishment of belief, faith and trust. There has also been a huge cost to religious institutions which have seen a decrease in the number of worshippers, reduced church attendance, and a drop in vocations to religious life. The RC Church in particular has also suffered huge financial cost through legal cost, financial settlements and compensation payments, as well as treatment cost for offenders.

The financial cost of legal actions and insurance claims has been manipulated by some RC bishops through threats of bankruptcy and the reduction of services. Some dioceses have threatened to reduce services, close nurseries and schools, and sell church properties to manage the costs of litigation. This adds insult to injury wherein victims are blamed again, and become targets of further abuse and hostility from parishioners.

Moving towards healing

To move towards healing victims and survivors must be listened to and heard, without judgement. The harm they have suffered needs to be recognised and acknowledged without prejudice. The '**ripple effect**' of RSA extends beyond direct victims but affects all faith communities, and the wider secular society. To facilitate healing it is essential to acknowledge errors made and lessons learnt. The way forward is to have a clearer understanding of all the factors that contribute to RSA. The following chapters aim to provide such understanding by looking at the RSA of adults, the nature and dynamics of RSA, and looking in more depth at those who have been affected and what is known about the abusers.

2 Religious sexual abuse of adults

The religious sexual abuse of adults is thought to be more widespread than the sexual abuse of children, but it has largely remained under-reported. As a result it has received less research or media attention. What is known is that RSA perpetrated on adults, especially women, is also denominationally blind and occurs across all denominations, religions and faith groups.[31] In contrast to the RSA of children, in the case of adult victims there is less recognition of the betrayal of trust and the abuse of power and authority.

This is due to the tendency of religious institutions and faith leaders to minimise, deny or cover up such sexual misconduct, and the consequent scapegoating by laity and the religious community. As a result, victims and survivors are less likely to disclose or report such sexual abuse so as to avoid personal shame and stigmatisation. In order to avoid another cataclysmic scandal, it is crucial that religious institutions and all faith leaders develop appropriate safeguarding policies and procedures to protect vulnerable adults as well as children.

The prevalence of RSA is largely unknown as it continues to be denied and remain hidden. Some reports suggest it is more than four times more common than the sexual abuse of children. Estimates suggest that between 10% and 20% of clergy, ministers and faith leaders engage in inappropriate sexual contact with adults.[29] Many of these incidents consist of repeated assaults involving multiple victims, sometimes over many decades. As ministers and clergy are often not admonished, or are moved to another ministry, they can continue to sexually abuse even more victims.

To date, there has not been enough systematic research across all faiths to draw robust conclusions about incidence and prevalence. Future research is crucial to fully 'identify and acknowledge the silent victims of RSA.

Adult females are most at risk of RSA and are considered to be the silent majority of victims. Most (96%) reported cases of adult RSA is perpetrated on females, with 4% on males.[26] However, these figures only represent known cases and are thus not representative of the actual scale of abuse. Adult male victims find it much harder to disclose or report sexual abuse and often suffer in silence.

REMEMBER Adult females and males are currently the silent victims of RSA.

Adult females

All adult females are at risk of RSA, including the most vulnerable – such as those with disabilities; those who are in distress or suffering from mental health issues; the ill and the elderly; and those who work within religious communities. There is considerable evidence that nuns are at risk of RSA by priests. This was highlighted during the Pope's worldwide apology in 2001[13] during which he apologised for the sexual abuse by priests of nuns and other church women in Africa. This apology was in response to reports that numerous priests and bishops in Africa, fearful of contracting AIDS from women in the community, turned to nuns and religious sisters as safer sexual partners.[14]

There is also evidence that RSA of adults occurs in seminaries, convents, retreats, religious colleges and in the religious community. There have been numerous reports of women who help clergy and ministers with administrative duties suffering RSA. In addition, housekeepers have been identified as being at risk of RSA by priests.[4]

Many women believe that they are in a consensual relationship with the abuser, not realising that they have been manipulated or groomed (see

The nature and dynamics of religious sexual abuse on page 32). There have been various estimates that up to 50% of RC priests do not observe celibacy and are sexually active. This is particularly the case in Latin America and Africa where it is not uncommon for priests and bishops to have sexual relationships with women, either as mistresses or as partners with whom they have children.[14] Estimates in Europe have found that between 30% (Germany) and 50% (Netherlands) of clergy have mistresses, while Rodriguez[14] found that 53% of RC priests in Spain had sexual relationships with women, and 12% were sexually involved with girls.

REMEMBER Many women believe that they are in a consensual relationship with the abuser, not realising that they have been manipulated or groomed.

READ *The Warrior Within* has more information about grooming and manipulation.

Such reports clearly indicate that celibacy is not observed and that clergy do have sexual relationships with women. What is less clear is how many of these are consensual. Given the power, authority and status that priests have over the laity, one wonders to what degree women can reject sexual advances made by clergy. The degree of religious duress and the fear of displeasing a 'man of the cloth' and the consequences of this in 'God's eyes' make it extremely hard for women to say 'no'. These women may feel flattered and honoured to be chosen by a member of the clergy, not realising that they are not able to make an informed choice due to fear and religious duress.

REMEMBER The degree of religious coercion and the fear of displeasing a 'man of the cloth' make it extremely hard for women to say 'no'.

When women fall pregnant they are commonly abandoned, rejected, hidden away or forced to leave the community. This creates secondary victims in their children who are usually conceived in secret, left unacknowledged, brought up without knowing their parentage and deprived of any financial support.

REMEMBER Children conceived in secret through RSA are unacknowledged secondary victims.

By far the largest group of women at risk of RSA are those receiving pastoral or spiritual support or counselling. There is evidence that Christian women are seven times more likely to seek help for marriage and family problems from pastoral rather than secular sources.[16] Often these women feel hurt and disappointed by male partners, and turn to a priest or minister who they respect and believe will not sexualise the relationship. This doubles the risk of their becoming victims, as abuse is twice as common in pastoral counselling than when provided by psychologists.[23]

Some adult females are at risk of RSA by nuns. Some of this occurs within convents where nuns sexually abuse novices or other nuns, but it can also occur within faith school, colleges and universities as well as in the faith community. Lack of research makes it hard to know to what extent females sexually abuse adults in pastoral counselling, in mentoring or when providing spiritual guidance. Female sexual abuse, both within the wider community and within a religious context, is notoriously under-reported and under-researched – and yet it represents a considerable part of RSA.

Adult males

All adult males are at risk of RSA – especially those in seminaries, or faith-based colleges and universities. The majority of this RSA is perpetrated by other males such as priests, ministers, or lay brothers, although there are some reports of males being sexually abused by nuns.[23] There has been no large-scale study of how many adult males are at risk of RSA, and this is a serious omission as it makes it hard to assess the scale of the problem. It is likely that there are many more adult male victims who suffer in silence.

It is estimated that around two-thirds of RC priests[24] and 30% of RC bishops[14] are practising homosexuals, many of them in active relationships both within and outside the Church. Rodriguez[14] found that 21% of RC priests in Spain had sexual relationships with males, and 14% with boys. While the majority of these relationships, except those with minors, are consensual, some may be as a result of manipulation, grooming or coercion.

Some homosexual priests and clergy are known to frequent gay bars and clubs in which they seek sexual encounters and relationships, which may not always be consensual. Like adult females, some adult males may not be able to say 'no' to the sexual attentions of clergy due to fear and religious duress.

Seminarians and fellow priests may also not be able to reject sexual advances especially when there is an imbalance of power, and the abuser has authority over them. Abusers often use their position in the religious institution's hierarchy to coerce their victim, either through promises of advancement or privileges, or through threats of limiting their role in the religious institutions. And added concern for victims is that a considerable number of active homosexual priests have been found to have died of AIDS-related illnesses, and are infected with HIV,[15] which puts sexual partners and victims at risk. The complexity of such adult homosexual relationships, the degree of consent and the risk of HIV and AIDS requires further research to protect future victims.

REMEMBER Like adult females, some adult males may not be able to say 'no' to the sexual attentions of clergy due to fear and religious duress.

The abusers of adults

The abusers of adults seem to be primarily males, although there is evidence of RSA committed by females.[23] Abusers, like victims, come from all denominations and faiths with quite a high representation in Protestant as well as RC Churches. There have been several reports[11] that have additionally implicated denominations such as the Southern Baptists, Presbyterian, United Methodist,

Episcopalian, Assembly of God, Evangelical and Evangelical Lutheran, as well as elements within Judaism.

Abusers who target adults are similar to those who sexually abuse children as they share a number of characteristics. In common with those abusers who prey on children, some sexual abusers of adults are predatory, with a smaller proportion non-predatory. Though they may not have been diagnosed, those that are predatory often display personality disorders such as borderline or antisocial personality disorder.

Common features seen in the predatory sexual abuser are impulsivity, distorted belief systems, and poor social judgement. The predominant personality trait is narcissism, in which the abuser has an inflated sense of entitlement, a self-centred focus, and pursues instant gratification. These predatory abusers commonly lack empathy and compassion, and are oblivious to the harm caused to others (see **Who are the abusers?** on page 53). In addition, they are highly skilled at manipulation, and at rationalising and justifying their actions and they are therefore good at getting out of trouble. Most chilling is the lack of remorse for harm done, a lack which is all too often replicated by the religious institution authorities involved.

In combination, this leads to sexual acting out and sexual impulse control disorders in which sexual or aggressive needs are met by inappropriate sexual actions. As many abusers are socially isolated, they typically become emotionally over involved with congregants, laywomen or seminarians whom they sexualise to fulfil their own unmet needs. This pattern of activity is frequently repeated, and it can become highly addictive.

Less common are religious sexual abusers who, during some form of psychological or spiritual breakdown, sexually abuse an adult. In such cases there is usually a single victim and the abuser is genuinely remorseful, not resorting to excuses, rationalisation or justification. Some sexual abusers are astoundingly naïve and have a distorted view of what constitutes a professional helping relationship or pastoral care, to the extent that they are unable, or unwilling, to distinguish between professional role and friendship, or to appreciate the importance of setting boundaries.

The role of religious institutions

Secondary abuse of adult victims is often committed by structural and systemic failures on the part of religious institutions through religious duress

29

and clerical culture. Religious duress and clerical culture exerts a powerful conscious and unconscious influence on the faith community and secular society. This religious duress makes it harder for individuals to have freedom of choice and to challenge religious beliefs and doctrine.

This is reinforced by clericalism in which religious institutions and clerics believe themselves to be superior to the laity, secular society and even the state.[8] This clericalism bestows special privileges to religious institutions and its clergy whereby they believe themselves to be above both civil and criminal law. Such grandiose beliefs provide a rational for canon law as seen in the RC Church and its resistance to involve the police and statutory agencies to investigate allegations of RSA (see **What is religious sexual abuse** on page 14).

The power in clericalism renders it vulnerable to allegations of corruption and abuse. When this is combined with failures relating to religious doctrine, lack of training and appropriate supervision, and the absence of clear safeguarding procedures, or proper implementation, of one can see how secondary traumatisation occurs. The sense of superiority associated with clericalism also leads to disbelieving victims and blaming them for having

seduced the abuser. The laity, who often takes their lead from the religious institution, further reinforce this in hostile attacks on victims for having brought shame to the church and the community. This is especially the case in religions and faiths that devalue women, or see them as sexual temptresses.

Blaming the victims commonly results in them being scapegoated and shunned as the faithful rush to defend the cleric. All the compassion goes to the abuser, who is seen as the victim of sexual exploitation. In some cases if the abuser is married his wife is blamed for not attending to the abuser's needs, thereby supposedly rendering him vulnerable to being seduced. This is often also reinforced in the legal system, when the motivation of the victim is the point of contention rather than the transgression of the abuser.

This scapegoating of victims by religious institutions, the faith community and the legal system makes it much harder to bring actions against abusers. This is magnified when religious institutions deny responsibility and refuse to accept accountability. The resultant reduction in the reporting and credibility of cases brought forward in turn reduces the pressure to develop and implement appropriate safeguarding procedures. This has led many states in America to criminalise RSA of adults in line with other professions who have a duty of care to vulnerable adults.[20]

Courts are not always sympathetic to adult female victims. Abusers who sexually abuse boys or adult males, rather than girls or women, often get much harsher sentences and are given much more coverage. This is due to that element of homophobia in which homosexual rape is seen as worse than heterosexual rape. This needs to be redressed as the traumatising and damaging effects of RSA is gender blind.

Healing can only take place when religious institutions, faith leaders, the laity and the criminal justice system understand and recognise that the RSA of adults as well as children is the same as sexual offences committed by any other professional, and that it constitutes a breach of trust and duty of care. Ensuring that RSA is seen as a criminal offence would place an increased demand on religious institutions to protect adults and children. Developing effective policies and procedures for recognising and responding to cases of adult RSA would provide adult survivors with some degree of justice and reparation, and would enable them to recover and heal.

Survivors of RSA need to be listened to and understood, and to be able to disclose without fear of shaming consequences. The next chapter aims to increase awareness and understanding of the nature and dynamics of RSA, how abusers seduce and groom their victims, and how this impacts on disclosure.

 WARNING If you know an adult male or female coerced into an inappropriate sexual relationship, make your concerns known to them or the relevant authorities, and encourage the victim to seek professional support.

3 The nature and dynamics of religious sexual abuse

RSA is not just about sexual assault, it is about the abuse of power and authority. It uses control, religious duress and deception to distort reality, to manipulate the victim and any bystanders. In addition, the abuser uses faith in God or doctrinal beliefs to silence victims and ensure secrecy. RSA involves a betrayal of trust by both individual abusers and religious institutions which can lead to what survivors often describe as a spiritual injury, or death. This abuse of power and trust resembles dynamics commonly associated with incest.

The abuse of power and authority

When abusers exploit their position of power and authority to sexually abuse those to whom they have a duty of care, they are in breach of ethical practice and thereby guilty of professional misconduct. Members of religious institutions who hold office are commonly accorded an elevated and protected status in society, and as such are invested with considerable authority over others. It is this protected status which allows some to lead a double life and remain undetected in what Rauch has called a 'wolf in God's clothing'.[31]

This abuse of power and authority is intensified when religious institutions prioritise the protection of the offender and themselves through denial and suppression of allegations. The net effect is a double betrayal, or institutional injury in which victims experience secondary traumatisation which deepens the wounding effect of RSA. In order to move towards healing it is necessary to acknowledge the individual and institutional abuse of power and authority so that survivors can name and legitimise their experiences.

REMEMBER To move towards healing it is necessary to acknowledge the individual and institutional abuse of power and authority so that survivors can name and legitimise their experiences.

Religious duress

Religious duress, according to Benkert and Doyle[8] is the power and authority that religious institutions, in particular the RC Church, have over the faithful through religious indoctrination. The faithful learn that to gain God's favour they need to please not just God, but also God's representative on earth, the clergy and the religious institution. This indoctrination is transmitted from the religious institution to the clergy, to the faithful, who in turn pass this in to their children (see **What is religious sexual abuse** on page 14).

Internalised religious duress distorts the reality of victims and bystanders. The fear and respect such religious institutions demand can prevent believers from accurately perceiving and evaluating abusive behaviour. This fear not only distorts the reality of the seduction of victims, but also makes it hard for victims to name and legitimise it as abuse. This confusion prevents the victim from making sense of his or her experience making it harder to process the traumatic impact of RSA.

REMEMBER Religious duress can distort the reality of victims and bystanders, making it easier to abuse.

This confusion is further reinforced when religious teaching deems sex outside marriage a mortal sin yet the victim is coerced into performing sexual acts by God's representative. This sin is intensified if the victim has been led into homosexual activity which the church sees as unnatural and disordered. Further confusion, guilt and shame occur if the victim experienced sexual pleasure. Abusers often use natural physiological responses such as pleasure in being touched to reinforce the notion that the victim is sinful, ignoring that they have led the victim into committing forbidden acts.

To atone for these sins, the victim must confess and seek absolution, despite the fact that this source of release is also the cause of the sin. As these paradoxes are irreconcilable the victim is paralysed to act which further intensifies feelings of guilt and shame. These are potent ingredients for developing complex trauma reactions (see **Understanding religious sexual abuse as trauma** on page 78). As the victim feels powerless and trapped with no means of escape he or she has no choice but to submit to the abuse. As the victim becomes more in thrall to the abuser they enter into a traumatic bond making it even harder to escape (see paragraph about **traumatic bonding** on page 34). This traumatic bonding makes it harder to disclose, or report the abuse or fear of causing displeasure to the abuser, church or God.

Religious sexual abuse is similar to incest

Clinicians have highlighted the parallels between RSA and incest wherein power, narcissism, denial and secrecy become potent forces that lead to sexually abusive behaviour[4] (see **Who are the abusers?** on page 53). This is especially so religions and faiths are seen to represent the 'spiritual family' in providing familial love,

33

communion, commitment and moral values.

The structure and hierarchy of the RC Church is an apt example of this concept, which is reflected in its use of language. The Pope is referred to as the 'Holy Father' and the Church is called the 'Holy Mother', while priests are referred to as 'Father', and consecrated ministers are called 'Brother' or 'Sister'. In addition, the power and authority held by the Church is regarded by many RCs as greater than that of the individual family, or indeed the state.

Families are like systems, and they can be functional or dysfunctional. When there are sharp imbalances of power between genders, parents or those *in loco parentis*, and children, and when this power is used to manipulate and sexually abuse children, the family becomes dysfunctional. The dynamics of incest are further replicated when there is a betrayal of an essential relationship, or attachment. As the child is utterly dependent on the parent to satisfy all of its needs, it cannot to refuse or reject the parent even if he or she is abusive. This can lead to '**traumatic bonding**'[5] in which the child submits to its parent's will in order to ensure survival. This entraps and immobilises the child.

This is especially the case when it is accompanied by beliefs in the shamefulness of sex, lack of open communication, denial and secrecy. These dynamics are commonly dictated by the head of the family (usually the father) who demands total obedience and loyalty to ensure no dishonour is brought to the family.

REMEMBER RSA resembles the dynamics of incest in which the betrayal of trust, denial and secrecy masquerades as care and protection.

Incest dynamics are also reflected in the sense of betrayal and anger felt by victims when the non-abusing parent – or, in the case of RSA, the religious institution – doesn't respond and fails to protect. The '**ripple effect**' of such multiple betrayals is that survivors of RSA commonly also feel angry with, and let down by, God. While this generalised sense of anger and betrayal is entirely valid, it is important to apportion the degree of responsibility for sexually abusive behaviour.

Identifying who is responsible for committing the sexual abuse, which individuals failed to protect the child from sexual offenders and which particular individuals imposed silence or neglected to act, can help the survivor to focus their anger more specifically and directly at those responsible (see **Understanding the impact on spirituality and faith** on page 140).

READ *The Warrior Within* has more information about managing reactions to trauma.

Narcissism is a common feature of both religious sexual abusers and incestuous fathers[8] (see **Who are the abusers?** on page 53). This narcissism is characterised by grandiosity, inflated sense of entitlement and lack of empathy. In both incest and RSA, the abuser is consumed with his or her own narcissistic needs and feels entitled to have these met by others at any cost. These narcissistic needs are not just confined to power and sex, but also include the need to be admired and adored, irrespective of their behaviour. Given the preoccupation with the self, there is little or no understanding of how their sexually abusive behaviour impacts on the victim or wider community. This permits offenders to minimise the sexual abuse, justify their behaviour and deny responsibility.

As in incest, if the victim discloses and is then not protected, blamed or scapegoated, they will experience a secondary traumatisation. In RSA this happens when both the faith community and the religious institution deny the

experiences of victims and survivors, and blame them for seducing the abuser. This leaves the survivor feeling ashamed and isolated with no source of comfort or protection as the very people who should have protected them also violated them.

This betrayal of trust is a central feature of incest and RSA. In using the power and authority invested in them, the abusers betray the trust of those they are supposed to protect. In addition, the abuser also betrays the victims, families and the rest of the community, as well as fellow clergy. All too often this betrayal of trust is not just confined to the individual abuser, but includes religious institutions and members of the faith community, who blame the victim and prioritise the reputation of the abuser or religious institution over the needs of the victim.

The role of deception

Sexual abusers in general are highly skilled in deception as this is necessary strategy in order to minimise detection. They are capable of deceiving not only children, but also other adults, their peers and their superiors as well as the criminal justice system and the mental health professionals who treat them. Rather than experiencing shame or guilt when telling lies, some abusers are aroused by their ability to deceive, known as '**duping delight**'.[4] Such abusers take pride in their deception and rarely feel apprehension or fear detection – even when an allegation is made against them.

Deception is made easier when abusers are protected by a hierarchical structure, and when a naïve congregation protects them at the expense of victims. Such protection allows paedophiles, and sexual abusers to lead double lives. To the outside world they are seen as someone who is dedicated to helping others, when in reality they are sexual predators.

Religious institutions have abetted this deception by covering up abuse allegations, relocating offenders to other diocese or parishes and silencing victims and all those who have spoken out against RSA. It is not uncommon to witness the removal or demotion of anyone within the religious institution who dares to speak out against the way sexual abuse allegations are managed.[14] The deception is often reinforced by inaccurate reporting and by policies and procedures not being properly implemented. This seduces the wider community into believing that children and vulnerable adults are safe and protected, when in reality they are not. That illusion is further bolstered by hollow and ineffective apologies that are not followed through with action when responding to the needs of survivors.

Distortion of reality

In order to deceive and assert power and authority over victims, religious sexual abusers need to distort the reality of the victim. These distortions commonly include beliefs about sexuality, responsibility for the abuse, and the consequences of disclosure. A potent form of distortion is the use of God and religious beliefs as a rationale to sexually abuse. This results in significant spiritual injury wherein the victim's and survivor's faith and belief in God is compromised. It also generates confusion in which everything is turned upside down making it hard to gain clarity or meaning.

Abusers who impose a distorted view of religious beliefs commonly imply that God is a co-conspirator in the victim's abuse. They often distort their perceived status with God, and use falsified theological beliefs to justify or excuse their exploitative behaviour. Distorted assertions about God's will or desire are often used to manipulate and groom the victim. The abuser may suggest that the sexual contact is 'God's will' or that 'God wants to teach the child about sex'. Such a distorted view implies that

God has a hand in the abuse and only values the victim as a sexual object.

Silence is ensured by instructing the victim that the RSA must be kept quiet even under the sacrament of confession, thereby co-opting the child into committing a further sin by not confessing. Another coercive strategy consists of telling the victim that 'God will punish you if you do not comply or if you tell'. As victims are made to feel responsible for the abuse and are prevented from seeking absolution through confession, they feel unworthy of God's love and forgiveness. In addition, if God has been made out to be a co-conspirator by the abuser, the victim will feel as though God has also abused them.

The grooming process

In common with incestuous fathers, and paedophiles, many abusers use deception to entrap and entice their victims so that they can groom. Before they can do this they need to deceive and groom any adults in the child's life and other adults in the community. Abusers are more easily able to manipulate people who have a strong faith. Such people are often more trusting, as they tend to see and emphasise the good in others, thus making it easier for abuse to be carried

on without suspicion. Moreover, when confronted with transgressions, people of faith tend to forgive more easily, sometimes at the expense of the victim.

Manipulation of attachment needs

Once the adults in the child's life have been manipulated, the abuser will begin to groom the child. To minimise the risk of detection and disclosure, abusers will target the most vulnerable victims who have unmet attachment needs such as those who are in care, those who have and absent parent, or those who come from large families (see **Who is at risk and who has been affected?** on page 45). The abuser will develop a 'special relationship' with the child in which he will meet any unmet needs so that the child becomes dependent on him.

This is made easier because the abuser is already seen by the victim, and family as being safe and trustworthy and a source of spiritual security. As the victim becomes more dependent on the abuser, he or she will be seduced into increasingly sexualised behaviour. Once in thrall to the abuser, the victim will fear the consequences of refusing the sexual behaviour, and will have no choice but to submit.

As in incest, this '**traumatic bonding**' entraps the victim, immobilises him or her, with no means of escape. This traumatic bonding leads to ambivalent feelings of towards the abuser and prevents the victim from disclosing the RSA. In addition, the victim is dependent on the abuser for spiritual security and remains trapped until the abuser discards him or her, or an event or circumstances ends it.

 REMEMBER 'Traumatic bonding' entraps the victim, immobilises him or her, with no means of escape.

Abuse masquerades as spiritual connection

The emphasis in grooming is on building a relationship which offers a special spiritual connection, or a greater degree of blessedness or sacredness. This is often presented as a personal gift from God which must be cherished and celebrated. The sacredness of this relationship is then used to justify secrecy on the pretext that others wouldn't understand, or would be envious of this special bond.

As the relationship becomes sexualised the child or adult begins to feel sinful and experiences a deep sense of shame.[6] When this is expressed, the abuser will manipulate religious beliefs to make the child feel that it is their

fault for having seduced the abuser or for not resisting temptation. Some religious sexual abusers invoke God as a co-conspirator in the sexual abuse by suggesting it is God's will, or punishment, or the only way to achieve spiritual enlightenment. This prevents the victim from experiencing God's unconditional love.

REMEMBER In RSA, abuse masquerades as spiritual connection.

Some religious abusers will use their power and authority to manipulate the child by making false promises. This strategy is often used with children who are in children's homes or schools: the child will be promised a return home or special privileges if he or she complies with the sexual abuse. This makes the child feel complicit in the abuse, leading to further shame.

The special relationship developed through grooming is associated with a range of other negative consequences. Not only does it make it harder to disclose, but it also isolates and alienates the child from his or her peers. Being singled out can elicit their envy and negative responses, putting the child at further risk from abuse. The abuser often encourages such isolation as it ensures the child's silence – or at least reduce the risk of disclosure. As the child becomes more entrapped it begins to accommodate to the abuse and becomes increasingly compliant. As the child is unable to avoid the abuse, it seeks positive attention from the abuser by being 'good', in the hope of reducing the frequency of the sexual abuse.

Predatory sexual abusers do not use grooming to entice their victims. Their sense of entitlement and absolute power renders grooming unnecessary as they force and threaten victims into submission. Their narcissism and belief that they are above reproach allows them to demand satisfaction of their sexual needs without the effort of developing a relationship. Such predatory abusers often appear charming and charismatic to their peers and other adults, in stark contrast to their sadistic sexually abusive behaviour. This allows them to conceal their abuse and makes it harder for the victim to be believed if the abuse is exposed.

Silence and secrecy

To ensure silence and secrecy the abuser will resort to a number of strategies. Some will use enticement and entrapment, while others use coercion. In entrapment the special relationship between the abuser and child ensures silence and secrecy as the child does not want to cause distress to the abuser. In addition, other inducements such as special privileges or becoming an altar boy are used. If these, fail the abuser resorts to threats and force to ensure the victim's silence. These threats can be so terrifying that some victims take their secret to the grave. Some survivors never disclose and die of old age, while some take their own life to end their suffering.

For some survivors of RSA the ultimate silence is suicide. While there is no statistical data on what proportion of survivors of RSA take their own life, clinical reports suggest that thoughts of suicide are not uncommon and that many survivors believe this is only way to end their pain and suffering.[17] This can be an agonising decision for them, especially if they come from faiths that have strong sanctions against suicide.

Silence is also enforced through distorting the victim's reality by using beliefs about God and religion to ensure secrecy. Victims and survivors are often made to feel that they have sinned and that not only will they will be punished by God, or their particular deity, but their family and wider community will as well. More chillingly, they believe that this punishment is not just confined to their present life, but will continue in perpetuity, into the afterlife.

 REMEMBER To ensure silence and secrecy abusers manipulate religious beliefs and faith in God.

Religious institutions

Religious institutions reinforce silence and secrecy by covering up allegations of sexual abuse, and by silencing dissenters and victims. Many victims and survivors have been silenced by being blamed for the abuse, or by means of out of court settlements.[30] This allows faith leaders to suppress allegations, avoid scandal and relocate abusers to other offices and countries where they can continue to abuse.

This conspiracy of silence is reinforced when, after disaffected clergy or ministers have spoken out, they are then side-lined or demoted, rendering them voiceless. The RC Church demands such vows of silence, or what has been called '**the Scarlett Bond**',[8] in order to protect the image and reputation of the Church and the transgression of the whistle-blower is punished.[8] The laity is also silenced by not having access to accurate information about abusers, abuse allegations or how these are handled. This allows them to continue not only to protect abusers, but also to continue to stigmatise victims and survivors.

Barriers to disclosure

The shame and self-blame felt by victims and survivors of RSA (see **Understanding shame, self-bame and self-forgiveness** on page 113) often prevents disclosure. Many victims fear that they will not be believed and stigmatised as liars. This shame and fear is heightened when they are made to feel complicit in their abuse and forced to believe that the RSA was their fault.

Some survivors are not able to disclose because they simply do not have the language, while others are just too frightened to do so. The lack of language means that the RSA cannot be clearly expressed and so it becomes shrouded, making it harder to legitimise. Some victims who have attempted to disclose have not been understood, so the abuse was ignored and continued. Many survivors do not disclose until many years later, sometimes not until their sixties or seventies.

All too often, victims and survivors are made to believe that RSA is their fault and that they deserved it, or that they are sick, perverted and sinful to accuse a man of God of rape. To add insult to injury, abusers, religious institutions and faith communities often believe that if RSA really did occur it was due to the victim seducing the abuser. This denial, blame and self-blame forces victims to minimise their abuse and suffer in silence. Many do not disclose until they feel safe to do so or no longer fear the negative consequences.

Some victims who did try to disclose as children, often during confession, found that rather than being protected, they went on to be abused by the person they disclosed to. Similarly, adults who seek pastoral counselling or spiritual guidance, sometimes for CSA or RSA, are further abused by the very person they sought help from.[23] In Ireland, it was not uncommon for children who disclosed to be labelled as psychologically disturbed or evil, and sent to reformatories or mental institutions. Once there they would be medicated or receive electroconvulsive therapy, or be subjected to further sexual abuse which often led to institutionalisation.[38] This re-victimisation destroyed all trust, preventing survivors from confiding in anyone, particularly professionals or those who has a duty of care.

Some victims and survivors may not be able to disclose until they feel safe or have the support of a partner, family or community. Survivors commonly feel they need to protect their families from the shame of RSA and so do not disclose until their parents are dead. Others wait until allegations become public, as these confirm and legitimise their experience, while still others wait until the abuser dies. Sadly, some survivors never disclose and so suffer in silence throughout their lives, taking the secret to their grave.

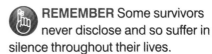 **REMEMBER Some survivors never disclose and so suffer in silence throughout their lives.**

Gender differences

Gender differences in disclosure of sexual abuse in the wider community show that girls tend to disclose more than boys. This appears to be reversed in RSA wherein more males appear to have disclosed. Many researchers and clinicians believe that this gives a false impression and that females represent the silent majority of RSA.[20] This is due to the additional sexual shame experienced by females, especially those from faiths that emphasise female sexual purity and chastity.

Some faiths place the responsibility for remaining chaste on females, even in cases of rape. When a girl or woman is sexually violated she is considered to have brought shame and dishonour

41

onto her family, and the community. This makes it particularly hard for victims from marginalised faiths or ethnic groups to disclose, sometimes with fatal consequences.

Stigmatisation

Some survivors find it hard to disclose for fear of stigmatisation by other faith members, families or the wider community. If their abuser was the same gender, some victims are afraid of a potential homophobic backlash. Disclosure is also made more difficult if the victim or survivor is marginalised on account of their sexual orientation.

A further fear is that they will be cast in the same light as their abuser. The fallacy of '**the cycle of abuse**' which contends that children who are sexually abused are more likely to become abusers, prevents disclosure for fear of being falsely labelled or not being able to find a suitable partner and have children. Survivors with disabilities also find it difficult to disclose, either because of their disability or because the abuser is also their carer whom they cannot afford to lose.

Institutional obstacles to disclosure

Institutional obstacles to disclosure arise when safeguarding policies and procedures are overly-complicated, or when there are no clear guidelines in place to respond to allegations. Where policies exist they are often difficult to access, and are written in language that is not easily understood. Religious institutions could simplify this by making leaflets which give clear guidelines, in plain language easily available in all places of worship, libraries and doctors surgeries. This would make procedures and the investigative process more transparent and aid disclosure.

In addition, the implementation of procedures and any investigation needs to be conducted in a timely manner. To manage the stress of disclosure, survivors require access to immediate support and spiritual affirmation while details of the allegations are investigated. Until religious institutions remove obstacles to disclosure, and simplify the process, they will remain complicit in silencing those whom they should have protected.

The role of sexuality and sexual shame

The control of sexuality features strongly in most religious teaching. Many faiths divorce sexuality from spirituality and debase sexuality rather than see it as a natural, healthy and necessary part of human experience. When sex is deemed evil and sinful it creates anxiety, and inflicts deep wounds that are hard to heal.

If the healthy expression of sexuality is prevented, as in celibacy, this natural drive can become corrupted or rechannelled into the abuse of power. Some critics of the RC Church have argued that the denial of sexuality through celibacy does not lead to a more spiritual life, but rather to an obsession and intoxication with power.[14,27, 33] The combination of the denial of sexual expression and the compensatory hunger for power is what drives religious sexual abusers to victimise children and vulnerable adults. The distortion of sex and power within some religions and faiths and the failure to understand the complexities of human sexuality is a significant factor in RSA.

Even more powerful are the contradictory messages around sexual abstinence and sexual abuse which is a source of great confusion for many survivors. On the one hand they are conditioned to believe that sexuality, sexual thoughts and actions are a sin and yet the uncontrolled sexual appetites of the abuser are permitted. This '**double bind**' means that the victim or survivor has difficulty in making sense of what it means

to be sexual. This is often reflected in their own ambivalence around sex and sexuality when they reach adulthood.

The concept of sin is also used to manipulate victims. In shaming victims for having sexual thoughts and blaming them for seducing the abuser, victims are convinced that they are sinful. This is reinforced when the abuser uses the victim's natural sexual responses and arousal as proof of sinful behaviour. If the victim and abuser are the same gender, a further sin is invoked: the sin of homosexuality. When these sins are deemed to be so wicked that even God cannot forgive them, the victim feels totally abandoned – even by God.

Denying sexuality and categorising sexual expression and masturbation as sinful, prevents any meaningful dialogue about sex. This makes it much easier for sexual predators and abusers. Many paedophiles state that the less a child or adult knows about sex the easier it is to abuse them.[7]

 REMEMBER The denial and institutional shaming of sexuality makes it easier to sexually abuse children and vulnerable adults.

The use of religious symbols and artefacts

Religious symbols and artefacts are a prominent feature in RSA. These are often present during RSA and become entwined with the abuse experiences. This inverts what should be symbols of spiritual comfort into powerful reminders of the abuse. Some sexual abusers introduce religious themes into RSA, or use crucifixes in a sexual way. If the abuse takes place in the presence of religious icons or rituals it will often make it impossible for the survivor to engage with or tolerate these in the future without triggering memories of the abuse (see **Understanding flashbacks, nightmares, intrusive memories and dissociation** on page 96).

Some abusers are known to make the sign of the cross on the victims forehead immediately after the sexual assault, or to pray during and after the abuse. Some abusers use Bibles, holy books, prayer cards, saints' medals or rosaries as gifts to seduce or reward the victim. As a result these objects become contaminated by the RSA and will no longer be a source of comfort or solace, but remain as powerful reminders of RSA.

The dynamics associated with RSA vary enormously with each experience. All of them leave a mark on the victim and survivor. While each experience is unique in terms of impact, there are commonalities. The chapters in **Part two** will look at the range of impacts to provide a deeper understanding of how these dynamics affect survivors long-term.

4 Who is at risk and who has been affected?

Given the secret nature of RSA it is not yet known how many children and adults have been victims, nor can it be estimated how many families, friends and communities have been affected. There is very little research or data collection into the scale of abuse, as many survivors are too scared to disclose what has happened to them. Some survivors may be reluctant to disclose as they are now very elderly, while others have died without ever having disclosed. On average survivors do not disclose until they are in their late thirties or forties. Tragically, many victims never disclose as the pain is too unbearable, and they end up taking their own lives.

Also, religious institutions and faith leaders are reluctant to reveal the number of allegations in order to protect their reputation. Most of the estimates and data come from allegations, inquiries and investigations, legal cases, and a number of published first-hand accounts (see **Resources** on page 208). Survivor organisations in Ireland, the UK and the United States believe that published data do not reflect the actual number of victims as much of RSA still remains hidden.[30]

Children and adults who are brought up in religious families look to their church or faith leaders for spiritual guidance and emotional support, especially when in need of pastoral care. Religious leaders and especially priests are held in high esteem, often higher than their parents, and are seen as the highest authority next to God. The most vulnerable children are those from troubled family backgrounds or large families in which emotional needs are not satisfied.

When such children are singled out for 'special' attention this is not seen as merely flattery but as a privilege, constituting unconditional love and grace bestowed by God's special chosen servant, and is considered to be evidence of worthiness. When this perceived, love and grace become an instrument for sexual gratification – a human impulse which the victim has been taught to think of as sinful – it is not only psychologically traumatising but also spiritually devastating.

Who is at risk?

Given the lack of data across all faiths this is hard to know, but it is important to recognise that both girls and boys are at risk, as are adults. In the case of the sexual abuse of adults, the evidence suggests that females are most at risk of RSA from males. There is however emerging evidence of same-sex RSA, with nuns sexually abusing other nuns, and priests coercing adult males into sexual relationships.[14]

It is likely that any data we do have is merely revealing the tip of the iceberg and that there are many more victims who remain hidden and still suffer in silence. As we have already seen, victims and survivors are often reluctant to disclose RSA for fear of the consequence of such revelations. Many victims do not disclose until many years after the abuse took place, having spent years suffering in silence. Clinical evidence suggest that some survivors abused as a young children or teenagers do not disclose abuse until they are in their late sixties or seventies.[19]

A major study in the United States investigating sexual abuse by RC clergy found that some 12,000 victims have reported offences.[26] This is likely to be a considerable underestimate, as the majority of sex crimes are not reported to authorities. In addition these are only allegations involving RC priests and does not include the many other faiths that have had allegations made against them.

So far there is very little data indicating how many children are currently at risk of RSA in England and Wales, due to low reporting rates and the lack of data recording. There is no centralised system for logging historic cases of RSA, and in the absence of a national inquiry or commission to investigate past cases of sexual abuse across faiths it is difficult to assess the extent of RSA in England and Wales (see **Appendix** on page 224 for more detailed data).

It must be remembered that in society at large as much as 95% of child sexual abuse goes unreported to police.[7] Few victims report their abuse when it happens, so the majority of RSA is never revealed, despite improved safeguarding procedures. In addition, of those cases that are reported less than 5% result in a custodial sentence.[30] These figures suggest that RSA is largely under-reported and that the prevalence is considerably higher. It is also likely that it is even more hidden in those faiths that have strict honour-based laws that prevent the faithful from talking about sex and sexual abuse, especially to those outside the faith.

Boys thought to be most at risk

As we have seen, the majority of victims of childhood sexual abuse by clergy appear to be boys. This is supported by the 2011 John Jay Study, commissioned by the United States Conference of Catholic Bishops, which found that 81% of victims were male and 19% female. In the case of male victims, 51% were aged between 11 and 14 years of age,

27% were between the age of 15 and 17, 16% were between age eight and 10 with 6% under the age of seven.[26]

This suggests boys are most at risk, although some priests do sexually abuse girls, and in 12% of cases both boys and girls are abused. It is important to remember that these figures are based on survivors who have come forward and made allegations, so they may not be representative of all victims. Females may be at equal risk, especially in other faiths, but may be more reluctant to disclose to preserve their reputations for chastity. It is interesting to note that there is considerably less data on the sexual abuse of girls, so this escapes scrutiny.

✊ **REMEMBER Both males and females are at risk of RSA, with boys between 11 and 14 years of age most at risk of sexual abuse by RC priests.**

Boys often look up to priests and religious leaders as role models, and for learning about the world. They are often seeking knowledge that that has not been provided by their parents who may be too beleaguered, uneducated or busy to satisfy the boys' search for intellectual, aesthetic, or spiritual fulfilment. Instead they learn sexual

indulgence and submission in the face of domination.

Religious-based homophobia and general homophobic attitudes make it extremely difficult and shameful for boys to be sexually abused by males. The fear of stigmatisation and being seen as gay makes disclosure even harder, especially when the sexual abuse has caused confusion and doubt around sexual orientation.

Girls thought to be most at risk

Girls most at risk are those who attend religious schools where they are vulnerable to sexual abuse by both priests and nuns. There is considerable evidence, especially from Ireland, indicating that many young girls were raped by priests, often with the collusion of nuns and the Mother Superior. Many of those raped ended up pregnant and were sent away to mother and baby homes, many of which were run by nuns. If these girls tried to report the rape they were silenced by both priest and nuns, and sent to other institutions including psychiatric hospitals.[23]

Sexual abuse by females in the wider community is largely under-reported and has not been fully researched. Similarly the sexual abuse by nuns, especially of girls, has not been investigated so the minimal data are derived from clinical reports and civil cases. Survivors of sexual abuse by nuns commonly report that this was often accompanied by severe physical and emotional abuse. Like boys who revere priests, girls often look to nuns for emotional reassurance, seeing them as powerful role models for a chaste and spiritual life. When this is eroded through sexual abuse, the child is left feeling betrayed and abandoned.

Pregnancy

It is not known how many of the girls raped by priests ended up pregnant, although clinical and anecdotal data suggests that this was not uncommon.[38] Often those girls who were sent to mother and baby homes had their child wrenched away from them and sold to wealthy couples in America. Usually the girls were told that their baby had died, and never knew that they had been adopted. Many of these adopted children have no idea about their birth mother or the circumstances of their conception and are therefore indirect victims of RSA.[21] The emotional and psychological cost to the survivors who lost their children or thought them to be dead is immeasurable.

Some of these young girls were allowed to keep their child but were vilified for having sinned. They were left to struggle with bringing up their child, feeling stigmatised and having to keep the identity of the children's father secret. As these children often grew up not knowing their father they too must be considered secondary victims of RSA.

Sexual abuse in the community, parishes or dioceses

Boys most at risk are those singled out for 'special' attention. These are often especially devout children who serve as assistants or express interest in taking religious orders. This increases the degree of access and the opportunity to carry out sexual abuse in which religious rituals and beliefs are perverted and used in justification. This is a potent example of abuse masquerading as love of God and the church. Many children are also at risk of sexual abuse in faith based community programmes such as youth groups, sports clubs, youth mission work and other faith based activities.

Religious schools and institutions

Boarding schools and convents have been particularly identified as institutional settings in which children have been physically, emotional and sexually abused. There is considerable evidence for sexual abuse in religious schools and reformatories across the globe, and in particular in Ireland. In England and Wales several cases currently under investigation include a range of religious orders such as the De La Salle Bothers, Christian Brothers, Jesuits, Benedictines, the Salesian Brothers, and the Rosminians[30] (see **Appendix** on page 224).

Physical and sexual abuse also occurs in other faith school settings, such as Madrassas, although these are more likely to be kept hidden due to the importance of maintaining honour and not bringing shame to the family or community. In religions where girls are praised for their modesty and chastity, and are taught to cover up and avoid eye gaze, to be sexually abused is particularly distressing, making it harder to disclose. Data on the incidence of sexual abuse in such faiths is hard to obtain as formal allegations, especially outside the community, are rarely made.

There is considerable evidence, primarily from Ireland, that children who were sent to Reformatories, Industrial Schools or orphanages were also subjected to brutal physical abuse alongside sexual abuse by both priests and nuns. Many of the girls who were sent to institutions such as the Magadalene Laundries suffered in this way and were traumatised by their experiences.

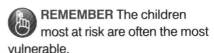 **REMEMBER** The children most at risk are often the most vulnerable.

The children most at risk are often the most vulnerable. Children in orphanages, children's homes, or convalescent homes, have been most at risk and were often silenced with promises of being helped to return home. Those who broke the silence faced being sent to psychiatric institutions where they would be heavily medicated, or given electric shock treatments. Such interventions exposed children to further abuse, the risk of institutionalisation, life-long dependency on prescription drugs and vulnerability to other psychiatric disorders. In some cases children in these religious institutions were prostituted to other adults in the community, often men in high positions of power.

Children with disabilities are known to be at a higher risk of being sexually abused, not only in the general community but also in religious settings. Such abuse is often even more hidden as, owing to their disabilities, these children are less able to disclose.

Migrant children

There is overwhelming evidence that migrant children who were sent from the UK to Australia, Canada and Zimbabwe during the World War II were often subjected to emotional, physical and sexual abuse. Often these children were told that their parents were dead and that they would have a better life abroad. These so called 'orphans' were sent across the globe, often to religious schools, only to be abused.

Secondary victims

Families of victims are also affected by RSA. Families are often overwhelmed with grief, anger and guilt for having failed to protect the child. This can lead to denial as a protection from feeling guilt. The shame of RSA forces some families to leave their communities for fear of being ostracised, increasing their sense of isolation as they are excluded and alienated from their community.

In turn the survivor may harbour anger and resentment towards their family for failing them. These rifts can only be healed through open, honest, and heartfelt communication. One further tragic impact is when survivors of RSA give up the struggle for survival and commit suicide. This can be devastating for families, partners and friends,

especially when they were not aware of the abuse or the pain that had been suffered in silence.

The families of abusers can also be affected by the sexually abusive behaviour of a beloved family member. Their hurt and betrayal is counter-balanced by a natural instinct to protect a loved one which can lead to denial and outrage in response to any allegations made, and misdirected anger at the victim.

REMEMBER There a number of secondary victims affected by RSA including the families of victims and perpetrators, partners and children of survivors, fellow non-offending clergy, as well as whole faith communities and society at large.

Partners of survivors are also most likely to be affected by RSA. Many survivors have complex and at times difficult intimate relationships in which sexual shame leads either to avoidance of sexual intimacy or sexually needy behaviour. These strategies are a way of dealing with the lack of power and control during the sexual abuse, and the need to restore this in their adult life. Many survivors find that their relationships turn into constant conflict, or end up in separation and divorce, which for them confirms their lack of relational worth (see **Rebuilding relationships** on page 154).

The children of survivors are also secondary victims, because the survivor is either over- or under-protective. If the survivor is plagued by overwhelming post-traumatic stress reactions, or self-medicates through alcohol, drugs or gambling, this can impact negatively on the children. In addition, children whose parents are separated or divorced due to the difficulties associated with RSA, as well as those who were actually the product of RSA, are also indirect victims, albeit unknowingly.

Religious communities, congregations, and ministry organisations are also deeply affected by RSA. In order to commit RSA, abusers need to groom other adults. This makes faith communities and congregations vulnerable to being deceived by abusers. Many sexual abusers find it easier to deceive those who have strong religious beliefs as they are more likely to accept moral lapses as they emphasise forgiveness, repentance and salvation.

Despite this, many devout followers feel that their faith has been shaken by abuse allegations, for they feel that if they cannot trust their priest or faith leader, then who can they trust? Those who were married by an abuser, or had their children christened by him, may feel tainted through this association and question the value of such rituals.

Many also fear that in continuing to pursue their faith and attend worship they may be seen as complicit in the cover up and denial of RSA. While they might not lose their faith in God, they may lose faith in a Church that fails to practice what it preaches. Arguably, this has drastically reduced the number of the faithful, especially among Roman Catholics, and affected church attendances.[18]

Furthermore, many devout worshippers become fearful of allowing their children to attend Sunday school or become involved with their religion. A potent concern for many congregants is that if RSA was kept so well-concealed, then this raises the question of what else may be being hidden. Such anxieties undermine trust in their leaders, causing them to doubt that future victims will be protected.

A further impact can be seen in the decline in young men and women wishing to enter the ministry, thereby diminishing the amount of new blood entering the Church or faith and potentially helping the healing process. It is estimated that there has been a 90% decline in seminarians since 1965, resulting in the closure of 86% of seminaries.[28] This has led to a shortage of RC priests, deepening the crisis within the RC Church.

Non-abusing ministers and clergy are deeply affected by sexually abusive colleagues as they feel they have been deceived by abusers. They feel betrayed and angry that this can have happened and that the church or religious leaders have not taken responsibility. This has led some to question their confidence in their church and has compromised their own role as a representative of their faith. Such doubts are often hard, if not impossible to reconcile, leading to disillusionment with their religious organisation or leaders.

Wounded perpetrators are heavily represented among religious sexual abusers, with many having been sexually abused themselves in childhood, often by religious figures or family members. While the majority of victims of CSA do not go on to abuse as adults, some are vulnerable to becoming abusers in adulthood. They may have entered religious orders to avoid sexual intimacy or as a way of covering up their own sexual difficulties, or confusion. As their own sexual abuse has never been processed or dealt with, it can render some of them more vulnerable to perpetrating sexually abusive behaviour, for they know that they will be protected by the power of their status and the authority of their church or faith.(see **Who are the abusers?** on page 53)

Society at large has also been affected by RSA in terms of the financial cost of supporting survivors who have had life-long struggles with depression and other mental health issues, or with physical illnesses. RSA also entails costs arising from substance misuse and the associated social problems including domestic abuse, abandoned children, broken relationships and in certain cases violence and other criminal behaviours. While some survivors are highly functional with good careers, others, as a result of their suffering, are unable to access employment opportunities for lack of educational attainment, or because of their impaired physical or mental well-being.

The following chapter will examine the profiles of abusers and explore the range of factors that contribute to their sexually abusive behaviour. If it becomes too overwhelming for survivors and families of victims and offenders to read, it is better to stop reading and return to it at a later point.

5 Who are the abusers?

Abusers come from all denominations and faiths and include both males and females. Reports of religious sexual abuse (RSA) have included most religions and faiths including the Roman Catholic, Anglican, Protestant, Jesuit, Church of the Latter day Saints (Mormon), Episcopal, Methodist, Lutheran, Presbyterian, Jewish, Greek Orthodox, Muslim, Hindu, and Buddhist. They have implicated rabbis, imams, pastors, monks, brothers, sisters, nuns, lay ministers, priests, and deacons as well as bishops and cardinals.

Although most faiths have received allegations of sexual abuse, most of the published research has been on males within the RC Church. As most of our knowledge about religious sexual abusers is drawn from this research it is important to be aware that this may not be representative of sexual abusers in other faiths, and that what follows is based on the limited research available.

Due to the hidden nature of RSA it is not known how many perpetrators there are. Estimates within the RC Church suggest that between 4% and 9% of priests sexually abuse children, although it is not known how many abuse adults. The largest study of RC priests by the John Jay College of Criminal Justice, commissioned by the US Conference of Catholic Bishops, suggests that only around 4% of priests sexually abuse children.[26] This estimate is felt to be artificially low and that there are many more abusers that have not yet been identified.[28]

As this research focused exclusively on RC priests it is hard to assess to what degree this is representative of other faiths, or of RSA by females. It is clear that more research is needed, especially across other faiths, to have a full understanding of the abusers.

 REMEMBER Our knowledge of religious sexual abusers is limited due to lack of research.

The spectrum of RSA offences

The spectrum of sexual abuse offences ranges from touching outside clothing, fondling, mutual masturbation and oral sex through to anal and vaginal penetration. It is estimated that the majority of sexual acts associated with RSA is penetration and oral sex (over 33%), followed by touching under clothes (15.8%), touching over clothes (9%) and sexual talk or use of pornography at 7.9%.[26]

The use of child abuse images or child pornography is of considerable concern as this fuels the fantasy and mastubatory arousal cycle which stamps in the sexual arousal to children. Many abusers believe they are doing no harm as there is no direct victim involved and do not acknowledge that by looking at child abuse images they are supporting an industry which does harm to children. Some religious sexual abusers have been found with thousands of child abuse images. While it is often rationalised that this is a substitute for sex it can lead to actual sexual abuse of children. In addition many abusers use child abuse images either to sexually arouse the victim, or as a way to normalise sexual activity between adults and children.[7]

⚠️ **WARNING** Child abuse images or child pornography is of considerable concern as this fuels the fantasy and masturbatory arousal cycle which stamps in sexual arousal to children.

RSA settings

RSA has been reported to take place in a range of settings with the majority (41%) taking place in the abuser's home, or on church premises (16%) or other places of worship such as temples, mosques, monasteries and ashrams. Victims are also abused in their own home (12%), in vacation homes (10%), in faith schools (10%) and in cars (10%).[26]

Abusers as paedophiles

The clinical diagnosis of paedophilia distinguishes between **paedophiles**, who are sexually attracted to children below the age of 13, and **ephebophiles** who are sexually interested in children over the age of 13. The 2011 John Jay College study of RC priests in the US[26] manipulated this distinction by defining paedophiles as those who are sexually aroused by children below the age of 10 and ephebophiles as those who are aroused by children above age 10.

In adopting this inaccurate distinction, the researchers were able to claim that the majority of clergy are not paedophiles. As the majority of RSA involves boys aged between 11 and 14 years of age they argued that the majority of abusers are ephebophiles, not paedophiles. The study found that 57-80% of clerical sexual abusers fitted their erroneous classification of ephebophiles while only 20-43% were deemed to be paedophiles. This has enabled the RC Church to reject the label '**paedophile priests**' and minimise the seriousness of RSA by failing to acknowledge the impact it has on children irrespective of their age.

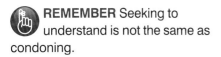

REMEMBER The impact of RSA on victims irrespective of age is more important than how abusers are labelled.

Factors associated with abusers

Factors associated with abusers include gender, age, sexual shame, sexual orientation and celibacy, as well as a history of child abuse including CSA, personality factors, mental health issues and psychological disturbance. In essence, abusers are as diverse as are the victims, and each will have a unique profile and a range of contributing factors. What is clear is that RSA is influenced by many factors – none of which excuse the abusive behaviour but are a way of understanding abusers.

REMEMBER Seeking to understand is not the same as condoning.

Gender of abusers

Male abusers are more common in faith settings and in the wider community. It is estimated that between 80 % and 95% of all CSA is committed by males, and between 5% and 20% by females.[7] These estimates mirror reports of RSA of both children and adults, where males are more highly represented than females. However, as many survivors of sexual abuse by females find it harder to disclose, current estimates do not necessarily reflect the true nature of sexual abuse by women. The taboo surrounding the sexual abuse by females is primarily due to cultural norms which prefer to see females are nurturing and sexually passive rather than sexually predatory.

Female abusers are much more hidden had have not received as much research as males. The little that is known is based on allegations that nuns and sisters have committed both physical abuse and RSA in a range of RC institutions such religious schools, convents, orphanages, convalescent homes, industrial schools and reformatories. While much of the RSA by females is perpetrated against girls, there are reports that some sexually abuse boys. There have also been reports of RSA by female ministers in other denominations of both children and adults of both gender.

There is some evidence that suggests that female abusers are themselves victims or survivors of CSA. One study of 36,000 nuns found that 62% suffered childhood abuse, with more than two thirds of these (70%) experiencing CSA.[23] To avoid adult sexual relationships and seek refuge from sexual abuse, some females who were abused in childhood may enter the sanctuary of religious orders. Despite this sanctuary they may not have the opportunity to work through, or resolve their childhood abuse. As a result a proportion may seek to satisfy their narcissistic needs for personal power and validation through the sexual abuse of children or other nuns, or novices.[23]

⚠ WARNING Nuns, sisters and female ministers also commit RSA although this is much more hidden.

The RSA by females is much more hidden especially in faiths where females are denigrated and where this sense of devaluation is discharged onto female children. Moreover, some female abusers use physical abuse and RSA as a way to break the girls' will and to ensure that they become submissive, passive and thereby virtuous females.

Age of abusers

Research into the sexual abuse of children by priests in the RC Church has found that the age range of abusers is between 25 and 90 years of age, with an average age between 30 and 39. This would suggest that religious sexual abusers exist across all age groups.

Number of victims

While the number of male and female sexual offenders is relatively low, each perpetrator may abuse multiple victims, sometimes as many as hundreds. This is especially the case when allegations have been made, suppressed, and the abuser has been moved to another community, diocese or country where they have been able to continue sexually abusing children. It is impossible to know how many victims have been abused as many have not come forward or who have died through old age or suicide.

Poor record keeping and documentation, or at times a complete lack of records, will distort any figures that are available. Some faiths have only recently started to keep records of allegations for auditing purposes, while others do not have any recording procedures in place at all. This would suggest that those figures that are available are merely the tip of the iceberg.

Sexuality and sexual shame

All religions contain guidance around the expression and management of sexuality and sexual feelings, with some religions more repressive than other. If the religious teachings and practices are excessively rigid, conservative or oppressive then this can lead to ambivalence about sexuality and the development of sexual shame. Many religions and faith leaders have no idea about current psychosexual research or understanding of sexuality. Lack of psychosexual knowledge and limited understanding leads to erroneous sexual beliefs and myths. These in turn lead to confusion, humiliation and shame around natural human instincts such as sex and sexuality. This sexual shame can be crippling and stigmatising which prevents any open dialogue about sexuality.

REMEMBER Sexual shame and lack of sexual knowledge makes children more vulnerable to RSA.

The lack of knowledge and open dialogue increases the power to sexually abuse. Abusers in the wider community often claim that the more naïve and lacking in knowledge of sex children are, the easier it is to entice or coerce them into sexual activity.[7] The less knowledge a child has, the easier it is for the abuser to impose a corrupted view of sex so as to normalise the sexually abusive behaviour. In addition, beliefs that sexual thoughts and masturbation are sinful increase sexual shame and make it easier for the abuser to manipulate such natural expressions of sexuality in order to sexually abuse.

This is especially the case in teenage boys and girls, whose emerging sexuality can feel overpowering and confusing. The abuser hijacks natural and normal elements of psychosexual development and corrupts these in order to sexually abuse the child or teenager. Abusers will use a variety of rationalisations for their sexual behaviour, such as RSA is 'God's will', or a 'special type of love' that brings the child closer to God, or that it is 'God's punishment' for impure sexual thoughts or behaviour.

The abuser will also use sexual shame to ensure secrecy by making the child feel guilty for natural sexual feelings. Thus teenagers who have sexual thoughts or who masturbate are made to feel ashamed and told they need to be punished for through sexually abusive activities. Alternatively this is used to blame the victim for seducing the abuser. This paves the way for self-blame and the belief that the RSA was the child's own fault, and that they deserve it. This adds to the sexual shame making it harder for the child to disclose. Many survivors do not disclose until late adulthood, or until they have a more adult understanding of psychosexual development and sexual feelings.

Sexual orientation of abusers

There has been considerable speculation that sexual orientation and homosexuality contributes to RSA. Despite such speculation there is no evidence that homosexuality leads to RSA. Abusers who sexually abuse children, including children of the same gender, are sexually interested in children, not homosexual. Although a large number of priests are thought to be active homosexuals, this does not mean that they are the ones responsible for sexually abusing children (see **The nature and dynamics of religious sexual abuse** on page 32).

REMEMBER Same-sex RSA of children arises out of a primary sexual orientation towards children who happen to be the same gender, not because of homosexuality.

Same-sex RSA of children arises out of a primary sexual orientation towards children who happen to be the same gender, not because of homosexuality. Sexual attraction to same-sex children is due to a variety of factors including identification with the child as a reminder of themselves when they were young, or a way of regaining personal power and control, or to triumph over the trauma of their own abuse.

Cultural, or religious attitudes with regard to gender also a play a significant role in same-sex RSA. This is most likely in religions that idealise virginity and purity, and devalue females. In such faiths sexual activity with same-sex children is seen as more acceptable or sublime than sexual relationships with females. In addition, opportunity and access also exerts a strong influence on the gender most likely to be abused.

Celibacy

Like homosexuality, celibacy has been proposed as a significant factor in RSA. There is very little evidence to support this as it is thought that the majority of celibate clergy do not observe their vows of celibacy.[14] In addition, there is evidence that RSA occurs across all faiths and denominations, even those that do not practice celibacy.

What is critical is that those faiths that promote celibacy should provide training to young seminarians and regular psychological and spiritual support to all clergy to enable them to manage their sexuality so as to remain celibate. This is especially necessary for those who seek refuge in taking religious orders as a way to avoid already existing sexual shame and sexual conflicts.

REMEMBER Celibacy does not cause RSA and occurs in other faiths that do not practice celibacy.

History of child abuse and CSA

There is considerable evidence that some men and women who enter religious orders have experienced conflicted and difficult childhoods. The John Jay study found that 6.8% of religious sexual abusers reported a history of child abuse, with 65% of these claiming a history of sexual abuse and 7% a history of physical and sexual abuse.[26] Abuser self-reports also show that some abusers come from large families in which emotional and psychological needs were not always met. Entering religious orders becomes a sanctuary and safe community in which to experience the status and power they lacked in childhood.

Research has shown that children who have been abused seek to '**triumph over trauma**' by finding ways of being in control and to feel powerful.[6] The status accorded to faith leaders, within the sanctuary of a religious institution, is one way of feeling empowered. In the case of those faiths that practice celibacy it is also a way of avoiding conflicted sexual feelings.

Many survivors of CSA have fears around sexuality, or that they might marry a potential abuser. Taking religious orders is a way of not having to process their sexually abusive experiences and of evading their sexuality. Religious life is seen by some as being part of a spiritual family in which they can get the support needed to regain self-esteem and value by dedicating their life to the needs of others. Through this they are able to hide away in shame and hope to atone for the CSA they experienced in childhood. It is also a place of safety, providing a clearly-defined hierarchical structure in which they are seen as valued members.

While entering religious life may initially provide respite from the trauma of CSA, over time survivors may find that as the CSA has not been resolved they are at risk of developing trauma reactions including post-traumatic stress disorder, dissociation, depression, and self-harming behaviours such as alcohol or drug misuse to numb the trauma. To minimise trauma reactions and acting out abusive behaviours, it is critical that those entering seminaries or undertaking religious instruction are given the opportunity to work through any history of child abuse, especially CSA, and receive appropriate psychological support so that they can recover from their abuse experiences.

Some religious sexual abusers who experienced CSA along with sadistic violence may suffer from extreme sexual difficulties which become entwined with sadomasochistic fantasies and practices. Such experiences prevent them from engaging in loving or caring relationships, or experiencing tenderness. It is more likely that they will experience their relationships, especially sexual ones, in terms of power and control, and domination and submission.

As adults in positions of power, they may feel compelled to re-enact their own childhood abuses by abusing children. In their attempt to triumph over trauma they become an abuser rather than remain a victim. Such abusers gain considerable satisfaction from taking away a child's innocence, or purity, as theirs was stolen from them. Moreover, defiling the child is seen by the abuser as a way of compensating for impure thoughts and shameful deeds.

This is not to say that a history of CSA leads to sexual abuse in adulthood, but rather that RSA is due to complex array of factors that may compel some to sexually abuse as adults.

⚠️ **WARNING** A history of CSA does not lead survivors to commit sexual abuse in adulthood. While a proportion of religious sexual abusers who have been abused go on to commit RSA this due to a multiple factors.

A history of CSA can lead some survivor-abusers to avoid any sexual expression through sexual abstinence or a compulsion to avoid sex, known as **sexual anorexia**, which can evolve into rigid and repressive sexual intolerance. As in anorexia, the suppression of appetite creates a heightened preoccupation with sex and the compulsion to avoid it. The denial and avoidance of sexuality is further legitimised by doctrinal moral judgements about sexuality and sexual shame. This can lead some to seek sanctuary and refuge from sexual challenges in secure and enclosed systems such as religious communities or the church, and in the practice of celibacy.

In contrast, some survivors of CSA who enter religious institutions are unable to control overwhelming sexual appetites and can develop addictions, or become **sexually incontinent**, Their preoccupation with sex and lack of control leads to a search for aggressive and dominant relationships in which they can wield power and control over others. These abusers are often passive and submissive among their peers yet are tyrannical when they have power over vulnerable others. To prevent such misuse of power it is critical that any childhood sexual trauma is worked through and resolved before the person ministers to vulnerable adults or children.

Sexual immaturity

Many men and women who enter religious orders or become faith leaders do so in late adolescence or early adulthood when they are still sexually immature or inexperienced. They often lack knowledge of sexuality and feel uncomfortable talking about sex. This means they have not fully explored their own sexuality, sexual orientation, sexual confusion or sexual conflicts. Those who enter religious orders may have little understanding of how to manage or express their sexual feelings, or how to observe celibacy. In essence their psychosexual development becomes arrested and fixed at a sexually immature level. This can result in a fear of mature, adult sexual relationships and a focus on sexually immature children or adolescents.

In some cases abusers may have been seduced as adolescents into religious orders without fully completing their psychosexual development. This arrested development may lead some to reclaim their sexuality by taking it from young children in their care, thereby repeating the cycle of their own abuse. To meet their affection needs some religious sexual abusers may seek refuge in inappropriate relationships with children, which they sexualise to compensate for a lack of intimacy, loneliness, social isolation or overwork. They may also use child abuse images or pornography to masturbate to which, over time, becomes increasingly less satisfying and can lead to actual sexual contact.

Personality factors

There is evidence that some abusers may suffer from personality disorders which have not been diagnosed. Some studies have found that 26.5% of clergy have personality related problems such as lack of emotional regulation with some identified as over-controlled, submissive and passive, while 8% have been identified with hostility problems.[32]

The most common personality traits are ones that are associated with narcissism and an inflated sense of entitlement, which under some circumstances can develop into antisocial personality traits, and lead to criminal offending, or coercive sexual activities.[33] Given such data it is essential that when individuals enter religious training that they are screened not just for personality disorders but also their ability to regulate their emotions appropriately.

The narcissistic traits exhibited by some perpetrators of RSA attest to a lack of empathy and compassion and the failure to understand how sexual abuse impacts on the child and later adult. It is not known to what extent clergy or nuns fit the diagnoses of narcissistic personality disorder, although many display narcissistic features. This is usually seen in the refusal to acknowledge their abusive behaviour, the maintenance of a self-image of perfection, a constant need to be admired and affirmed, excessive intolerance of criticism, and the use of scapegoating to vilify others and to deflect from their own abusive traits. Some abusers develop pathological narcissism in which they feel entitled to use children to soothe themselves.

In addition, they are often masters of dissimulation, highly manipulative, and extremely skilled in deceiving others. This deception allows them to deceive their peers and colleagues by appearing to be pious and virtuous while living a double life in which they dominate and control others. Like all narcissists, their sense of entitlement makes them greedy in satisfying their own needs with no real regard for the harm or hurt caused to others. Their deception extends to faith communities and congregations in which they seek to hide. There are numerous examples of sexual abusers leaving prison having found a faith who then infiltrate faith communities knowing that they are more likely to be accepted.

WARNING Abusers are often masters of dissimulation, highly manipulative and extremely skilled in deceiving others.

Addiction and mental health

Research has found that many clergy suffer from a range of mental health disorders and addictions, which are not always diagnosed.[21] Most common is the misuse of alcohol to self-medicate feelings of loneliness, anger or frustration. Abusers may also seek refuge in sexual addiction as a form of self-soothing to manage feelings of guilt, shame and self-loathing. As these feelings emerge the abuser is drawn into sexual thoughts and fantasies which in turn give rise to further shame and guilt. As these obsessive thoughts increase so does the compulsion to act upon them. The initial relief is only temporary and almost immediately replaced by disgust and self-loathing. As these negative feelings build up again the only relief is to repeat the cycle. Thus RSA begins to resemble an addiction.

Cognitive distortions

Alongside personality factors and mental health, the way an individual thinks, or their cognitive style also has an impact on abusing behaviour. Commonly, people who hold strong religious views, including many clergy, believe that having a sinful thought is equivalent to perpetrating a sinful action or behaviour. This gives rise to cognitive dissonance, whereby if a person can be condemned for a sinful thought he or she may as well carry out the sinful action. Such distorted thinking patterns if left unchecked can develop into inappropriate sexual behaviour.

Distorted thinking patterns are also used to groom the child into believing that the RSA is part of God's will. Many abusers use God and religious beliefs to increase the power and authority over the victim and to justify their behaviour. This justification is further supported by the abusers belief in forgiveness. In believing that God will forgive them, abusers can continue to sexually abuse with impunity as their relationship with

God will not be compromised. Some abusers also believe that their good work in the community cancels out any moral lapses such as the RSA making it easier for God to forgive them.

The role of power

For some individuals, entering the priesthood or a religious institution is an escape from poverty, family abuse or a sense of disempowerment. The power and status that priests and other faith leaders have will attract those who feel personally disempowered. To compensate for this lack of personal power they will exploit the power associated with their religion or faith and use their status to control and dominate others. Such power is intoxicating and potentially corrupting.

 WARNING The pursuit of power is intoxicating and potentially corrupting, leading to the control and domination of others.

Abusers who are assigned power and status, and yet lack personal power, live in perpetual fear of having this power taken away from them. This fear leads them to continually feed their need for power through persuasion, intimidation, or control and domination over others, either physically or sexually. The result is that these individuals need a constant supply of others that they can feel power over. This thirst for power can become insatiable leading to an endless search for victims.

In order to physically or sexually abuse others the abuser needs to dehumanise the victim, not realising that he or she is also personally dehumanised in the process. This has vampire like overtones whereby the abuser feeds on the life force, purity and innocence of the victim to salve his or her own sadistic and sinful behaviour. As the life force is sucked out of them, the victim is left feeling empty. In contrast the abuser's life force is temporarily restored only for it to dissipate leading to repeated acts of sexual or physical abuse.

Secondary perpetrators

Those who knew and did nothing

Many survivors of RSA feel that those that knew about the abuse and did nothing colluded consciously or unconsciously with the abuser. Many survivors report being removed from classrooms and dormitories for no reason and returning in a distressed state yet other priests, ministers or nuns did not question, challenge or stop this. Similarly, housekeepers who saw children being invited into the abuser's home, or bedroom, and who changed soiled sheets nevertheless remained silent. Members of the faith community who had suspicions or heard stories of RSA also closed their eyes and ears, as did the families of some victims, even after a disclosure was made.

This attests to the power of religious institutions in which the laity, and other clergy fear the consequences of challenging the integrity of priests or ministers. The need to protect and idealise priests and ministers becomes paramount especially if this ensures spiritual development and salvation. As forgiveness is one of the fundamental principles of religious doctrine, those who knew but did nothing feel that to be good Christians they had to forgive abusers rather than hold them to account for RSA.

Religious institutions

Abusers do not abuse in isolation and are often supported, consciously or unconsciously by the institution they belong to. As a result many survivors of RSA see religious institutions as secondary perpetrators, or accomplices. Many such survivors believe that Church institutions and faith leaders are co-conspirators in RSA in neglecting their duty of care to the most vulnerable, both at the time of abuse and when allegations are made. They also feel wounded by how allegations have been handled, or mishandled and how the protection of the abuser has been prioritised over the needs of victims and survivors. The lack of open communication, secrecy and lack of accountability only adds to survivors' sense of betrayal and represents secondary traumatisation.

The lack of an appropriate response from faith leaders, and in particular the RC Church, can be seen as a form of malignant institutional narcissism in which the church believes itself to be so powerful that it is above the law. This is encapsulated in the RC Church and canon law which overrides criminal law. Institutional narcissism is also seen in the emphasis on protecting the reputation and perfection of the Church and Pope at all costs. To ensure this, priests, bishops and cardinals are required to take a vow of silence to keep secret anything that might bring harm or scandal to the Church, including the sexual abuse of children. If a priest or minister dares to break this vow of silence to speak out on behalf of victims, he or she is silenced, relocated or discredited. Like Narcissus, the need to be seen as perfect is paramount.

It is critical that faith leaders recognise their lack of understanding and accept responsibility for their failure to protect. To restore faith and promote healthy physical, emotional, cognitive and spiritual development faith leaders need to ensure that they no longer indulge in institutional narcissism and acknowledge the harm done not just by the individual abuser but also the institution that failed to protect the most vulnerable.

Insurance companies

Insurance companies may also be considered secondary perpetrators in their role of protecting religious institutions from compensation claims. In trying to minimise claims and limit payouts, many insurance companies can appear ruthless and uncaring towards victims. In addition, it is likely that insurance companies drive the adoption of safeguarding procedures not through a desire to protect future victims, but for the purposes of compliance with insurance policies. This casts doubt on the motivation of the religious institution, giving rise to the suspicion that they implement safeguarding procedures purely for insurance purposes rather than out of compassion for the victim or survivor.

Some survivors also feel re-traumatised by the responses from faith communities and the legal system. The laity and faith communities often take their lead from their faith leaders, and may unwittingly cause harm by stigmatising victims and survivors. This is often extremely wounding as survivors feels excluded from their spiritual family. The legal system can also fail victims and survivors by not fully understanding the nature and dynamics of RSA and finding in favour of the abuser or religious institution, and not the victim.

Treatment of abusers

Treatment of abusers requires specialist evaluations and planning which cannot just be left to the church or faith leaders. Therapeutic treatment and interventions need to be administered by specialist clinicians unswayed by religious considerations preferably in secular treatment centres. While pastoral treatment is valuable in terms of the spiritual dimension it is not sufficient to address all the dynamics involved in sexual offending against children and adults. The treatment of sexual offenders is extremely complex and difficult, with no known cure. As most sex offenders and sexual abusers of children can be taught to manage their sexual predilections, it is essential that treatment also addresses the need for power and control which underpins sexual offending.

Given that there is currently no effective cure for CSA, it is critical that abusers are consistently monitored by either faith leaders or the criminal justice system, or both. This is especially the case if they are laicised, or released from ecclesiastical control and returned to the community without criminal intervention. Laicisation without such consequences often exacerbates the situation, especially if they are not monitored, as the offenders can continue to abuse within the community. In addition shame and isolation is known to increase the risk of re-offending.

Reparation and prevention can occur only when faith leaders take personal responsibility for their role in RSA. There has to be an end to making excuses, and this has to be evidenced by providing unreserved and genuine apologies that are supported by action (see **How faith leaders and religious institutions can help survivors to heal** on page 180). What can also help some survivors is to have a face-to-face, professionally-facilitated meeting with their abuser. Some survivors report that such a meeting can help them regain personal power through confronting their abuser.

In addition, to prevent RSA in the future, faith leaders need to face the problem head on and develop better screening to assess the psychological disturbance and personality characteristics of those entering the ministry. Furthermore the training of priests and faith leaders must include a more open dialogue on sex and sexuality from a secular as well as spiritual perspective.

The following section aims to increase awareness and understanding of how RSA impacts on victims and survivors. It is hoped that all readers will find this useful to deepen their understanding of the aftermath of RSA.

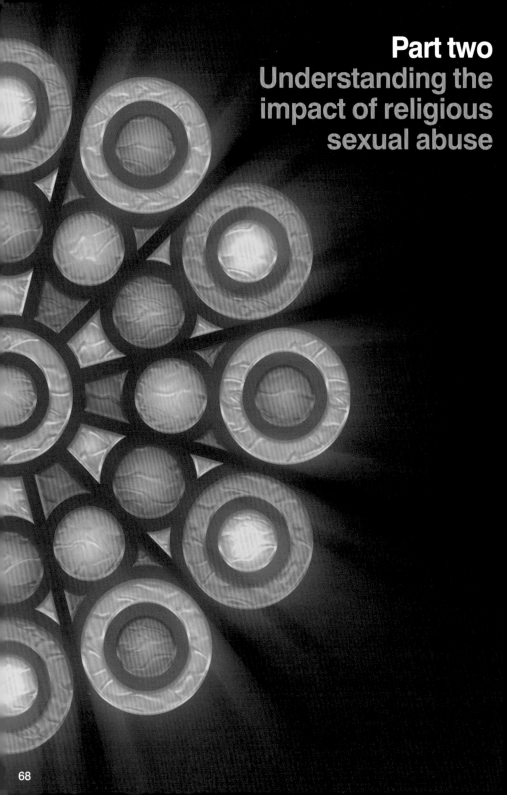

Part two
Understanding the
impact of religious
sexual abuse

6 The impact of religious sexual abuse

RSA impacts on the victim and later survivor in a number of significant ways. It can disrupt biological, psychological, emotional and intellectual functioning, as well as spiritual experiencing. To manage the trauma of RSA, survivors often disconnect from painful feelings and their abuse experiences. This disconnection from self can extend to disconnecting from others which can lead to difficulties in relating to others. Over time this can lead to a disconnection from the world and the spiritual self.

One of the biggest impacts is on the sense of control such as seen in traumatic stress reactions which are outside of conscious control. These are often very frightening and make the survivor feel as though they are going crazy. It is important to have an understanding of these trauma reactions and find a way of restoring control over them (see **Understanding religious sexual abuse as trauma** on page 78 and **Understanding trauma reactions** on page 87).

RSA can also erode the sense of personal power and control, distort reality, and give rise to a number of losses, especially loss of sexual pleasure, and loss of faith.

Factors in impact

It is important to acknowledge that RSA affects each individual differently. Some survivors will experience considerable difficulties while others may not feel particularly affected. This will depend on a variety of factors such as: age when the abuse occurred; gender; the relationship to the abuser; the frequency, duration and type of abuse; and the number of abusers and the degree of social support.

Age

The age of the victim at the time of the abuse is a highly significant factor. The younger the child the harder it will be to separate the metaphysical concept of God from God's representative on earth, namely the cleric committing the abuse. This is especially the case when the child is told that this is what God wants, or that this is what God does to those who obey, or defy him.[18]

Younger children are not able to reason symbolic and metaphysical concepts and so are more likely to internalise distorted beliefs and messages imposed by the abuser. This can lead doubts about the benevolence of God and cause greater spiritual injury whereby the survivor feels robbed of their faith and spiritual identity.

Gender

Gender is another crucial factor with research suggesting that more males than females experience RSA. Reports suggest that 80% of victims of RSA are boys and 20% are girls. However this only represents known cases of abuse and it may be that females are the silent majority of religious sexual. In terms of the sexual abuse of adults, females do seem to be more at risk, but equally this could be due to reporting rates with adult male victims less likely to report their sexual abuse. This is especially the case in those faiths and religions which deem homosexuality a sin.

The gender of the abuser will also have considerable impact. Sexual abuse by females is much more hidden and remains largely taboo. In the wider community, survivors of CSA by women find it much harder to disclose their abuse and are often not believed. RSA by nuns and female ministers leads victims and survivors feel less safe and to question perceptions around females as being more caring and nurturing.

The relationship to the abuser

The relationship of the child or adult to the abuser is also an important factor in impact. The more the abuser is a part of the victim's life, and the more he or she has invested in the abuser, the more damaging the sexual abuse becomes. If there are multiple abusers then the victim will experience more negative consequences.

The frequency, duration, and nature of the abuse

The frequency, duration, and nature of the abuse will also have an impact on the victims and survivor. The more frequent and prolonged the abuse, the more likely it is that the victim will experience traumatic reactions. This is also more likely if the sexual abuse involves oral, genital or anal rape, or is accompanied by violence and sadistic or ritualistic abuse.

Social support

There is considerable evidence that social support can significantly reduce the negative impact of abuse, both at the time of the abuse and in adulthood.[5] If the victim has access to support from family or friends they are more able to legitimise what has happened to them as abuse. Such social support is rarely available due to the secret nature of RSA. This means that victims often feel abandoned by families and friends, and those who should have protected them, including God.

Impact on sense of control and powerlessness

Like all forms of interpersonal abuse, RSA reduces survivors' sense of personal power and control. The lack of control is experienced both internally and externally. Trauma reactions that occur outside of conscious control can activate a range of bodily responses that seem uncontrollable. These can be terrifying in that they resemble the bodily reactions during the abuse (see **Understanding trauma reactions** on page 87). This can lead to a lack of trust in their bodily responses.

The loss of control and sense of powerlessness is also experienced in not feeling in charge of one's life. This is often seen in difficulties in psychosocial functioning and relationships. Problems in relationships can render survivors more vulnerable to re-victimisation and further sexual exploitation. Instead of harmony, relationships are often riddled with conflict as abuse dynamics of power and control are re-enacted.

Relationships become opportunities to replay, or test capacity for power and control. This can veer between passivity, submissiveness and crippling dependency, and aggression, dominance, and fierce independence. As a result, relationships become the arena to restore either personal power or reduce feelings of powerlessness.

Some survivors try to do this through active control of their social relationships by being controlling and demanding, while others become overly compliant and develop strategies to avoid conflict so they do not risk feeling overwhelmed and powerless. These survivors divert authority to external sources of control and seek sanctuary in dependency which replicates their abuse experience. Some survivors constantly switch between dominance and submission which can be confusing and exhausting for partners and friends.

Whichever position is taken it must be understood within the context of the abuse experience. Both positions use denial, dissociation and cognitive distortions to ward off painful emotions as a way of managing the abuse. This rollercoaster way of managing emotions is also often accompanied by substance abuse or compulsive behaviours which can give a temporary sense of power and control during times of vulnerability and stress.

Traumatic impact of religious sexual abuse

The impact of RSA – just like CSA – must be understood within a trauma

71

framework. There is considerable evidence that CSA can lead to a range of trauma reactions including post-traumatic stress disorder (PTSD) and complex post-traumatic stress disorder[5] (see **Understanding trauma reactions** on page 87). These complex trauma reactions are also seen in survivors of RSA.[4]

REMEMBER The impact of RSA is traumatic and must be understood within a complex trauma framework.

Common trauma reactions include **alterations in emotions** such as hyper-arousal, irritability, mood swings and preoccupation with suicide; **changes in consciousness** such as flashbacks, intrusive memories and dissociative episodes; **alterations in self-perception** such as shame, guilt, self-blame and sense of helplessness and powerlessness; **chronic self-destructive behaviours** such as substance misuse and self-injury; **changes in relationships** in which dominance and compliance and approach and avoidance are used to regain a sense of power and control; and **alterations in systems of meaning** such as shattered assumptions about the world, lack of purpose in life, sense of hopelessness and loss of faith and spirituality.

These trauma reactions are further complicated in RSA which need to be considered. The spiritual injury associated with RSA and the loss of faith can lead to a range of theological conflicts and existential dilemmas. Survivors end up reluctant to feel, and fearing life and death – especially if they believe in an afterlife, where they might meet their abuser.

The existential impact of RSA is an invisible wound which, although hard to identify, significantly affects the way the survivor experiences the world. The world become drained of colour, the sky is no longer as blue, the sun seems less bright, birds sing with less exuberance and the sense of time becomes blurred between past, present and future. Reality becomes distorted and inverted wherein night is day and day is night, and nothing seems to be the way it appears – leading to an inability to trust self-perception and experiencing.[17]

The impact of secondary traumatisation

In addition to the original trauma, many survivors are re-traumatised by insensitive responses from religious institutions. They can also be further traumatised by negative and hostile reactions from their families, other faith members and the wider community, as well as insurance companies and the criminal justice system. These secondary traumas re-trigger the original trauma which intensifies trauma reactions. As these become more overwhelming, the survivor feels increasingly out of control and less able to cope. In attempting to restore control the survivor may shut down or seek escape through self-medication such as alcohol, drugs, food, exercise, gambling, sex or shopping. For some survivors the only escape is suicide.

The physical impact of RSA

The physical impact of RSA results in trauma reactions that release stress hormones such as cortisol into the body (see **Understanding religious sexual abuse as trauma** on page 78). Prolonged release of stress hormones can impair physical health and give rise to stress-related illnesses. Survivors often do not recognise that compromised health is strongly associated with the RSA. In making this link, and finding ways to regulate their physiological arousal and traumatic stress responses, they can significantly reduce the impact of RSA on their physical health and prevent chronic fatigue.

READ *The Warrior Within* has more information about managing reactions to trauma.

Impact on psychosocial functioning

The terror of RSA and the inability to process the experiences has a huge impact on psychosocial functioning. As the victim and survivor's resources are diverted to managing overwhelming trauma reactions, there is often little energy left for cognitive processing and gaining mastery over other skills. This is often seen in not reaching educational or academic potential. As the victim is preoccupied by the abuse experience they are not able to concentrate or focus sufficiently on educational attainment. This is made worse if they are at a religious or faith school, and their abuser is on the teaching staff. Many survivors who were physically and/or sexually abused in faith schools or religious institutions report that they were too terrified to learn.

This legacy often extends into adulthood preventing them from going to college, or university or to take vocational courses. This has a significant impact on access to career and employment opportunities. Survivors who have not reached their educational or career potential often believe – falsely – that they are stupid and inadequate, which further contributes to their sense of shame. In reality, the majority are highly intelligent and more than capable, but do not realise that their lack of attainment is linked to RSA.

Some survivors find sanctuary and escape in educational and academic pursuits, or throw themselves into successful careers. Such survivors often appear as highly confident and functional in their careers although this is not always easily translated to their personal life or relationships. The ability to compartmentalise the RSA, and shut off from it allows them to concentrate and focus on psychosocial functioning. However, the impact of the RSA will seek expression and is more likely to emerge in personal relationships making these a source of conflict.

Impact on the self

RSA has considerable impact on the self and self-perception. Many survivors suffer from low self-esteem and a crippling lack of self-worth. They also feel a deep sense of shame especially if the abuser blamed them for the abuse. If the survivor became aroused, or responded to sexual touching, they may feel an increased sense of shame and self-blame as they feel their body betrayed them. These negative self-perceptions lead to negative thoughts about the self, such as '**I deserved to be abused**' or '**I am sinful, evil or wicked**'. Such self-loathing leads many

survivors to punish themselves through self-harming behaviours.

The lack of control over their body and overwhelming sensations and feelings can further lead some survivors to disconnect from the self as a way to avoid experiencing emotions. They often split off all feelings, especially pleasurable ones, through the process of dissociation. In locking away their feelings they reduce their ability to be fully in contact with their experiences, not realising that this can make them vulnerable to further re-victimisation and abuse.

Impact on relationships

The sense of shame, betrayal and stigmatisation leads to withdrawal and social isolation. This makes it hard for survivors to reach out to others for fear of being abused or betrayed again. Although the survivor wants to be loved and cared for, closeness and intimacy is associated with fear and anxiety. This results in '**approach and avoid**' behaviours in which the survivor wants to be visible and yet needs to hide and become invisible. This makes it hard to enter fulfilling relationships which can lead to a deep sense of loneliness. Some survivors avoid relationships altogether, or they have relationships that are so full of conflict that they consistently fail. Some survivors are fortunate in finding a stable loving relationship that is sustaining which makes the impact of RSA easier to manage.

Impact on sexuality

The mixed message around shame, abstinence and sexual abuse is a source of great confusion for many victims and survivors. On the one hand, they are conditioned to believe that sexuality, sexual thoughts and actions are shameful and sinful and yet the uncontrolled sexual appetites of the abuser are permitted. This double bind makes it hard for the victim or survivor to make sense of what it means to be sexual. This is often reflected in their own ambivalence around sex and sexuality in adulthood.

The impact on survivors fluctuates between a compulsive need to be sexual, as proof that their sexuality has not been compromised, and an avoidance of anything sexual. Compulsive sexual behaviour is most commonly seen in sexual addiction which is characterised by an endless pursuit of multiple sexual partners. In contrast, sexual avoidance, or sexual anorexia, is facilitated by focusing on the flaws of partners as an excuse to remain sexually unavailable. This can evolve into rigid sexual intolerance, condemnation of others, and religious based moral judgements about sexuality.

The impact of loss

There are many losses associated with RSA, both actual and symbolic. There is the loss of childhood and right to protection, the loss of family and friends through shame and isolation, and the loss of the sense of achievement educationally or professionally. Survivors also feel a sense of loss around their physical and mental well-being and their capacity to have healthy relationships, as well as their sexuality, faith and spirituality. Each survivor will experience a range of losses unique to them, and these need to be grieved as part of the healing process. It is through the mourning of these losses that the survivor can integrate the losses and move towards healing.

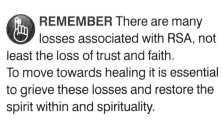

READ *The Warrior Within* has more information about managing reactions to grief and loss.

REMEMBER There are many losses associated with RSA, not least the loss of trust and faith. To move towards healing it is essential to grieve these losses and restore the spirit within and spirituality.

Impact on spirituality

The spiritual injury accompanying RSA is deeply wounding, not just to victims and survivors but also to families, friends, partners and the wider community, as well as to other non-offending clergy. It can lead to the loss of faith, loss of a spiritual family and loss of identity. Some survivors lose their belief in God which can lead to a alienation and an aching sense of aloneness and spiritual disengagement. Some survivors may try to fill this spiritual vacuum with alcohol, drugs, violence or sexual promiscuity.

Many survivors feel ashamed of their loss of faith, and continue to attend their place of worship. However they often feel false and hypocritical as they go through religious rituals feeling increasingly empty as their integrity is compromised. Some survivors do not lose their faith in God, but lose trust in religious institutions and their official representatives.

Forgiveness becomes conflicted, which is further source of despair for some survivors. Many faiths emphasise the importance of forgiveness for healing, and yet some survivors may not feel able to forgive. Moreover, if forgiveness is through religious practice, such as the confessional in the RC Church,

survivors could be at risk of being abused and shamed again. In religions that believe in an afterlife, forgiveness is a particular source of terror because if the abuser is forgiven the survivor will be condemned to meet them in the afterlife. This creates enormous anxiety around whether there will be protection from abuse in the afterlife. Some survivors so desperately fear meeting their abuser in the afterlife that they do all in their power to avoid entry into heaven. This fear of life and death creates significant existential anxiety.[18]

Prayer and contemplation are also compromised in RSA. The negative associations around the rituals of prayer and worship make it hard to engage in them, or to truly believe in their value. Many survivors prayed and appealed to God to make the abuse stop, to no avail. These unanswered prayers have left many survivors feeling abandoned by God. As a result prayers are seen as hollow, which is why many survivors do not feel that the prayers offered by faith leaders in response to RSA are sufficient for healing.

Loss of faith also results in shattered assumptions about the world, the meaning of life in the here and after, and a loss of purpose. This, along with the traumatic effects of RSA, can lead to a disconnection from self, others and the world. While this is devastating for many, it is possible to heal. To do this requires an acknowledgement of the traumatic impact of RSA and sensitive responses to the pain and harm caused (see **Healing and support for survivors** on page 179). When the spirit within is revived and allowed to emerge, it is possible to reclaim personal faith and spirituality to allow for post-traumatic growth.

The following chapters will explore the impact of RSA in more detail and depth. Those readers familiar with *The Warrior Within* may wish to skip these and go on to **part three**. Readers not familiar with *The Warrior Within* will find these chapters helpful to gain a deeper understanding of the effects of RSA.

READ *The Warrior Within* has exercise and activities to aid recovery from the effects of RSA.

WARNING If reading the book triggers overwhelming feelings and trauma reactions, stop reading and do something that is comforting and grounding.

7 Understanding religious sexual abuse as trauma

Trauma is usually defined as an overwhelming threat to life, serious injury or physical integrity involving intense fear, helplessness or horror. Trauma consists of a single event or multiple and repeated traumatic events. RSA abuse commonly consists of repeated traumatic experiences over prolonged periods of time usually involving multiple violations such as sexual assaults, emotional or physical abuse, and the distortion of reality.

In order to understand survivor's reactions to trauma it is important to have some knowledge of how the body responds to trauma. This section will include some scientific information which can appear quite complex to begin with.

What makes RSA traumatic

What makes RSA traumatic is that the experience is emotionally and psychologically overwhelming and cannot be processed in the normal way. In addition to this, the sense of betrayal, secrecy and silence associated leads to fear, self-blame and shame. When the trauma occurs in childhood, is repeated and chronic and is characterised by entrapment, deception and distortion of reality, the child is not able to process the experiences and become vulnerable to complex traumatic stress reactions.

These include the symptoms of PTSD with additional features such as the ability to regulate emotions, alterations in self-identity and consciousness, and changes in meaning and spirituality.

To fully appreciate the impact of RSA it is crucial that it is understood within the context of trauma and complex trauma. This is a much more accurate reflection of the seriousness of RSA which has the capacity to traumatise victims and survivors. Even if the abuse was not violent, the distortion of reality and the anticipation of the abuse make it traumatic. It is not until RSA is classified as trauma – or complex trauma as CSA is – that the impact on victims will be legitimised and appropriate treatment provided. To gain greater understanding of the traumatic impact of RSA it is necessary to understand how the body reacts and responds to trauma.

The impact of trauma

RSA can consist of a single event, or repeated events over many years. It may be perpetrated by a single abuser or involve several perpetrators. Its impact differs for each survivor, and factors that affect it include: age; the type of abusive acts; the frequency and duration of abuse; and the relationship with the abuser. What is common to all, is the neurobiological, or bodily responses and psychological reactions that are activated to protect the individual from the trauma. These reactions are like an **emotional immune system** which instead of fighting invading bacteria or viruses, fights to protect from sexual, physical, emotional or psychological assault.

The emotional immune system

When in the presence of danger the brain releases a cascade of neurochemicals which start a complex chain of bodily reactions to protect the individual from trauma. These not only protect the person from the harmful effects of the trauma but also aid survival. The emotional immune system cushions the trauma, but cannot prevent it from happening or totally anaesthetise emotional pain.

In the presence of trauma, the individual is not in control of the emotional immune system, as it acts outside of conscious awareness just like the physical immune system. It is vital to acknowledge that any reactions during the trauma are outside of conscious control and therefore the person cannot be blamed for how they responded. Recognising this can vastly reduce survivor's feelings of shame, self-blame, or guilt which can often feel paralysing.

REMEMBER Reactions to trauma are outside of conscious control and survivors should not blame themselves for how they responded during the RSA.

The body's alarm system

In the presence of danger the body's **alarm system** is tripped and goes on red alert. Once on red alert the alarm system sends signals to the body to prepare for **fight**, **flight** or **freeze**. This sets off two crucial biological defence systems: the **sympathetic nervous system** and the **parasympathetic nervous system**. The sympathetic nervous system requires a high level energy necessary for fight or flight, while the parasympathetic nervous system slows down the heart and metabolic rate resulting in the freeze response.

The body's alarm system is regulated in an area of the brain called the **limbic system** by two structures: the **amygdala** and the **hippocampus**. The role of the amygdala is to detect threatening information through external senses such as touch, taste, sound, smell, or vision. The amygdala is responsible for determining whether the incoming stimuli is desirable, dangerous or benign. To maximise survival, this evaluation is instantaneous but crude and primitive. It does not use deeper analysis, reason or common sense. This is why it is often referred to as the '**fast and dirty route**'.

If the stimulus is life-threatening, stress hormones such as adrenaline and cortisol are released which send messages through the nervous system to the muscles and internal organs to either attack, run or play dead. The amygdala is highly sensitive to any danger and is easily activated to increase readiness to attack or defend (**fight**), run (**flight**) or submit (**freeze**).

In contrast to the 'fast and dirty' route of the amygdala, the hippocampus takes a much slower route. It evaluates the external threat through deeper analysis using conscious thought, memory, prior knowledge, reason, and logic. The hippocampus is also critical in laying down new memories and experiences. If the danger is truly life threatening, the hippocampus will send messages to continue with appropriate responses. If however the deeper analysis concludes that the stimuli are not dangerous it will send messages to deactivate the responses. These two structures usually work in concert to promote a balanced response to the situation.

Breakdown of the system

Breakdown of the emotional immune system occurs after prolonged and repeated trauma common in RSA. The feedback loop that controls these two systems malfunctions and floods the body with high levels of stress hormones. These hormones are highly toxic and are only designed to circulate for short periods of time so that the person can get to a place of safety or remain safe until the threat is over. In the case of RSA, where the child cannot fight or run to safety, the only option is to freeze or submit. This means that the stress hormones cannot be discharged and so remain in the system, which can have a number of negative consequences.

Evidence shows that high levels of cortisol that are not discharged can destroy brain cells which affects the function and size of the amygdala and hippocampus. This malfunction leads to increased fear and anger responses, as well as memory impairments.

Alarm system default setting constantly 'on'

When the brain and body is flooded with chronic levels of stress hormones, the hippocampus goes 'offline' and is unable to evaluate the degree of threat or danger accurately. It cannot assess whether the danger is internal or external, or whether the traumatic incident has passed or is continuing. As a result it cannot send the appropriate messages to the amygdala to deactivate the alarm system. This leads to the alarm being on constant red alert and the continued release of stress hormones.

This means that the body will continue to respond as though the trauma is on-going, even after the threat or sexual assault is over. As the alarm remains on a default setting of 'on', the person feels and acts as though he or she is being repeatedly traumatised. This leads to a heightened or continuous state of danger, known as **hyper-arousal**. This hyper-arousal forces stress hormones to continue to flood both body and brain, which results in the tyranny of post-traumatic stress responses.

Storing new memories

As the hippocampus does not regulate the alarm setting, or stop the release of chronic levels of stress hormones, its ability to store new memories is reduced. This means that the trauma is not stored within context or time, making it seem as though it is continuous and neverending. This in turn prevents the processing of the trauma, keeping it 'online' with the same vividness and intensity as when the actual assault happened.

Not being able to process the experience will make it harder for the person to store it as memory or recall it. This leads to fragmented and incomplete memories, or a lack of memory of the experience. It is for this reason that recovery from the trauma of RSA has to include bringing the hippocampus back 'online'. In doing this, it can resume regulation of the alarm system, accurately evaluate danger, and differentiate between internal and external threat.

READ *The Warrior Within* has more information about managing memories.

Damage to physical well-being

High levels of circulating stress hormones can also impact on physical well-being leading to hypertension, physical exhaustion, chronic fatigue syndrome (CFS), sleep problems, or digestive, respiratory and endocrine problems. In addition, chronic fear reactions and high levels of adrenaline can result in tsunami-like anger which cannot be expressed for fear of consequences. This means the survivor has to suppress his or her anger thereby creating even further stress. Hyper-arousal also affects the ability to concentrate and the processing of information, making it hard to gain meaning from the experience, and how it has impacted.

The role of the freeze response

While the emotional immune system activates three alternative reactions, fight, flight or freeze, in most cases of RSA there is only one option – to freeze. The freeze response is designed to conserve energy so that the person can escape when the danger is over. A young child cannot outrun or fight an adult effectively, so the only option is to freeze. While the freeze response protects the person from the greater threat of the consequences of fighting back or running away, it can feel like passive submission. This can lead to self-blame and guilt, making the survivor feel as though he or she was weak in not fighting back or running away.

In reality, a child can never fully escape the abuser, especially if they are a significant figure in the child's life such as a priest, nun, or lay minister who has power and authority over them. In the presence of the abuse the child is powerless and feels helpless. However, this feeling of submission often haunts the survivor, leaving the survivor feeling ashamed that he or she did not do more to prevent the sexual assault.

The freeze response is also designed to protect from fully experiencing the physical and emotional pain of the sexual assault itself. As the parasympathetic nervous system comes online, a sense of calmness descends on the brain. This slows everything down, and the body begins to feel numb in order to cushion the anticipated pain and the emotional terror of the sexual assault. Once the experience is over, these reactions fade and the stress hormones are discharged through movement.

In RSA in which there is no escape, these hormones cannot be discharged and so continue to circulate. This leads to increased numbness, paralysis, dissociation, psychological deadness or collapse. Thus the terror and distress cannot recede, instead growing stronger over time and causing even more intense distress, which the mind tries to block through avoidance or numbing

REMEMBER Freezing is **not** giving up or a passive act of submission. It protects from further harm and is not a conscious choice but part of the alarm system. It is activated when in danger with no means of escape.

Post-traumatic stress disorder and complex post-traumatic stress disorder

Approximately one third of survivors of repeated sexual assault develop symptoms of post-traumatic stress disorder (PTSD) or, more often, complex PTSD. The most common PTSD symptoms are divided into the following three categories:

- **persistent re-experiencing of the trauma** – this can be in the form of: recurrent and intrusive memories; recurrent distressing dreams or nightmares; reliving of the traumatic experience through flashbacks; or intense psychological reactivity to internal or external cues that resemble the trauma;

- **persistent avoidance of stimuli associated with the trauma and numbing of responsiveness** – this manifests as: avoidance of thoughts, feelings, activities, places and people associated with the trauma; an inability to recall aspects of the trauma; diminished interest in activities; feeling detached and estranged from others; a restricted range of feelings or emotional anaesthesia; and a sense of foreshortened future; and

- **persistent symptoms of increased arousal** such as: difficulty falling or staying asleep; irritability or outbursts of anger; difficulty concentrating; hyper-vigilance; and exaggerated startle response.

Continual re-experiencing of the trauma can be triggered by both internal and external cues. This means that even if the person is no longer in actual external danger, internal feelings and sensations may trigger a range of PTSD reactions. Given that the person is already in a high state of anxiety, it is easy to set off the highly sensitive alarm system on the basis of internal physiological arousal.

This can be potentially dangerous as the survivor may not be in touch with external reality and therefore cannot judge the degree of danger objectively which means that actual danger is not recognised, and safety cannot be fully evaluated or achieved. Given the nature of RSA, many survivor are vulnerable to developing complex PTSD.

In the case of complex PTSD the symptoms become chronic as they start to affect the very core of the self. Complex PTSD is commonly seen in people who have experienced prolonged sexual or physical abuse, or torture. Although complex PTSD is currently not recognised in psychiatric diagnostic manuals such as DSM-IV-Tr or the proposed DSM V as a distinct category, it is a more accurate reflection of the range of symptoms seen in survivors of CSA and RSA.

Like PTSD, complex PTSD results in hyper-arousal, and powerful out-of-control physiological reactions to emotionally evocative experiences, and difficulties in calming or soothing these. This results in difficulties in managing anger, fear and sadness. It also impacts on how individuals think and feel about themselves, and how they relate to others. Complex PTSD can also result in a distortion of reality awareness, stigmatisation and a deep sense of shame.

In addition to the many PTSD symptoms, complex PTSD also includes:

- **difficulties in regulating emotions** with extreme emotional reactivity and difficulty in calming these;

- **chronic destructive behaviour** such as drug and alcohol abuse, eating disorders, risky sexual behaviours, self- injury and suicidal behaviour;

- **somatisation** in which psychological pain manifests as physical pain;

- **alterations in relationship to the self**, including shame, self-hatred and self-loathing.

- **alterations in relationships with others** including difficulty functioning at work, romantic and marital relationships, difficulties with parenting, social isolation, and low perceptions of social support; and

- **loss of faith and sustaining beliefs** including loss of spirituality.

To manage such strong reactions survivors commonly try to avoid all feelings, even pleasurable ones, and withdraw from others leading to social isolation. In order to avoid shame, they retreat from the world and feel as though they live in a bubble. One of the most potent features of complex PTSD is changes in meaning and belief system. This is especially the case in RSA, in which religion and faith are manipulated and eroded by the abuser leading to changes in spirituality.

READ *The Warrior Within* has more information about PTSD and complex PTSD.

PTSD and complex PTSD can produce a range of other psychological disorders, especially anxiety disorders such as **agoraphobia** and **social** phobia, depression, obsessive compulsive disorder, borderline personality disorder and chronic fatigue syndrome. It can also give rise to a number of physical complaints including headaches, irritable bowel syndrome, and unexplained aches and pains which are all ways in which the body expresses trauma and emotional distress.

Distortion of reality

Religious sexual abuse can also disrupt sensory perception, whereby internal and external reality is so distorted that the survivor is fooled into thinking that danger is present when it is not, and vice-versa. As trauma reactions are beyond conscious control, survivors commonly feel betrayed by their bodies, making it even harder to trust themselves or their reality. This lack of trust emphasises the need to avoid feelings, people and certain situations which reinforces the sense of alienation from self and others. An important part of recovery from RSA is to restore reality through more accurate sensory perception and interpretation. This will enable the survivor to gain a better balance between internal subjective reality and external objective reality.

External reality is monitored by the sensory system which uses sight,

sound, smell, touch and taste, while internal reality is monitored by sensations such as heartbeat, pulse rate, muscle tension, and breathing. In addition, **proprioception** – how the body monitors its location in space – is necessary to retain a sense of bodily self. The distortion of external and internal reality is most noticeable when the abuser makes the child or adult feel special, or tells them that what is happening is pleasurable despite feelings of shame or revulsion. This can cause tremendous confusion especially when what is happening is unpleasant, or shameful, and yet the body responds physically with sexual pleasure.

Such distortion of reality can lead the child to believe that sexual abuse is normal, or that it has had no harmful or damaging effects. If the survivor has incorporated this belief, it is likely that the abuser deliberately distorted his or her reality by normalising the abuse, making it a part of God's will, or by performing sexual acts that he or she experienced as pleasurable. This will have minimised the perception of the traumatising effects of RSA making it harder to legitimise it and recover from it.

REMEMBER Even if the RSA was subtle and non-violent it can still be traumatising and confusing in distorting reality, especially if religious beliefs are used to groom and manipulate the child or adult.

The following two chapters aim to increase understanding of the loss of control experienced by survivors and how this can be restored, and the range of trauma reactions.

READ *The Warrior Within* has more information about managing the symptoms of trauma.

ONLINE The One in Four website has a selection of relevant exercises and activities to help manage symptoms of trauma.

8 Understanding trauma reactions

Trauma impacts differently on each individual and are normal biological responses to overwhelming threat in which escape is not possible. Post-traumatic stress reactions are largely due to avoidance or lack of emotional processing which means they are not fully integrated. There is considerable evidence which shows that when survivors avoid feelings or thoughts, these will intensify and are twice as likely to recur, generating even more distress.

There are number of common post-traumatic stress reactions that are associated with trauma which survivors need to be aware of in order to understand how RSA has affected them. The most common trauma reactions associated with RSA are **hyper-arousal**, **hyper-vigilance**, **avoidance** and **loss of control**.

Hyper-arousal

Hyper-arousal is when the survivor is in a constant of state of high alert due to the increased levels of stress hormones such as adrenaline and cortisol flooding the body, which results in feelings of restlessness, anxiety, irritability, or out of control emotions. High levels of adrenaline lead to physiological responses such as increased heart rate, palpitations, and sweating. It is also associated with episodes of uncontrollable anger or rage, and wild mood swings when the nervous system becomes overloaded with stress hormones and the survivor swings between high levels of agitation and total exhaustion.

As the emotional alarm system is on high alert, the survivor's energy and resources are diverted to survival mechanisms and to manage stress reactions. Such high arousal makes it harder to think clearly, evaluate external or internal cues accurately, process or make sense of the experience. This makes it harder to regulate emotional reactions making it difficult to maintain control over the body, thoughts or feelings.

Hyper-arousal can also disrupt sleep, rest and eating patterns which prevents the body from being able to recuperate through rest and healthy nourishment which can result in exhaustion and chronic fatigue. Some survivors get so accustomed to being in a state of hyper-arousal that they cannot relax and often pursue stressful activities through confrontation, arguments, or punishing work schedules.

As hyper-arousal is normalised the survivor loses any conscious awareness of its origins, or its link to abuse. Knowing the origins of hyper-arousal – and recognising it is not a sign of going 'crazy' – is the first step in taking control. It is vital to release the trapped energy and discharge the high levels of stress hormones so that the body can rest and reset the emotional alarm system.

REMEMBER Post traumatic stress reactions occur outside of conscious awareness and are not signs of going 'crazy'.

READ *The Warrior Within* has more information about how to release stress hormones through movement and exercise.

Hyper-vigilance

Hyper-vigilance, which is a symptom of hyper-arousal, makes it hard to relax. In hyper-vigilance, survivors constantly anticipate threat and are on high alert to monitor the environment for any signs of danger. This is can lead to an increased **startle-response** in which the survivor is in a constant state of watchfulness and jumps at any loud noise or stimuli. Alternatively, some survivors become so preoccupied by internal sensations that they '**tune out**' from the environment, and become hypo-vigilant. This detachment and dissociation puts the survivor at risk of threat as he or she is unable to identify external dangers.

Avoidance

One way of managing trauma is through avoidance. This can include avoidance of trauma cues, people, places or activities associated with the trauma including intimacy and sexual relationships. All of these can lead to social isolation and a deep sense of aloneness. Some survivors avoid feelings and thoughts through numbing or dissociation as a form of anaesthesia. Alternatively, feelings and thoughts are avoided through distractions, sleep, watching mindless television, relentless work schedules or keeping busy at all times. Survivors of RSA also find it hard to visit places of worship, or tolerate being in the presence of any faith related iconography.

Survivors also avoid emotions through the soothing or numbing effects of food, alcohol, drugs, or self-injury. While distractions and blocks provide short-term relief, avoidance actually intensifies negative feelings and thoughts. Every time these are avoided they become '**stamped in**' as they remain unprocessed and unintegrated.

Loss of control

As post-traumatic stress reactions occur outside of conscious awareness the survivor is unable to control them.

This loss of control is not just over negative emotions but can radiate out to pleasurable feelings and experiences. As a result even pleasurable feelings or activities which share the same internal sensations as fear are experienced as dangerous and can set off the emotional alarm system.

To regain control of emotions and trauma reactions survivors may resort to self-injury or self-medication through food, alcohol or substance misuse, sex addiction, or gambling (see **Understanding harmful behaviours: self-harm and self-medication** on page 104). Some survivors use such behaviours to dissociate, numb or release the emotional or psychological pain. Another way to restore power and control is through trying to control others. This usually leads to power struggles in relationships which re-enact the power dynamic associated with RSA. To triumph over trauma, some survivors will seek to control others, or control their environment through obsessive compulsive behaviour. Other survivors are so used to feeling powerless that they unconsciously seek relationships in which they can submit themselves to a more powerful, dominant partner.

Whichever methods are used to regulate emotional distress, these are commonly accompanied by chronic feelings of ineffectiveness, shame, despair or hopelessness and feeling permanently damaged. Ultimately such methods can put the survivor at risk of further harm and re-traumatisation. In addition, distorted perceptions which result in negative thoughts such as self- blame, self-loathing and shame can lead to defensive tactics such as avoidance or hostility, and a lack of belief in a safe or benign world.

Restoring control

Loss of control is a significant effect of RSA This includes loss of control over feelings, thoughts, actions and behaviour as well as the body. In addition, the RSA reduces control over autonomy and the survivors perception of reality. Over time, the ability to make informed choices and live life to the full becomes limited. A key aspect of recovery is to regain control over emotional reactions and sense of reality.

Resetting the emotional alarm system is vital to regaining control and limiting the impact of trauma reactions. This means changing the default setting, so that the alarm is not so easily tripped. This will allow the crucial areas of the brain to come back online and restore physical and emotional balance. Deep breathing and reducing stress levels will restore a sense of safety and reinforce control over traumatic reactions.

Feeling more in control

Regulating emotions will help survivors to feel more in control of them. It can help to find healthier substitutes to manage trauma, such as grounding techniques and physical exercise which will help to the survivor to reconnect to his or her body. This will decrease dependency on external sources of comfort such as food, alcohol, drugs or other people to regulate emotional distress. This can be immensely liberating as the survivor reclaims trust in him or herself and control over previously uncontrollable reactions.

REMEMBER In RSA, someone else controls the survivor's body, thoughts, feelings, and behaviour, as well as their reality, preventing them from acting autonomously. To recover it is vital to restore control so that survivors can choose what is right for them.

Restoring control over trauma reactions necessitates a full understanding and processing of the trauma and abuse experiences. Avoiding distressing sensations and feelings can result in a

vicious cycle. The emotional content of flashbacks, nightmares, and intrusive memories, or suppressed, or moved away from conscious thought and as such remain as raw as when you first experienced them. Since they were not processed they are twice as likely to re-emerge with greater intensity and vividness.

REMEMBER Avoiding or suppressing traumatic experiences means they are twice as likely to recur with greater intensity and vividness

Understanding feelings

Emotions and feelings are essentially signals and communications about experiences, which represent a rich database. They are an essential part of experiencing and help individuals to understand themselves. While it is important to listen to emotions it is not always necessary to act upon them. Suppressing emotions requires considerable psychological energy and can cause considerable pressure and reduces the sense of well-being.

REMEMBER Feelings are valuable signals that need to be attended and listened to. They are not facts and do not have to be acted upon.

Emotional processing helps to balance emotions and develop internal harmony. Many survivors of RSA are so overwhelmed by their emotions that they become hyper-aroused leading to irritability, extreme mood swings and uncontrolled outbursts of anger. This **hyper-arousal** can create an emotional rollercoaster for both survivors and anyone in their orbit. Not only are such uncontrolled emotional outbursts exhausting, they tend to prevent getting close to others, and generate hostility and aggression.

In contrast, some survivors avoid all feelings and emotions and become shut down. This usually involves disengaging from self and others, and an unshakeable sense of detachment, or dissociation. This dissociation and disengagement, or **hypo-vigilance** renders the survivor vulnerable to further re-traumatisation as they are not able to recognise danger in the external world.

It is vital to restore the natural balance of feelings by recognising that feelings ebb and flow and do eventually subside. If the natural flow of emotion is blocked, the survivor will lose contact with the natural, biological regulation of emotions. It is crucial that survivors of RSA are able to restore balance and harmony to their emotions through being able to regulate them.

READ *The Warrior Within* has a range of exercises and activities to help with the regulation of emotions.

Balancing emotions enables the flow of positive feelings and restores spontaneity, richness and colour to emotional experiences. Emotional harmony can improve the functioning of the emotional immune system and reduce being flooded with uncontrollable, tsunami like emotions. It will also restore a sense of control. This is critical as during RSA the child, or adult does not have control over what is happening to them, or how their body responds.

Restoring control over feelings and the body is extremely empowering as the survivor regains a sense of taking charge of his or her life. Mastering control over emotions also helps when processing the traumatic impact of RSA and allow the survivor to become more aware of their banished, or suppressed needs. Processing the trauma and accompanying emotions will release the energy needed to deal with all aspects of the trauma while opening up new creative opportunities for your life.

Restoring reality

Processing the trauma and restoring control over emotions will also free up energy to challenge distorted perceptions and beliefs. Survivors who are still in survival mode and consumed with uncontrollable feelings have little or no energy to challenge the distorted beliefs imposed by the abuser. Once they regain control over traumatic reactions and release trapped energy, survivors can begin to explore distorted perceptions and restore their reality. This will allow them to identify how they were manipulated by the abuser and how he or she contaminated their religious beliefs and faith in God.

 WARNING Emotional processing can only begin once the survivor is safe, has mastered grounding and breathing techniques, and has gained confidence in using them to soothe and calm.

Breathing

Breathing fully and deeply soothes, calms and restores control. All too often, survivors of RSA breathe shallowly or quickly as a response to heightened anxiety. As the body takes in less oxygen, panic sets in – which triggers the emotional alarm system. As fear responses are activated, dizziness and shakiness takes over, which only serves to increase panic. Breathing more slowly and more deeply to increase the intake of oxygen will decrease anxiety and reduce the risk of panic attacks.

READ *The Warrior Within* has a range of breathing exercises.

Bodily sensations

Breathing helps to reconnect to the body making the survivor more aware of bodily sensations. This is vital as it enables the survivor to identify internal cues more precisely and objectively, and prevent internal stimuli overriding current external reality. This allow survivors to be more in touch with reality. It also enables the survivor to discriminate between bodily sensations. Sensations of fear and pleasure have common aspects of physical arousal, causing confusion in people whose emotional processing has been altered.

Excitement, pleasure, physical exertion and fear all involve an accelerated heart rate, which can trigger reminders of the traumatic experience. As a result, many survivors of RSA are unable to experience or tolerate pleasurable sensations in their body as the increased heart resembles the fear and anxiety associated with the sexual abuse. Consequently, many survivors of RSA actively avoid positive feelings or pleasure to minimise triggering traumatic fear responses.

REMEMBER To be truly safe and protected from danger survivors must remain in touch with both internal and external reality.

Tolerating pleasurable sensations allows the survivor to enjoy the full spectrum of bodily sensations including pleasure and relaxation, rather than just panic and pain. Relaxation is often difficult for survivors as the release of tension reduces alertness, or **hyper-vigilance** making them feel more vulnerable. As relaxation can induce fear, panic, nausea or disorientation in some survivors, they may need to find alternative ways of staying in contact with the body such as muscle tensing.

READ *The Warrior Within* explains various methods and exercises to help stay in contact with the body.

Releasing emotions

Emotional regulation allows survivors to release feelings and emotions more effectively. A very good way of achieving this is through physical activities such as martial arts, tai chi, kick-boxing, playing tennis, squash, jogging, riding a bike, or swimming. Emotions can also be discharged by listening to invigorating music, drumming, dancing, vigorous cleaning, throwing bottles

into a bottle bank, tearing newspaper, punching or screaming into a pillow or cushion. To minimise the risk of harm, these must always be released in a safe, contained environment.

READ *The Warrior Within* explains various methods and exercises to help release emotions.

Grounding techniques

Grounding techniques can help to regain control over traumatic aftershocks it is helpful to find activities that help to keep the survivor in the present and connected to his or her body. There are a number of grounding techniques that are useful to manage the traumatic afters effects of RSA, and which reinforce feelings of safety and security. Grounding techniques are particularly useful to manage a number of traumatic aftershocks such as anxiety, intrusive memories, flashbacks, dissociation, and panic attacks which will be explored in the next chapter.

READ *The Warrior Within* has more information about grounding techniques and their uses.

Mindfulness

Mindfulness is an excellent strategy that helps with grounding by tracking sensations, thoughts, and emotions to enable greater awareness and control over the body and physical being. Mindfulness enables the survivor to become more consciously aware of current feelings, thoughts and experiencing without judging these. This keeps the channels of communication open between mind and body making it easier to link experiences. It also allows the survivor to restore reality by trusting his or her subjective experience rather than relying on others to define these a the abuser did.

External stimuli

Regulating and balancing exposure to external stimuli such as television, music, reading or conversation is helpful to restore inner peace and calm. Reducing the sensory overload from excessive external stimuli will regulate the emotional alarm system and prevent over-arousal. Survivors can balance the build-up of external stimuli by regularly taking time to sit and focus on just being present.

The role of stress

Given the heightened level of arousal and stress experienced by many RSA survivors, it is crucial to find as many ways as possible to reduce stress. Simplifying and streamlining daily routines and rituals such as meal times and bedtimes can reduce stress and restore a sense of control. In addition, having more structure in the survivor's daily life counteracts the chaos that trauma has brought. Regular meal times, and a healthy balance between relaxation, exercise and sleep is also important to manage stress and restore control over everyday life.

 READ *The Warrior Within* has more information about ways that you can reduce stress.

The stress associated with RSA can lead some survivors to crave stress in their adult life. There is evidence that early childhood stress can make some children vulnerable to seeking stress in adulthood.[5] This is partly due to familiarity, and partly due to becoming accustomed to an over-aroused and emotional life. The hormones released during stress, in particular adrenaline can become addictive leading some survivors of RSA to seek stressful situations. It is also a way of feeling more alive which is appealing to some survivors, especially those that believe themselves to be emotionally dead.

Releasing stress hormones through physical exercise is an extremely efficient method of maintaining a connection to the here and now instead of the past. It also counteracts the response by discharging trapped energy by sending a message to the brain to switch off the alarm system as the trauma has passed. Releasing built up stress hormones which have become toxic, will renew energy levels and regulate current stress.

Exercise releases good hormones, known as **endorphins** into the brain, so when the stress hormones are expunged and new ones released a sense of well-being spreads throughout the body. A further benefit of physical exercise is the increase in muscle tone. There is research that shows that increased muscular strength promotes greater emotional strength, and that improving muscle tone can be better than relaxation in dealing with trauma. Physical exercise also helps to regulate breathing and restore control over the body. Older survivors will need to choose their preferred form of exercise carefully so as not over stretch themselves.

READ *The Warrior Within* has more information about the use of physical exercise to help manage stress.

WARNING Before engaging in regular physical exercise it is important to seek medical advice.

Altering the emotional alarm system

Altering the emotional alarm system through breathing, grounding techniques and physical exercise restores control and allows for the release of trapped energy which indicates that the trauma is over and **freezing** is no longer necessary. Restoring control is the first step to recovery as it will reset the emotional alarm setting making it easier to regulate emotions and trauma reactions. This will prove invaluable for managing some of the classic trauma reactions such as flashbacks, nightmares and intrusive memories, which will be addressed in the next chapter.

WARNING Strenuous exercise which increases heart rate and respiration can mimic the arousal during sexual abuse which can trigger trauma reactions.

9 Understanding flashbacks, panic attacks, nightmares, intrusive memories and dissociation

Flashbacks, **nightmares**, **panic attacks**, **intrusive memories** and **dissociation** are the aftershocks of trauma, increasing feelings of helplessness because they can occur at any time. Because they are spontaneous, the fear of them can leave survivors of RSA feeling paralysed, incapable of leaving the house or even sleeping. To manage these trauma reactions, survivors need to understand them and regain control over them. Emotional processing, breathing and grounding techniques discussed in the previous chapter will help to restore control. To help the survivor to manage these it is important to understand the function of these trauma reactions and the cues that can trigger them.

READ *The Warrior Within* has a range of grounding techniques and action plans to help manage flashbacks, nightmares, panic attacks, intrusive memories and dissociation.

ONLINE The One in Four website has a range of grounding techniques and action plans to help manage flashbacks, nightmares, panic attacks, intrusive memories and dissociation.

Understanding flashbacks

Flashbacks are very intense and vivid recollections of traumatic experiences that have not been fully processed and integrated into the survivor's memory system. Flashbacks are essentially just that – flashbacks to the past. They are unprocessed experiences that manifest as extremely vivid and intense sensory memories. They are usually accompanied with intense physiological arousal such as increased heart rate, palpitations, constricted breathing, sweating, muscle tension and an overwhelming sense of terror. These physiological responses are the same as the physiological arousal at the time of the sexual abuse and activate the same cascade of biochemicals and stress hormones as the original trauma. As the intensity resembles the abuse experience, survivors feel as though the sexual abuse is happening to them all over again in the present.

During the flashback the body often takes on the same posture and survival reactions such as freezing, cowering and submission. However, despite mimicking the trauma, flashbacks do not represent what is actually happening in the present. They are powerful signs that parts of the trauma have not been dealt with properly or incorporated into memory.

 **REMEMBER** Flashbacks are very intense and vivid

recollections of traumatic experiences that have not been fully processed and integrated into the survivor's memory system.

Recognising flashbacks and identifying the sensory cues that trigger them is the first step in dealing with flashbacks. These sensory cues can come through any one of the sensory channels: smell, sound, sight, taste, or touch. Each survivor will have a different set of triggers depending on their experience. It is important to identify the unique triggers so as to prepare for the flashback and find ways to prevent these from being activated.

Common triggers for flashbacks

Common triggers for flashbacks in survivors of RSA usually include sights, sounds and smells that are associated with religious practices, rituals or icons. In the case of visual cues, these tend to include any visual stimuli associated with the abuse, such as the colour of the robes worn by the abuser or the sights associated with the place in which the RSA took place. Survivors are abused in range of settings including places of worship, religious institutions, schools, in cars, in houses including their own homes. Each of these will all have specific sensory cue associated with them.

If the RSA occurred in a place of worship, **sights** such as lighted candles, sun streaming in through stained glass windows, religious iconography such as the cross, altar, pulpit, rosary, prayer mat, incense burner, chalices or any one of a range of religious images can become triggers. The sight of the confessional, altar or choir boys, or holy book can also be powerful cues that can trigger flashbacks.

In the case of **sound**, common triggers are the language used in worship, the peal of church bells or call to the mosque, the sounds associated with prayer or mass, choral music, hymns, or chanting can all trigger flashbacks. Any sounds associated with the location where the RSA took place also act a powerful triggers.

Smell is also a potent sensory cue that can trigger flashbacks. This commonly includes the smell of incense if that was present at the time of the RSA, the smell of the abuser, including their scent or aftershave, the smell of the communion wine or the bodily fluids associated with the sexual abuse.

Certain **tastes** such as sacramental wine or bread can trigger flashbacks, as can foods and drinks associated with the RSA. The taste and smell of alcohol is a particularly powerful trigger if this was present during the abuse, as is the taste of semen or other bodily fluids.

Touch is a further trigger for flashbacks, this includes not only sexual touch but any touch associated with religious rituals, such as making the sign of the cross on the forehead.

Other common triggers in RSA include dates and season in the faith calendar such as holy days, or religious celebrations as well as church events such weddings, baptism, confirmations, special mass or prayer meetings as well as funerals. Times of day when worship normally takes place can also become a source of anxiety. Rituals associated with worship, such as receiving communion or confession, can also triggers flashbacks.

Managing flashbacks

As flashbacks are so powerful and have the capacity to seemingly transport the person back in time to the abuse, many survivors avoid cues that might trigger trauma reactions. The paralysing effect of flashbacks means that some survivors will no longer be able to enter a place of worship or consecrated location. It is for this reason that any pastoral counselling or guidance, including reporting RSA should ideally take place in a neutral setting. Similarly, being in the presence of a faith representative who is dressed in religious garments can also induce terror and render the survivor speechless. Religious institutions and faith leaders must understand how such sensory cues trigger post-traumatic stress reaction and be sensitive to the impact these can have on survivors.

To manage flashbacks, survivors will need to develop strategies such as reassuring internal dialogues as well as action plans and grounding techniques. As flashbacks drain vital energy and leave the individual exhausted, it is really important that survivors are able to soothe and nurture themselves in the aftermath of the flashback.

Nightmares and vivid dreams

Nightmares and vivid dreams are a common after effect of trauma and an important part of the survival system. In essence, nightmares are the night time equivalent of flashbacks and therefore represent unprocessed aspects of the traumatic experience. Nightmares also symbolise emotional aspects of the trauma such as feelings of shame, humiliation and anger. Like flashbacks, nightmares and vivid dreams help the survivor to sort through experiences so that they can be integrated into memory. Nightmares are often more terrifying than flashbacks because the survivors resources and coping strategies are '**offline**' making it harder to manage them.

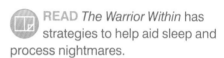 **REMEMBER** Nightmares are the night-time equivalent of flashbacks. They are the brain's way of processing experiences and filing them into the memory system.

The effects of nightmares

The fear of nightmares can make it difficult to fall asleep or even go to bed, leading to insomnia. Even once asleep, the restless unsatisfying nature of the sleep can leave the survivor feeling drained and exhausted. Not sleeping reduces energy levels and leaves the survivor tired and irritable. As it is impossible to sleep for any length of time the survivor cannot process new experiences or recharge his or her batteries. This can lead to poor concentration, confusion and a sense of not being able to manage even the simplest of tasks.

Dealing with nightmares

Developing strategies that can aid sleep and processing the content of the nightmares can restore control over disturbing dreams and nightmares. It critical that the content of the

nightmares are processed to ensure they do not recur.

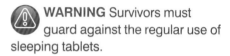 **READ** *The Warrior Within* has strategies to help aid sleep and process nightmares.

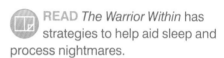 **WARNING** Survivors must guard against the regular use of sleeping tablets.

Panic attacks

Panic attacks are characterised by a sudden surge of intense anxiety which can be triggered by something specific that is frightening, or spontaneously. As they can happen at any time, survivors may fear leaving their home or avoid places or situations in which the panic attack first occurred. The fear of having a panic attack can lead to social withdrawal and anxiety, social phobia and open spaces, or agoraphobia.

Signs of panic attacks

Signs of panic attacks include shortness and shallowness of breath, pounding and irregular heartbeat, a sense of feeling 'unreal', pains or tightness in chest similar to heart attack, unsteadiness, trembling and dizziness, and the feeling that the world is spinning around. The survivor may also experience excessive sweating, feeling faint and light headed, a fear of losing control, going crazy or even dying. This is often accompanied by tingling in the hands and feet, choking or sense of being smothered, flushed skin, an urgent intense need to run away, nausea or a powerful urge to scream. The intensity of the symptoms can make the survivor feel as though he or she is having a heart attack.

Managing panic attacks

Survivors of RSA often experience panic attacks without being aware what has triggered them. It is important to identify triggers and link these to the sexual abuse experience. Many survivors report the symptoms of a panic attack while visiting places of worship, watching religious ceremonies or services, or seeing representatives of their faith. Although panic attacks appear life-threatening and overwhelming they can be managed once the link is made between RSA and unprocessed feelings.

 REMEMBER Panic attacks do pass, and can be controlled and managed.

Memories and intrusive memories

Memory is a necessary aid to survival as it stores both positive and negative experiences. Positive or pleasurable experiences are stored so that they are repeated while negative or unpleasant experiences are stored so that they can be avoided. Memory is very complex, and dynamic in constantly reviewing, evaluating, adding and subtracting experiences. Memories can only be stored if experiences are fully processed and made sense of, otherwise means that they remain '**online**' waiting to be processed.

 REMEMBER Unprocessed experiences are harder to store in memory because they are still 'online', demanding constant attention. This means they will remain as frightening as when they were first experienced.

Traumatic memories

Traumatic experiences are less easily processed as they are so terrifying and are most likely to remain online, yet not always in conscious awareness. If traumatic memories are not processed they cannot be integrated or stored. If this is accompanied by dissociation, or avoidance it is even harder to store the experience. As a result the memories are stored and remain '**online**' at the same intensity as when first experienced. While they are online they continue to demand attention and are triggered by sensory cues leading to flashbacks, nightmares and intrusive memories.

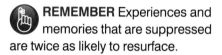 **REMEMBER** Experiences and memories that are suppressed are twice as likely to resurface.

Intrusive memories

Intrusive memories are usually so distressing that the survivor will try to avoid them, not realising that this makes them even more vivid and frightening, and twice as likely to recur. The more the survivor tries not to think about them, the more they will spontaneously recur and demand attention. Survivors commonly try to block recurring memories through dissociation, the use of alcohol, drugs, food or self-injury. Alternatively, they resort to distraction by keeping busy or working constantly.

Lack of memories

When experiences are so overwhelming that they cannot be understood, or processed, the survivor cannot store them in memory. This leads to fragmented memories which commonly consist of fleeting images, sounds or smells which lack context or coherent narrative and are detached from any meaning. The degree of memory recall will vary from survivor to survivor with some able to access all memories, some with only partial recall, and others with no recollection at all of the abuse. What is remembered and forgotten is not always subject to conscious control and is rarely actively decided upon by the survivor. Moreover the absence of full memory does not invalidate the RSA.

Restoring memories

There are a number of ways that memories can be restored although if they were not stored originally this will be much harder. Some survivors of RSA may never restore full memory of the RSA and will need to balance trying to restore memories with restoring well-being.

Drugs that block memories

There are now a number of drugs that can block memories at a biochemical level, which can be administered either pre- or post-trauma. While such drugs sound appealing it is vital to recognise that currently their effects are only partial and may not work for each individual. More importantly they may have a negative effect as blocking memories which signal that something is wrong will prevent emotional processing. As these drugs merely block the memory without processing it, they may be most helpful in the short-term until emotional regulation is mastered.

 WARNING Drugs that block memories will not integrate a survivor's experiences, which could result in lack of continuity and confusion. Ultimately this could interfere with the recovery process and the potential for post-traumatic growth.

Dissociation

Dissociation is often referred to as 'mental flight when physical flight is not possible'[6] and is a highly adaptive response to inescapable trauma. It provides a 'mental shield' to allow the person to detach from feelings, bodily sensations and reality. The signs of dissociation include feeling spaced out, or being in a dazed or dreamlike state. Attention is more narrowly focused as the person tunes, or screens out, the external world.

Survivors who dissociate find that the external world appears unreal or surreal, and that time has slowed down, or speeded up. In dissociation, familiar places, people or objects appear alien, or seem not to exist – known as **derealisation**. Survivors are commonly plagued by unusual body sensations as if floating away, or as if the body is split off from other parts. In addition,

survivors who dissociate report that they feel as though they are looking at themselves from a distance, usually from above, and the abuse is not happening to them but someone else.

During dissociation experiences are not processed which results in huge gaps in memory, or complete amnesia of the trauma. As the mind blanks out part or all of the experience, survivors lose their sense of continuity of who they are, and their reality, known as depersonalisation.

 WARNING To ensure the survivor is safe it is not advisable to drive or operate machinery while dissociating, and that young children, pets or any dependents are safe.

Everyday dissociation

Everyone dissociates to some degree – through daydreaming, being on autopilot or when absorbed in a good book or activity, such as gardening or watching a film. These are all normal and healthy forms of detaching from reality, although some survivors detach through alcohol or drug misuse, binge eating, or self-injury which can put them at further risk of harm.

Dissociation can become dangerous when survivors become so out of contact with their body that they retreat into their head, and lose contact with all external sensations. Alternatively, they armour their body to such an extent that they are unable to feel or be aware of the internal cues that signal something is not right. Another danger of sealing off all feeling is that others perceive the survivor as cold and unfeeling, which reduces opportunities for intimacy in caring or loving relationships.

If survivors 'tune out' too much they will lose contact with their surroundings and can no longer monitor threat or danger. Alternatively, if they dissociate during an experience they will have no recollection of what happened. While this emotional anaesthesia initially aids survival, over time it can result in changes in the survivor's sense of reality, time and memory.

⚠ **WARNING** Although dissociation is a normal response to trauma it can interfere with everyday functioning.

Repeated dissociation not only compromises reality but also gives rise to uncertainty about whether the RSA happened to them or someone else. Lapses in reality can also leave the survivor feeling like a shadow of a person, rather than a real human being. Dissociation can become so habitual that eventually survivors dissociate from all feelings, including pleasurable ones, leading to emotional and psychological frozenness in which nothing is felt at all.

Dissociation is immensely exhausting and physically draining as it requires enormous reserves of mental energy to block out feelings and sensations. In essence, dissociation becomes less effective over time, as the survivor is not able to process experiences and thereby increasing the need to dissociate which can interfere with recovery.

Dissociative identity disorder

Under certain circumstances, frequent and continuous dissociation can result in such fragmentation that several separate personalities are formed to support the person. This is known as **dissociative identity disorder** (formerly known as **multiple personality disorder**) wherein the survivor no longer possesses a single functioning personality, but is inhabited by a number of other distinct personalities. Such severe dissociation can interfere with everyday functioning and needs professional attention.

10 Understanding harmful behaviours: self-harm and self-medication

Survivors of RSA may resort to self-harming behaviours in order to manage their emotional pain, overwhelming thoughts and PTSD symptoms. Self-harm comes in a variety of forms, from passive self-harm as seen in self-neglect, to active self-injury, eating disorders and substance abuse.

Passive self-harm can encompass lack of self-care, poor hygiene, lack of boundaries, self-neglect, not being able to say 'no' or not being able to express basic needs. In addition, the avoidance, or repression of pleasurable feelings can be considered a form of self-harm.

Deliberate or **active self-harm**, by contrast, consists of direct self-injury such as cutting, self-mutilation, burning or persistent suicide attempts. Alternatively, some survivors may regulate their mood or limit their emotional pain through alcohol, drugs, food or addictive behaviours such as gambling, shopping or sex. It is essential to identify such self-harming behaviours and to replace these over time with more affirming ways of regulating emotions.

READ *The Warrior Within* has more information about how to identify and replace self-harming behaviours.

Function of self-harm

Self-harm and self-injury serve a number of purposes and these will vary from survivor to survivor. It is important for each survivor to identify not only self-harming behaviours, but also to understand their function and link these to their RSA experiences. Such knowledge will enable them to replace self-harming behaviours with more self-affirming behaviours.

Passive self-harm

Passive self-harm – which is evident in self-neglect, poor self-care and lack of boundaries – commonly represents lack of self-worth and lack of self-esteem. In many respects it is a reflection of how a survivor feels internally. Lack of self-care and poor hygiene is an external manifestation of how dirty the survivor feels on the inside. It is also an unconscious form of protection to ward off people.

If the survivor looks unkempt and does not bathe regularly people will not attempt to be close to them or want to be intimate. Many children who have been sexually abused use this as way of repelling their abuser and some continue to use this strategy in adulthood.[7] In contrast, self-neglect for some survivors is a way to elicit care and attention from others. It is a non-verbal, or symbolic way of saying 'Please take care of me' – much as a child elicits caring behaviour from others.

Difficulties with setting boundaries and being unable to say 'no'

This represents the lack of boundaries and inability to say 'no' during the RSA. The sense of powerlessness and helplessness associated with the RSA prevent the survivor from saying 'no'. In addition, survivors lack any sense of entitlement to set boundaries or express their needs. Many survivors also fear negative consequences if they assert themselves and feel compelled to remain submissive and compliant. To reverse this, survivors need to develop self-respect and the confidence to assert themselves alongside self-assertion skills to express their needs and set appropriate boundaries.

READ *The Warrior Within* has exercises to help with self-assertation and self-respect.

Active self-harm

Self-injury and self-medication

Self-injury and self-medication is commonly used to regulate uncontrollable and overwhelming emotional states. Survivors use self-injury in a variety of ways ranging from a way to escape emotions, to cope with crises, or to calm and self-soothe. In addition, self-injury is also a way to manage trauma reactions, in particular flashbacks and intrusive memories, and to create opportunities for nurturing.

Survivors often try to block out intrusive memories using alcohol, drugs or a combination of the two – or also to aid sleep or to avoid nightmares. Self-injury is also a way to numb any pain or manage tension or anxiety, or it can bring the survivor out of a dissociative state, or to feel more real and alive. Self-injury may also be used to verify the survivor's existence, externalise inner pain, see blood, or as a method of cleansing toxic feelings.

Some survivors use self-injury as a form of control. As they had no control over the RSA they seek to restore control in the only way they can which is through their body. Self-injury is a way of taking control over the pain, or the body that was out of control during the RSA. It is also a way of punishing the body for responding to the sexual abuse. In the case of eating disorders, food is used to lose or gain weight, to protect against and avoid sexual advances and relationships.

A danger of self-injury is that it can become addictive and compulsive to the point that the survivor no longer has control over such activities. Whatever the function or motivation for self-injury, survivors will need to examine its purpose and develop alternative strategies to regulate emotions.

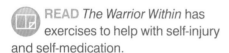 **READ** *The Warrior Within* has exercises to help with self-injury and self-medication.

WARNING A danger of self-injury is that it can become addictive and compulsive to the point that the survivor no longer has control over such activities.

The cycle of self-injury

To enable survivors to find alternative ways of regulating emotions, survivors will need to understand the **cycle of self-injury**. To do this, it helps to identify the warning signs that signal the need to self-injure. These commonly include: feelings of being engulfed by mental pain; intense feelings of anger; sadness, or despair; out of control physical sensations; or negative self-beliefs. These feelings quickly become overwhelming, and as panic and terror take over the survivor feels compelled to self-injure. The physical response to self-injury is the release of **endorphins** – the body's natural opiates – which deaden and numb the physical pain and promote feelings of calm and relief. This 'rewards' the harm by giving a feeling of control and relieves the anxiety allowing the survivor to cope and function more effectively.

Alternatively, some survivors are so out of touch with their feelings and dissociated that self-injury is the only way to exit dissociative states and feel. This creates a sense of 'aliveness' and thereby confirms the survivor's existence. As a result the survivor feels more grounded and, as endorphins are released, they are able to experience a sense of euphoria. However, once the immediate positive aspects of the self-injury have worn off, feelings of shame, guilt, self-hate and self-disgust begin to emerge, which escalate until the need to self-injure recurs. To interrupt the cycle of self-injury, survivors need to identify the triggers that lead to either dissociation or an overload of emotion, and find alternative ways of managing overwhelming emotional states.

READ *The Warrior Within* has information on identifying dissociation triggers, and finding alternative ways to manage emotions.

REMEMBER The need for self-injury is a signal of unexpressed feelings which do not have to be acted upon.

Alternative ways to regulate emotions

To reduce the compulsion to self-injure, survivors must find other ways to manage feelings. The familiarity of self-harm and its past effectiveness can make this transition difficult. Survivors commonly find it difficult to stop self-injurious behaviour and may initially focus on harm minimisation until alternatives are found. This can be achieved by ensuring that cutting instruments are sterilised and that wounds are cleaned and dressed to reduce the risk of infection. To avoid increased risk of tissue damage and cutting too deeply, it is essential to avoid self-injurious behaviour while under the influence of alcohol or drugs.

Useful strategies to reduce self-harm and self-injury

Useful strategies to reduce self-harm and self-injury are to replace blood with a red marker pen, or to simulate the pain of cutting by snapping a rubber band on the wrist or ankle. To exit dissociative states it helps to squeeze an ice cube or hold a cold aluminium can. A cold shower or chewing strongly-flavoured food stuffs such as chilli, ginger root, raw onion or lemon can simulate the sensations associated with self-injury and help the survivor to feel more grounded.

It is vital to master a range of **grounding techniques** using all five senses. Survivors need to find which are most effective for them, and engage with the full range of emotions. It is also helpful to connect with trusted others by phone, email, text or face-to-face. Survivors need to try staying in the present reality and finding a way to absorb themselves in a task. If the survivor feels controlled by a powerful internal critical voice, it is helpful to engage it in a dialogue to change any negative messages into more compassionate and encouraging ones.

A highly effective strategy is the **15 minute technique**. When the urge to self-injure occurs, survivors need to try and delay the urge initially for 15 minutes, and distract themselves with simple tasks such as doing a crossword puzzle or sudoko, or journal writing. Survivors often find that writing down lists of favourite paintings, plays, poems, films, books or songs can be beneficial. Once these 15 minutes are over, survivors can attempt another distraction technique, and so on. Whilst engaging in these distractions, the need to self-injure will lessen and hopefully self-injury will be avoided altogether. Most importantly, it allows the survivor to restore control over the compulsion to self-injure.

READ *The Warrior Within* has a full range of grounding techniques and action plans to help survivors.

Negative thoughts and negative beliefs

Managing negative thoughts and negative beliefs can reduce the need for self-harm. RSA renders survivors more vulnerable to distorted and biased thinking. Negative beliefs usually consist of negative thoughts about the self, others, the world and the future. While some of these beliefs may have been inserted by the abuser they often become automatic and seem to occur outside awareness.

Common negative self-beliefs such as 'I am to blame', 'I am bad' or 'I am worthless' represent an inner critical voice which constantly undermines the survivor stripping him or her of any self-esteem. They also lead to the false belief that the survivor is to blame for the abuse and deserves all the bad things that has happened to him or her.

Survivors also hold negative beliefs about others as being untrustworthy, rejecting or potentially abusive. These negative beliefs emphasise that the world is hostile and full of danger and disappointment. Such beliefs emphasise survivors lack of safety and trust which leads to defensive reactions and disconnection from others.

Intense emotions are often driven by **emotional reasoning** in which feelings are assumed to be facts, and an accurate reflection of reality and truth. Common examples of this are assuming that if one **feels** bad then one must **be** bad, or because one **feels** guilty then one must **be** guilty. Such emotional reasoning can lead to **personalisation**, when the survivor assumes responsibility when there is none. A good example is assuming that because the survivor had an erection or an orgasm during the sexual abuse he or she must have wanted it.

Believing that feelings are facts often underpins self-harming behaviours especially if survivors believe they are to blame and to take responsibility for things that really are not their fault. When this is combined with a harsh **internal self-critic** who constantly reminds them that they are '**useless**' or '**stupid**', they feel compelled resort to self-harm as a self- punishment. Such thinking, if left unchallenged, can lead to thoughts suicidal thoughts and behaviour.

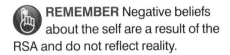 **REMEMBER** Negative beliefs about the self are a result of the RSA and do not reflect reality.

To compensate for perceived flaws survivors impose unrealistic expectations on themselves and become perfectionist in their thinking and behaviour. As these expectations are unrealistic and virtually impossible to achieve, survivors experience a repeated sense of failure. This leads to even more guilt and self-criticism, and a greater need to be perfect. High expectations are often also placed on others and, when they are not met, results in a repetitive cycle of being disappointed in them. This reinforces the belief that others cannot be trusted.

Reducing the impact of negative thoughts and beliefs

To reduce the impact of negative thoughts and beliefs, survivors need to identify them and then replace these with more accurate and objective thoughts. Some common biases in thinking are:

- **all or nothing thinking** – in which only extremes are seen rather than the full range of possibilities;

- **over-generalisation** or **mislabelling** – whereby a totally negative image is created on the basis of one single, minor deficiency;

- **catastrophisation** – the tendency to predict and expect the very worst in any one situation based on one minor difficulty;

- **mental filtering** or **disqualifying the positive** – in which a positive aspect of self, others or a situation is downgraded, rejected or dismissed as unimportant;

- **magnification and minimisation** – in which negative events are exaggerated in importance and positive events are underestimated; and

- **jumping to conclusions** – in which negative conclusions are drawn which are not justified by the facts.

Two further types of distorted thinking are **mind reading**, in which the survivor is preoccupied with reading the minds of others rather than staying with his or her own thoughts and feelings, and **fortune telling**, in which the survivor believes he or she can predict the future. Neither of these are based on objective evidence but are driven by fear and projection. It is a form of 'psyching yourself up' for the worst case scenario so as not to be disappointed or to be prepared for the worst possible outcome.

To reduce self-harm and create a more positive view of the self it is important re-evaluate such thoughts with more realistic appraisals and not be restricted by negative biases that serve to undermine self-esteem and self-worth. This allows survivors to develop more self-compassion and empathy. It will also minimise self-blame, guilt, and shame and reduce the need to self-harm and allow survivors to feel more control over their recovery.

READ *The Warrior Within* explains ways to identify and replace negative thoughts and beliefs.

ONLINE The One in Four website explains ways to identify and replace negative thoughts and beliefs.

Alternative methods of communication

Once ways to manage self-injury have been identified, these can be used to support alternative ways of communicating distress. Practising more effective communication skills can help when talking to and connecting with others. In communicating with others and sharing fears and vulnerabilities, unexpressed feelings can be released which will reduce the sense of shame and loneliness. This will lead to more effective emotional processing and thereby reduce the need to self-injure and self-medicate.

Self-medication

Self-medication is a common way for survivors to manage overwhelming emotions. Alcohol, drugs and food are a way to numb distressing feelings and suppress painful memories. Some survivors associate alcohol with RSA, especially if it was used to intoxicate them or formed part of the abuse ritual, such as sacramental wine. Alcohol addiction is a common long-term effect of RSA, with some survivors becoming addicted from a very young age. Other forms of addictive behaviours such as sex, gambling, shopping, internet gaming, or watching pornography, over-exercising and punishing work schedules are also ways to avoid negative feelings, or thoughts.

Survivors who are dependent on alcohol or drugs rarely link their addiction to the RSA and find it hard to seek specialist support, as this may become another source of shame. There is also a real fear that, if they become sober, deeply buried feelings may re-emerge. Linking self-medication to the suppression of emotions and the trauma of RSA is essential as this will help process the abuse experience in a more effective way.

 WARNING Many survivors use alcohol or food to numb feelings which can become addictive and lead to alcoholism, anorexia, bulimia or obesity.

Depending on the degree of self-medication it may be necessary to consider a residential detoxification or rehabilitation programme to aid recovery. Alternatively, 12 step fellowship programmes – such as Alcohol Anonymous (AA) or Narcotics Anonymous (NA) – provide support and help. There are now a number of specialist 12 step fellowship programmes to help with a vast range of addictions including food, gambling, shopping, the internet, love and sex.

Eating disorders

Eating disorders are also common among survivors of RSA. Some survivors seek comfort in food to numb negative feelings, or overeat to the point of obesity to avoid intimacy. In cultures that emphasise slimness, being overweight reduces sexual attention and enables the survivor to avoid sexual relationships. Thus their weight adds an extra layer of protection to ward off others. Some survivors avoid food altogether as a way of controlling the only thing they feel that they are able to control – what goes into, and comes out of their body. This is most evident in bulimia wherein the survivor over-indulges in food and then punishes him or herself through purging.

Giving up self-injury

Giving up self-injury is not easy and can feel like a loss which needs to be mourned. Self-injury, alcohol, food or drugs will have become a reliable and predictable way of controlling mood and avoiding feelings. Losing or giving up these behaviours can be like losing a reliable friend or non-judgemental companion and can revive a sense terror.

This can lead to internal resistance, or a fear of further loss of control. Before working on self-harm and self-injury it is essential that survivors master other ways of regulating emotions and have restored some degree of control. Most importantly, survivors must pace their recovery in order to optimise success in replacing self-injury behaviours with healthier alternatives.

Suicidal thoughts

Self-injury and self-harm can also be a way of managing suicidal thoughts and suicide attempts. In order to ward off suicidal feelings, or as an alternative to suicide, self-injury becomes an immediate and less terrifying prospect. Some suicidal thoughts and feelings are masked and resemble '**Russian roulette**' where risky behaviour such as reckless driving or stepping out in front of traffic is a way of inviting death without actively committing suicide. Here the cessation of pain is the primary goal rather than to die. If the survivor is preoccupied with recurring thoughts of suicide, or is actively suicidal, it is vital that he or she seeks professional help.

WARNING If self-injury is out of control or the survivor has persistent thoughts about suicide he or she will need to seek professional help.

Safety plan

It is essential that a safety plan is put into place if suicidal feelings persist. Any safety plan must include a list of people that can act as a support network, both personal and professional, as well contact details of a doctor or GP and a list of specialist services such as Samaritans. It helps to draw up a safety contract with a trusted friend and agree to contact them when suicidal thoughts become too overpowering.

READ *The Warrior Within* has advice on how to devise a safety plan.

ONLINE The One in Four website has advice about how to devise a safety plan.

11 Understanding shame, self-blame and self-forgiveness

Shame

Shame is a virus that infects the soul. It is often seen in survivors of RSA alongside guilt and self-blame. Shame affects the core identity of survivors and is difficult to resolve. Guilt and shame are commonly confused despite their many differences. Guilt is something that can be dissolved through apologising for harm done and/or making reparation. As shame affects the whole of the person, not just actions, it is much more difficult to manage. Shame is also one of the most difficult emotions to resolve because it does not have a specific channel for release. Unlike sadness which can be discharged through tears, shame remains trapped within.

 WARNING Shame is a virus that infects the soul.

Understanding shame

Understanding the function and impact of shame can help survivors to manage it more effectively. In the words of Nietzsche – '**Everyone needs a sense of shame, no one needs to feel ashamed**'. Shame is important for survival because it indicates that an experience or behaviour feels wrong for some reason. It highlights that the abuse was wrong not due to the actions of the survivor but those of the abuser. In committing RSA, the shame lies solely with the abuser who has acted in a shameless way. During RSA the victim is unable to challenge the shameful behaviour of the abuser. As the abuser feels no shame, the victim takes on his or her denied shame as their own.

REMEMBER A survivor is not responsible for the RSA that they experienced.

Incorporating the shame of the abuser intensifies any shame felt during the RSA. Survivors often feel shame for submitting to the RSA; or for not telling someone about it; or for having an erection or becoming aroused during the abuse. It is **essential** to recognise that shame lies with the abuser that coerced and entrapped the survivor into submission. Abusers often perform sexual acts on their victims that are arousing and pleasurable so that they feel complicit in the abuse and feel too ashamed to reveal the experience.

Abusers often amplify this by blaming the victim and making them feel as though they seduced the abuser. This is often the case in RSA where sex is seen as sinful and bad. Any arousal on the part of the victim becomes a source sexual shame. In addition, religious duress makes it hard for victims to see

113

their abuser as capable of sin as they are God's representative on earth. This leaves them with no choice but to see themselves as sinful in order to preserve the sacred image of the abuser. To release themselves from this imposed sense of shame, survivors need to redirect it back to its original source – the abuser .

READ *The Warrior Within* has useful exercises to help deal with redistribution of shame.

Talking about shame

As shame is a social emotion it can be alleviated through talking to trusted others who will not judge the survivor. One function of shame is to regulate behaviour and ensure acceptance within families, tribes, cultures and social groups. As a result, shame leaves the individual feeling isolated and excluded, and needing to hide physically as well as psychologically. This reinforces the sense of shame and a vicious cycle of withdrawal and exclusion begins. This compromises the basic human need for connection and sense of belongingness.

Survivors experience a further conflict in the desire to be seen by others, yet needing to be invisible in order to protect themselves from further shame or abuse. This paradox can be paralysing and explains why victims and survivors find it difficult to disclose or report RSA. Shame renders them voiceless and invisible and reinforces suffering in silence.

Shame attacks the very core of the survivor and has the capacity to destroy his or her identity through self-hatred and self-loathing. This is further reinforced by such negative beliefs as '**I am a bad or shameful person**', '**I am a mistake**' or '**I am defective**'. The emotional effects of this shame manifest in different ways. Survivors of RSA commonly experience feelings of self-contempt, loss of dignity or honour, or feel like '**damaged goods**'.

WARNING Shame attacks the very core of the survivor and has the capacity to destroy his or her identity through self-hatred and self-loathing.

In contaminating religious beliefs and making God a co-conspirator in the abuse, survivors begin to question their value and worth in God's eyes. This undermines their value in this life and the afterlife. As they cannot atone for or be absolved of their shame, their very existence is threatened in undermining their right to exist. This can lead to feelings of vulnerability, anxiety, neediness and dependency. These further reinforce the sense of shame and can lead to suicidal thoughts and behaviour.

Shame and the body

Many survivors of RSA focus their shame on the body, as they see it as defective and an object of scorn. This results in an extreme dislike of the body and revulsion, which in some cases can develop into **body dysmorphic disorder**. In order to control **body shame**, survivors commonly wear shapeless clothing or resort to extreme exercise regimes or cosmetic surgery to resculpt the body into a state of perceived perfection. Some survivors punish themselves with deliberate disfigurement through self-injury or by depriving themselves of any bodily pleasure.

This body shame generates extreme self-consciousness in social situations. Some survivors are unable to eat or drink in public or in the presence of others. This is often because they are preoccupied with how others will perceive them if they are seen to express or indulge basic bodily needs. This crippling shame can lead to social phobia and avoidance of others.

Body shame is also seen in the constant need to be in control of bodily movements, actions and performance.

Survivors of RSA are usually very self-conscious of how their body appears to others. They are often terrified of being embodied or allowing themselves to engage in spontaneous movement. Many survivors are reluctant to move their bodies along to music or to dance for fear of losing control and appearing to take pleasure in their body. They are also terrified to be seen to express any sensuality or sexuality through their body in case this is seen as evidence of sinful sexual expression. As a result they become extremely inhibited physically and come across as rigid and stiff.

Sexual shame

Sexual shame is particularly common in survivors of RSA. This is associated with the instilled sense of sexual shame which denies bodily pleasure, sensuality and sexuality that underpins a lot of religious doctrine. It is also as a result of the RSA in which the body has become a source of overwhelming confusion and shame. This is particularly the case if the body responded or became aroused during the sexual abuse. The link between physical pleasure, sin and shame is conditioned and reinforced by the abuser. Many abusers manipulate religious beliefs such as sexual shame and sin as part of the grooming process, or during the sexual activity itself. This leaves the survivor feeling morally and spiritually flawed. The self-hatred of the body and its 'sinful' responses can lead to the denial and avoidance of all bodily pleasure.

REMEMBER Many abusers manipulate religious beliefs such as sexual shame and sin as part of the grooming process, or during the RSA itself.

This can have a significant impact of relationships as survivors avoid sexual intimacy. Alternatively, some survivors cover up their sexual shame with sexual promiscuity in which the body and sexuality is devalued through repeated meaningless sexual encounters. The shamelessness in sexual promiscuity is reminiscent of the shamelessness of the abuser and thus represents a re-enactment of the abuse experience. Given the range of reactions to sexual shame it is crucial that survivors are aware of how shame has impacted on them, their relationships and sexuality.

Dissolving shame

Human contact is a powerful way to dissolve shame. Shame thrives on isolation and concealment, and dissipates through connection to others. Connecting to supportive others who are non-judgemental and accepting is a powerful antidote to shame. Shame dissolves in the presence of human contact, compassion and empathy. It is only when the survivor is respected, affirmed and made visible that shame can be released and eased.

READ *The Warrior Within* has useful exercises and activities to help deal with shame.

ONLINE The One in Four website has useful exercises and activities to help deal with shame.

REMEMBER Shame thrives on isolation and concealment and dissipates through connection to others.

Self-blame

Self-blame supports shame. Many survivors of RSA blame themselves for submitting to the abuse and not fighting back harder. This self-blame must be challenged, and evaluated within the context of trauma reactions. Freezing and submitting are instinctive reactions in the presence of danger and trauma and occur outside of conscious awareness and voluntary control. They are the body's way of ensuring survival and should not be a source of self-blame.

Similarly not being able to say 'no' was not a choice but enforced by the power dynamics in the RSA. Survivors who sought contact with the abuser did so not to because they wanted to be sexually abused but as a way of feeling more in control of when the abuse took place and thereby ensuring a degree of predictability. These are merely examples of coping strategies that aided survival rather than sources of self-blame.

REMEMBER Survivors who felt aroused or experienced pleasure or orgasm during the abuse are not responsible for their abuse. Arousal is the body's natural response in the presence of sexual touching.

Self-blame is also a strategy to reduce the sense of helplessness and lack of control. In blaming themselves survivors feel that they had an element of control over the abuse, and this illusion of power enables them to reduce their feelings of helplessness. This is especially the case in male survivors who are socialised to be active and dominant rather than passive and submissive. Hope is also preserved through self-blame because if the survivor feels that they had some control over the abuse, then they believe that they will be able to prevent future abuse. Whilst self-blame produces feelings

of control the cost is amplification of self- loathing and shame. If survivors can let go of self-blame and find self-compassion they will be able to develop a more empathic view of themselves, and release the crippling sense of shame.

Self-forgiveness

Self-forgiveness plays a vital role in reducing self-blame and shame. In reminding themselves that they had no power or choice whilst being abused, or the way they responded can allow survivors to transfer responsibility firmly onto the abuser. In addition, self-forgiveness can release any other guilt or shame that is associated with RSA. By linking their reactions and behaviours to the abuse, survivors can gain a greater understanding of some of their more negative responses and see them as defensive strategies to manage the aftermath of RSA.

Forgiveness can also help to reduce shame for some survivors of RSA providing they have chosen to do this and it has not been imposed. Forgiveness is an intimate and personal choice and should only take place if the survivor believes it to be helpful in their healing. Religious beliefs usually emphasise the notion of forgiveness, and imply that this is crucial for recovery.

This may need to be challenged, as forgiveness is choice that lies with each individual survivor and should not be determined by others (see **Restoring spirituality and forgiveness** on page 164).

Survivors who view forgiveness as a kindness to themselves, rather than absolving the abuser, find that it is an important milestone in their healing that permits them to let go of anger and hurt. Although this may be healing for some survivors, it does not apply to all. Each survivor needs to find their own way of recovering from RSA and explore what is healing for him or her.

The fear of being exposed and visible makes it very difficult for survivors to engage in personal and intimate relationships. The impact this has on relationships and its links to RSA will be explored in the following chapter.

12 Understanding the impact on relationships

As RSA involves a betrayal of trust, survivors often find it extremely difficult to trust others or get close to them. This betrayal of trust is not confined just to the abuser but also extends to faith leaders, religious institutions and even God – all of whom failed to protect. Some survivors also feel betrayed by their families and the faith community in not recognising or believing that they were being abused.

REMEMBER The betrayal of trust is not just confined to the abuser but also includes faith leaders, religious institutions and God, as well as the family and the larger faith community.

The fear of being hurt again, or that getting close to someone may become sexual, may result in avoiding intimacy. This method of survival can seem effective, but carries a high price, not least agonising loneliness or unsatisfying and disappointing relationships. This presents a real paradox as survivors are in constant battle with a yearning for closeness, and the need to avoid intimacy. This can be extremely damaging in itself, as the fear of future betrayal and abuse leads to the avoidance of relationships, isolation and alienation. In contrast, some survivors are too trusting and their deep need to feel close to someone compels them to rush into intimacy too quickly. Each of these is fraught with danger and can lead to persistent difficulties in relationships.

WARNING Avoiding relationships or rushing into them too quickly can lead to persistent difficulties in relationships.

Relational worth

Relational worth – or how individuals rate themselves to others – is determined by early experiences, and shape future relationships. This is more often sensed, felt or known rather than explicitly expressed. When abuse masquerades as care and attention, it can be difficult to distinguish between genuine care and nurturing, and coercion and manipulation. Survivors who were groomed by their abuser and seduced into a 'special' relationship will experience subsequent relationships as confusing and turbulent, rather than a source for comfort or security. The dehumanisation in RSA in which the survivor was objectified, results in the belief that he or she exists solely to serve and satisfy the needs of others. This can lead to paralysing wariness of relationships and inability to connect to others whether family, friends, partners or children, in addition to professionals or work colleagues.

Most survivors of RSA are consumed with relational fears such as a fear of showing vulnerability, dependency, fear of reaching out in case they are rebuffed, as well as a fear of saying 'no' or expressing needs. Allowing these fears to predominate can result in excessive self-reliance and self-sufficiency, or overwhelming and paralysing dependency needs. These give rise to a range of relationship dynamics including prioritising the needs of others, anticipating their needs through mind-reading, controlling them, whilst detaching from their own feelings and needs. While these are most obviously seen in actual relationships, they can also manifest in symbolic relationships such as with God, or one's faith.

The relationship with the religious institution

RSA can impact negatively on the survivor's relationship with the religious institution and God that failed to protect him or her. This is intensified if the religious institution denies the abuse or refuses to act upon any allegation made. Many religious institutions do not respond sensitively to allegations and are known to blame the victim or make them feel guilty for damaging the reputation of the abuser and the faith. This secondary betrayal makes it hard for survivors to continue to practice their faith within their usual place of worship and trust the religious institution to protect others. This can compel some survivors to reject the religious institution and in some cases their faith. In contrast, other survivors continue to worship but with little enthusiasm and merely go through the motions.

Some survivors find that RSA destroys their relationship with God. This is especially in cases where the abuser distorted religious beliefs and implicated God in the abuse. As a child, the survivor may have prayed to God to put an end to the abuse or punish the abuser, to no avail. This will lead the survivor to doubt God's power or ability to protect them. As God's grace and power is questioned, the survivor will feel ashamed for such doubts. Many survivors of RSA feel abandoned by God which reinforces their lack of self-worth, in that even God does not value them enough to protect them.

This threatens the survivor's relationship with God to the extent that some will lose their faith altogether. This loss of faith can lead to what feels like a spiritual death, in which they lose not just deeply-held beliefs, but also to the loss of their spiritual identity and the loss of a relationship to their spiritual family. These losses need to be mourned in order to restore faith and spirituality (see **Understanding trauma reactions** on page 87). Survivors can be helped in this by acknowledging that it may be easier and safer to be angry with God or the religious institution than the abuser. This is evidence of how much the actual abuser is still feared.

Relationships within families

Relationships within families can also be destroyed through RSA. Many survivors feel emotionally isolated and abandoned by their family as a result of RSA. Survivors may feel angry with their family for not having recognised the signs of abuse, or if they were disbelieved when they disclosed. This is especially the case if the abuse took place in the family home, or if they were not given a choice to avoid the abuser. Many religious parents see it as an honour if a faith leader pays them, or their children, special attention and would have insisted that the child be grateful and respectful to the abuser. Survivors often report being sent to the abuser despite their protestations. This can lead some survivors to believe that the family colluded with the abuser.

Alongside this, the survivor will have learnt that their trust in their parent to protect them was futile. RSA gives a clear message to victims that the abuser is all-powerful, indeed so powerful that not even parents, faith leaders or God can stop him or her. This undermines a sense of trust in the family which intensifies the victim's fear of the abuser. When this cannot be expressed because the abuser is held in high esteem by the family, communication becomes impaired which reinforces the sense of abandonment and isolation.

Keeping the RSA secret prevents open communication and some survivors distance themselves from the family for fear of disclosing the abuse. Some survivors are so conscientious in protecting their parents or family from discovering the abuse that they need to reject the family as a source of comfort making them feel even more isolated. As communication is inhibited the relationship begins to break down making it harder to communicate as the child grows up. Many survivors find that this lack of communication becomes so embedded that it they find it hard to have any meaningful conversation with family members even when the abuse has stopped and they are adults.

The lack of communication is exacerbated if the survivor has doubts about their sexual orientation or discovers that they are gay, lesbian or bisexual. This is especially the case if their faith sees homosexuality as a sin.

In order to protect the family the survivor will not be able to express sexuality which forces them to keep yet another secret. This will create considerable barriers to the relationship.

Some survivors become overprotective of their parents and younger siblings, especially if they fear that they could be abused too. The child is consumed with fear and guilt and becomes over-compliant and over-responsible. In many respects this is a role reversal, where they become the carer rather than being cared for. The role of carer is often taken into adult relationships in which the survivor is overly responsible and adopts the role of carer in relationships, and is never able to say 'no'. The fear of being vulnerable and its association with abuse prevents them from allowing themselves to be taken care of.

In contrast some survivors are so angry about the abuse and lack of protection that they become aggressive, defiant and hostile. This hostility is an effective way of avoiding closeness and intimacy which keeps the secret safe. Often labelled as a 'problem child' who seeks negative attention, such survivors become increasingly withdrawn to hide their hurt and pain. Their aggressive and hostile behaviour can lead to antisocial traits in adulthood, leading to problems

with authority and the police. As they are unable to reach out to others they are more susceptible to self-harming behaviours, self-medication and addiction to manage overwhelming feelings.

The only way for some victims to manage the RSA is to become detached from the world and their family. By entering into a fantasy world through daydreaming, reading, computer gaming or watching television, the victim escapes from this or her reality. As they become more 'lost' they stop communicating with their family, finding it hard to voice feelings or experiences. As an adult, the survivor is often shy and avoids relationships, and becomes lost in a fantasy world. They are often seen as loners and excluded from activities where they can meet others and develop relationships.

REMEMBER To avoid closeness and keep the secret of RSA, survivors can become compliant and overly responsible, hostile and angry, detached and shy, or a figure of fun.

Some survivors manage their abuse by minimising it and becoming the joker or storyteller. In order to relate to others they seek attention through laughter or telling amusing stories. Here they receive attention but closeness is blocked through humour. As adults they are often seen as lively and fun without realising that this masks a depth of pain and agony, and a need to be rescued.

RSA can split families apart, especially if they do not believe the survivor or if some family members do believe and others do not. This can cause deep ruptures within and between families. It is important that all family members recognise that this is precisely what gave the abuser the power to abuse. To minimise the risk of disclosure and to increase the power of the abuser, it is necessary to divide the victim from the family and any caregivers. Being able to restore and rebuild these damaged relationships is a crucial step in the process of recovery and healing (see **Understanding trauma reactions** on page 87). If family relationships seem irreparable it is important not to give up hope and consider seeking family therapy.

 WARNING It is in the abuser's interest to destroy family relationships as it increases his power. Restoring and rebuilding these is a crucial step to recovery and healing.

Whichever way survivors manage their abuse and family relationships, these are often highly adaptive at the time but exert considerable costs which

reverberate into adulthood. The focus is on avoiding closeness and intimacy as a way of keeping the survivor safe. These patterns of relating become conditioned and are often replayed in adulthood in relationships not just with friends, partners and their own children, but also work colleagues and peers.

Relationships with others

Relationships with partners, friends, children, work colleagues and professionals are also commonly impacted by RSA. The loss of control and sense of powerlessness experienced during the RSA commonly results in difficulties in psychosocial functioning and relationships. Some of these problems can render some survivors more vulnerable to re-victimisation and further sexual exploitation. Instead of harmony, relationships are often riddled with conflict as abuse dynamics of power and control are re-enacted.

Power and control dynamics

Many survivors of RSA feel compelled – often unconsciously – to replay, or test capacity for power and control. This can veer between passivity, submissiveness and crippling dependency, and aggression, dominance, and fierce independence. As a result relationships can become the arena to restore either personal power or reduce feelings of powerlessness.

Some survivors try to do this through active control of their social relationships by being controlling and demanding, while others become overly compliant and develop strategies to avoid conflict so they do not risk feeling overwhelmed and powerless. Survivors who resort to control may do this in obvious ways through anger, hostility and domination. Or they may adopt more subtle controlling behaviour patterns, such as never revealing themselves in their relationships, not allowing others to get close, always being the carer, or through obsessive-compulsive behaviours such as cleanliness, tidiness, being busy all the time or working excessively.

Survivors who are compliant tend to divert authority to external sources of control and seek sanctuary in dependency which replicates their abuse experience. While this dependency can be overt in always deferring to their partner, it can also be seen in less obvious ways of behaving. Such survivors often appear very childlike in constantly asking for reassurance or permission to do anything, their inability to make any decisions, not being able to trust their instincts, or by leading highly chaotic lives that need others to help them sort out. The risk of such high-level dependency is that the survivor may attract controlling partners who are likely to abuse them, or re-victimise them. Some survivors constantly switch between dominance and submission which can be confusing and exhausting for partners and friends.

When this is used as a way of relating to the survivor's own children it can be frightening for the child and be seen as abusive. Many survivors feel shocked and mortified that they may be doing harm to their children and fear not being able to control how they are with them. This needs to be carefully monitored in terms of child protection concerns. If survivors or partners are concerned by such behaviour patterns they may need to seek professional advice.

⚠️ **WARNING** Survivors need to monitor the impact of power and control dynamics in their relationship with their own children and, if necessary, seek professional advice.

The need to control and dominate, or be submissive and compliant, can cause considerable relationship difficulties with friends and work colleagues. Survivors who are domineering, controlling or hostile are perceived negatively and actively avoided, whereas survivors who are submissive and compliant are often taken advantage of and exploited. This can lead to a sense of betrayal or resentment on the part of the survivor which prevents them from developing an equal or respectful relationship. When survivors switch between control and compliance, friends and work colleagues become confused making them wary of entering into a relationship. The lack of predictability and mood swings leads to avoidance and the survivor is left feeling isolated and rejected.

Whichever position is taken, it must be understood within the context of the abuse experience. Both positions use denial, dissociation and cognitive distortions to ward off painful emotions as a way of managing the abuse. This rollercoaster way of managing emotions is also often accompanied by substance abuse or compulsive behaviours which can give a temporary sense of power and control during times of vulnerability and stress.

⚠️ **WARNING** Power and control dynamics in relationships are a replay of the RSA in which the survivor

re-enacts either being the abuser or the victim.

Switching between 'approach and avoid' behaviours

Related to power and control is switching between what is known as '**approach and avoid**' behaviour This is a common pattern for relationships, where any instance of opening up is followed immediately by the urge to withdraw. This is usually seen in the survivor inviting or welcoming intimacy and contact, and then immediately feeling violently angry or rejecting. Many survivors develop this pattern during the abuse, where they are forced to satisfy the abusers needs to their own detriment. In the environment of abuse any physical closeness meant danger, and expressing needs or saying 'no' resulted in punishment or distance. This severely undermine the survivor's ability to trust.

The role of trust

RSA's repeated betrayal and distortion of awareness robs survivors of the ability to trust others. When survivors become aware of this, they may try to overcompensate and invest their trust too easily, not realising that this renders them vulnerable to further abuse, exploitation or betrayal. Commonly the need to be accepted, liked and understood overrides the lack of evidence that the other person is trustworthy.

Trust must be measured in degrees and seen on a **spectrum** rather than polarised between 'trust' or 'no trust'. The level of trust in others will depend to a large extent on the course and development of the relationship. This will vary from relationship to relationship and person to person, and must be closely monitored. It is important that survivors do not invest trust too quickly or on flimsy evidence. This includes trusting authority figures and professionals, especially when the survivor was abused by someone who had power and authority over them. It takes time to develop trust, and survivors need to choose how much or how little to trust rather than being compelled or coerced into it.

REMEMBER Trust must be measured in degreees and exists on a spectrum – **not** all or nothing.

To facilitate trust, survivors need to learn to trust themselves before they can trust others. This will take time and should be paced carefully. Once survivors are able to trust and value themselves more they will be able to be more open to others and seek relationships rather than avoid them. This will need to be combined with the ability to set boundaries and being more able to express their needs assertively. By expressing feelings and revealing relational needs, and communicating more effectively survivors will find that they will be able to risk closeness and intimacy without feeling threatened or suffocated. Equipped with these new skills, survivors will be able to rebuild relationships that have been damaged by RSA (see **Rebuilding relationships** on page 154).

READ *The Warrior Within* has useful exercises and activities to help facilitate trust.

13 Understanding sexual difficulties and sexual shame

RSA can lead to a number of sexual difficulties which affect sexual relationships. Some survivors find that their sexuality has not been compromised and experience virtually no sexual difficulties whereas others find that their sex lives are irrevocably damaged. The range of difficulties can extend from complete avoidance of sexual activities, or sexual anorexia to sexual promiscuity or sexual addiction.

Some survivors are so terrified of sex that they avoid all sexual intimacy and sexual contact as it reminds them of the RSA and triggers traumatic reactions. This is especially the case in the presence of certain sexual touches, specific sexual acts or sensory cues reminiscent of the abuse. As these can trigger flashbacks of the RSA, survivors find it extremely difficult to experience sexual pleasure. For these survivors sex is contaminated and tainted by guilt and shame.

 WARNING RSA can lead to a number of sexual difficulties ranging from complete avoidance of sexual activities, or sexual anorexia to sexual promiscuity, or sexual addiction.

In contrast, some survivors will engage in indiscriminate sexual behaviour which lacks any real sexual pleasure and is generally unsatisfying. Such sexual promiscuity may be the only way the survivor knows how to get their need for affection met. Some survivors believe that they are not entitled to love, care and affection and that the only way to access these is through sex. RSA and early childhood sexual experiences can lead to traumatic sexualisation in which the victim's identity is organised around sex. As a result some survivors see themselves as sex objects and believe that this is their only worth or value. This can lead to sexual addiction in which survivors seek to medicate the effects of RSA through sex.

Alternatively, some survivors try to prove that they are not sexually damaged, or to cover up sexual confusion, by engaging in indiscriminate sex. Survivors who fear that their sexual orientation has been shaped or compromised by the RSA will try to cover this up through heterosexual promiscuity in the hope that this proves that they are not gay, or lesbian. This prevents the survivor from really exploring their sexuality and giving themselves permission to express their true sexual orientation. This is especially the case when they have been influenced by homophobic faith-based beliefs.

Traumatic sexualisation is also manifest in other forms of sexual behaviour such as compulsive masturbation wherein the survivor feels compelled to masturbate many times a day without relief or satisfaction. This is often accompanied by distressing images or memories of their sexual abuse which are confusing. In such cases, survivors fear that this is evidence of their seduction of the abuser not realising that the compulsive masturbation is a way to triumph over the abuse.

A small proportion of survivors attempt to triumph over trauma by becoming sexually controlling or predatory in their sexual encounters as a way of empowering themselves. These usually manifest in sexually-demanding behaviours, such as insisting on sex irrespective of whether the partner is willing or not and the need for constant sexual reassurance. This can lead to dangerous and unhealthy sexual behaviour which is not only damaging to others but also to the survivor. If survivors are affected in this way it may be necessary to seek professional or specialist help. Alternatively, some survivors manipulate and control their partners by withholding sex.

Some survivors end up being involved in indiscriminate sexual behaviour because they cannot say 'no' when others demand sex. This can be dangerous as it leaves them open and vulnerable to abusive relationships in which elements of abuse and love become intertwined and resemble the RSA experience.

⚠ **WARNING** Traumatic sexualisation can prompt sexually controlling and predatory behaviours in a small proportion of survivors which is damaging to others as well as to the survivor.

Some survivors find that they experience physical complications such as erectile dysfunction or pain upon penetration. Many survivors fear that they have been physically damaged by the sexual abuse and that this will prevent them from having children. It is important that if survivors fear that they have been physically damaged that they seek medical advice to allay any fears they may have. Female survivors who have been sexually abused and vaginally penetrated will fear that their hymen has been broken and that this will cause complications when they marry as they are no longer virgins. This can be an enormous source of shame and humiliation and a fear of getting married.

The impact of RSA on sexuality

RSA hijacks natural psychosexual development and prevents survivors from discovering their own sexuality and imposes negative associations with sex which can colour all future sexual relationships. This is compounded by the sexual shame that is associated with many faith-based beliefs and which prevent an open dialogue around sex. The abuser may have further contaminated these beliefs during the RSA in order to maximise their control and power over the survivor and to reduce the risk of disclosure. These distorted beliefs will have influenced the survivor's attitude towards sex and sexuality, and intensified his or her shame. Survivors will need to identify any distorted beliefs and replace these with more accurate knowledge to reclaim their sexuality.

READ *The Warrior Within* has practical exercises and activities to help reclaim sexuality.

Sexual shame

Religious teachings often depict sex as shameful or sinful. This is intensified if sexual shame was used to manipulate the survivor and if it involved sadomasochistic overtones. This can lead to submissive and/or dominant sexual behaviour, preventing the survivor from relating to partners in a healthy, loving or caring way. Many survivors are unable to take pleasure in non-sexual physical contact as they fear that it will lead to sexual demands. This can be extremely confusing and makes casual sexual relationships easier as there is no expectation love or affection. RSA also prevents survivors from saying 'no' to sexual advances without feeling guilty or ashamed, or from regulating their natural desire when to have sex.

The betrayal of the body

Sexual shame is also felt if the survivor experienced any sexual pleasure during the abuse. In responding to sexual touch, becoming aroused or having an erection or orgasm, many survivors feel as though their body has betrayed them. It is important that survivors realise that the abuser may have intentionally performed these sex acts in order provoke arousal. This is designed to make the survivor complicit in the abuse and to feel as though he or she was to blame. The shame associated with sexual arousal significantly reduces the chance of disclosure and allows the abuser to remain undetected.

Bodily responses

Survivors need to be aware that physical responses to sexual touch, having an erection or becoming lubricated are all natural. Erections may be involuntary and occur as a result of fear or stress as well as arousal. Equally, vaginal lubrication in females is an automatic response, and a natural protection from tissue damage. Neither response specifically indicates sexual desire or arousal. These reactions may occur for purely non-sexual reasons, in the same way that nipples become erect due to fear and cold.

The sexual arousal cycle

If sexual stimulation continues after the sexual arousal system has been activated it naturally tends to lead to orgasm. Experiencing involuntary ejaculations or orgasms does not mean that the survivor encouraged or desired the sexual encounter. Moreover, it does not make the survivor responsible for the RSA. It also does not mean that the survivor is dirty or sinful. The body is merely responding to the sexual stimulation not the abuser who has exploited these responses to induce shame and minimise the risk of disclosure.

REMEMBER The body is biologically programmed to become aroused, experience pleasure and orgasm in the presence of sexual stimulation. It responds to sexual stimulation, not the person.

Sexual arousal and sexual desire

It is essential that survivors distinguish between **sexual desire** and **sexual arousal**. Sexual desire and sexual arousal are two separate and different things. Individuals can become aroused without the desire to be sexual and such arousal is natural response to sexual stimulation. The only inappropriate behaviour is that of the abuser in coercing the victim into sexual activity.

Physical pain during sex

Some survivors experience physical pain during penetration. This is primarily due to tensing the muscles in the vagina or anus as a way to protect themselves from unwanted sex. This tensing becomes automatic in the presence of sex in adulthood – even if it is with a loving partner. Many survivors fear that sexual pain is evidence of physical damage to external or internal sexual organs. A medical examination by a sensitive specialist can reduce some of these fears. Survivors may also consider discussing any other anatomical or body image concerns they might have including the size and shape of their penis, clitoris or vagina. Whilst most RSA does not lead to long-term damage or deformities, survivors should seek medical advice and take any concerns seriously.

Muscular tension is often a reaction to fear, leading to pain during intercourse. A common problem that female survivors encounter is **vaginismus**, in which the vaginal muscles contract making penetration virtually impossible. While lubricants can help, it is better for survivors to recue their fears and learn to relax the muscles. Male survivors with very tight foreskins that make intercourse and even erections painful should also seek medical advice.

Emotional reactions

Fear can also affect the emotional temperature of sexual relationships. During sex, survivors often feel overwhelmed by strong feelings of shame, terror, anger or humiliation which are difficult to contain. Sexual stimulation can induce intrusive memories or flashbacks that can compel the survivor to tune out, or dissociate. This is because the sexual contact has triggered the same sensations or sensory cues as experienced during the abuse. The fear of flashbacks or unexpressed anger about the abuse can initiate defensive reactions like detachment, withdrawal or aggression. This can scare both the survivor and his or her partner, particularly if this has not been linked to the RSA. This is a conditioned response to the sexual abuse, and does not mean that the survivor does not love or care for his or her partner. By identifying the triggers and sensory cues that induce flashbacks, anger, fear or dissociation, the survivor can begin to take control of them.

 READ *The Warrior Within* has useful exercises and activities to help identify triggers.

Changing sensory cues

To minimise trauma reactions, survivors will need to replace negative sensory cues with more pleasurable ones that link to the present, loving relationship. It is helpful for the survivor to explore these with his or her partner to make the necessary changes. Couples could consider changing where and when they have sex, and experiment with different sexual positions and sexual behaviours. Many survivors find adding pleasant smells either through body oil, lotions or candles can change the sensory cues sufficiently to reduce flashbacks. A couple might also explore new ways of experiencing sexual pleasure that do not mimic the stimulation of the abuser.

Altering the light by using scented candles, or changing the environmental stimuli such as sounds and visual cues can also help. If the abuse took place in silence it may help to talk quietly or to put on some music. Similarly if the abuse took place in a bedroom, then it may help to have sex in other locations. In essence, the survivor needs to change as many sensory cues as possible including varying who initiate sex in order to reclaim control over their sexuality. Trying a range of sensory cues will help eliminate old associations and defensive physical responses and give permission to enjoy sex without shame or guilt.

Body shame

The sexual shame associated with RSA can also extend into body shame which in turn impacts on sexual feelings. Survivors often hate parts of their body especially of certain parts were fetishised by the abuser. Negative feelings about the body, or not being able to control bodily responses, reinforces the survivor's sense of confusion and body shame.

Body shame is often seen in a survivor's need to cover up their body or disguising their appearance. This may be through gaining excess weight or disfigurement, or wearing baggy unattractive clothes to ward off sexual advances. Poor personal hygiene is also a powerful way to repel others. Alternatively, some survivors do the

opposite by dressing in a sexually provocative way, or by using excessive amounts of makeup in order to compensate for not feeling attractive. These are attempts to define sexual identity and prove that sexuality has not been compromised. Some survivors may resort to starving themselves or to diet to excess in order to eliminate curves and hide sexual maturity. Survivors who binge and purge food may be unconsciously recreating the bodily pleasure and pain experienced during the RSA.

Male survivors may engage in excessive body building to compensate for feelings of vulnerability, and to protect themselves from further abuse. Similarly, female survivors may exercise obsessively to gain control over the body that betrayed them during the abuse. To reclaim their sexuality, survivors need to nourish and care for their body by eating healthily and regularly, and exercise appropriately. In this way they can begin to take more pleasure in their body. They may also wish to indulge their body more by having regular massages and applying scented oil or lotion to nourish the skin.

Reclaiming sexuality

To reclaim their sexuality, survivors need to re-learn to take sensual pleasure in their body by rebuilding a safe sexual foundation. This will require a better understanding of sex and sexuality which is not contaminated by sexual shame. In addition, they need to feel more comfortable in talking about sex. In discussing their sexual fears, as well as their desires with their partner can significantly improve the quality of their sexual relationship.

⚠ **WARNING** It is critical for survivors to pace themselves when reclaiming their body and sexuality and avoid rushing it.

Sensate focus

A powerful way to reclaim both body and sexuality is through a series of exercises called **sensate focus**. This will enable survivors to explore their body and its responses either alone or with a partner. Through self-exploration or with a partner survivors can get to know their body and identify what they do and don't like.

📖 **READ** *The Warrior Within* has useful exercises to help survivors explore sensate focus.

🖱 **ONLINE** The One in Four website has useful exercises to help survivors explore sensate focus.

Mood and its impact on sexual relationships

Mood can affect sexual relationships by increasing or decreasing **libido**. Survivors' libido can be affected by stress or unresolved anger, which can impact on the desire to have sex, as well as levels of sexual arousal. Some female survivors find that their monthly hormonal cycle has a significant impact on their libido – as do conflicts, arguments and unresolved anger.

Lack of control and unpredictability also exerts a powerful influence on sexual relationships, especially if this is reminiscent of the RSA. Many survivors find that it helps to be more in control of when to have sex and feel more comfortable with some advance warning so they can get into the right mind set and mood. A degree of knowledge about when sex might occur can help survivors to feel more comfortable instead of feeling put upon. Although this reduces sexual spontaneity, it does give the survivor some control over when to have sex. Many survivors resort to alcohol to lower inhibitions or combat sexual fears. While small amounts of alcohol may help to relax the survivor, they must remember that too much alcohol will affect sexual performance and the ability to experience pleasure.

Being free from interruptions

Feeling safe and eliminating the possibility of interruptions will increase sexual desire and arousal. This is particularly the case with survivors of RSA who would have been **hyper-vigilant** during the abuse in case someone found out what was happening. This hyper-vigilance is often taken in adulthood making it hard for survivors to relax sexually.

Sexual trust

A healthy sexual relationship requires sexual trust. For this to grow survivors and their partners must define and implement sexual boundaries and ground rules. Open and honest communication will create this trust and allow the survivor express their feelings and sexual needs without worrying about upsetting or rejecting their partner. Boundaries and ground rules are essential for healthy sexual relationships.

Survivors will also need exchange regular affirmations of love and compliments and know that they can say 'no' with feeling humiliated, hurt or rejected. Survivors also need to know that not **all** hugs and cuddles lead to sex and that they are expressions of affection.

In reclaiming their sexuality survivors can significantly improve the quality of their sexual relationship. Alternatively some survivors may decide to be celibate for a period of time or choose not to enter into sexual relationships. This should not be judged and needs to be respected providing the survivor has worked through the RSA and is sure that he or she is making an informed choice. In making such a choice the survivor may benefit from counselling or psychosexual therapy. If they do decide to refrain from expressing their sexuality, survivors must remember to grieve the loss of their sexual expression.

The importance of grieving losses, including sexual losses, is addressed in the following chapter which looks at the grieving process.

14 Understanding grief and loss

RSA and the trauma that accompanies it are linked to a sense of loss, both in the present and the past. Self-blame, negative self-beliefs and shame prevent survivors from feeling they deserve to grieve. RSA induces losses across a wide spectrum, including physical, psychological and spiritual losses. Recovery is only possible if survivors can identify the full extent of their losses, from the past to the present. Once identified these losses can be validated and subsequently mourned.

The losses associated with RSA can be both symbolic and actual losses. Common examples of losses include loss of childhood, loss of protective parent(s), loss of nurturing family, loss of self, loss of control and autonomy and loss of self-esteem and self-worth. One of the most damaging losses associated with RSA is the loss of faith, religious beliefs, and trust in God. The loss of faith can lead to spiritual death in which the survivor feels they have lost their spiritual identity as well as a sense of belongingness to the spiritual family.

REMEMBER The losses associated with RSA can be both symbolic and actual losses.

Other losses may involve a loss of control over the body, loss of continuity, loss of healthy relationships, loss of well-being and loss of belief in a benign world and a better future. Some survivors experience a loss of hope of ever recovering from RSA, which can lead to such despair that suicide becomes the only option. This can present an enormous dilemma to those survivors whose faith deems suicide to be sinful. For some survivors suicide is preferable, as they would rather die in sin than risk entering to heaven where they may encounter their abuser.

Survivors who are unable to legitimise the RSA of self-blame or shame face additional obstacles in their grieving. To prevent these blocks to grieving, survivors need first to work through residual self-blame, shame and negative self-beliefs so that they can fully legitimise their abuse. To do this will require self-compassion and empathy so that the survivor can allow the hurt and pain to be released and begin the grieving process.

The grieving process

While it is essential to grieve all the losses incurred, survivors will vary enormously in how they grieve. Each survivor's grieving process will be unique and cannot be determined by others. Despite these unique differences, counsellors have found that there are some common phases that most bereaved people go through. The sequence and length of time each phase takes will vary from survivor to survivor, as will the eventual outcome.

Phases of grief

Survivors will go through a number of phases of grief and experience as wide range of emotions. These commonly include **denial**, **numbness** and a **preoccupation with – and yearning for –what is lost**. This will give rise to feelings of **sadness** for what has been lost, **anger** for what was taken from them and **jealousy** of those who were not abused. It is important to express both sadness and anger in order to be able to accept the loss and readjust to life. Accepting the loss is not the same as accepting the RSA, it is an acknowledgement and validation of the abuse. This allows survivors to integrate the losses rather than avoiding them and readjust to life.

The release of accumulated grief can feel overwhelming, and survivors must pace themselves, and make sure that they nurture themselves throughout the process. It is important to take time to work through the losses and to go at a manageable pace. The grieving process can feel excruciating at times and survivors will need to persevere

to reduce the ferocity of the pain does reduce over time. While most of the pain will be released some survivors will find that they are left with a small nub of sadness or a sense of loss.

 REMEMBER The release of accumulated grief can be overwhelming and survivors need space to grieve and give themselves time to mourn each loss.

As survivors examine each of their losses they will begin to understand of how RSA affected them at the time and how this still affects them in the present. It is important to mark each of the losses with a small memorial ritual to honour each loss. This can be done individually for each loss or to mark many losses at once.

 READ *The Warrior Within* has useful exercises to help manage the grieving process.

Expressing feelings

Survivors need to allow themselves to feel whatever emotions emerge – be that anger or sadness – without judging them, or feeling ashamed. This can be very difficult for some survivors especially if they have been taught to see tears as a weakness, or were if their tears were ridiculed, punished or ignored during the abuse. Some survivors will have forced themselves not to cry during or immediately after the abuse and will find it very difficult to allow themselves to cry. This is often true of males who have been socialised to not show their feelings and to be stoical in the presence of adversity.

REMEMBER Survivors need to allow themselves to feel whatever emotions emerge, be that anger or sadness, without judging them or feeling ashamed.

Releasing suppressed sadness and anger

Anger may also have been suppressed by survivors, both at the time of the abuse and subsequently. To express anger at the time of the abuse would have been dangerous and been associated with negative consequences. As anger cannot be expressed it is internalised and intensified. Many survivors of RSA bury their anger so deeply that they turn the anger against themselves through self-blame and shame. Such internalised anger can become toxic and lead to depression. Releasing the anger through the grieving process and redirecting it back onto the original source is a powerful way of externalising pent-up anger.

If sadness and anger have been suppressed for many years they will take on tsunami-like proportions. Survivors who have never been able to cry or allow themselves to feel their sadness will fear that they will be deluged by tidal waves of tears; that they will be submerged and swept away in their grief. This fear, while very real, is then used to rationalise the survivor's reluctance to grieve. These blocks to grieving only serve to intensify the sadness and increase unshed tears. In such cases, survivors need to trust in the process of grieving and allow themselves to release the suppressed sadness and tears in small, manageable doses. If they fear doing this on their own then they need to consider doing it with a trusted other or their counsellor.

Some survivors find it easier to release their sadness and are terrified by their anger. This is often the case for female survivors who have been conditioned to believe that anger is unacceptable in females. Many female survivors cover up their anger with sadness as this is seen as more socially acceptable and are only able to access anger or rage once they have fully expressed their sadness. As anger emerges, many survivors fear that it will erupt in volcanic proportions and consume them. As a result survivors fear that if they externalise their anger that they will either explode or implode. To avoid such annihilation survivors feel compelled to suppress their anger again and block the grieving process.

Many male survivors are only able to feel anger which commonly masks their loss and sadness. Although they are in touch with their anger they are not necessarily expressing this in relation to the RSA. Their anger may be more generalised resulting in conflicted relationships and explosive outburst of aggression or violence. The grieving process allows the survivor to link their anger to the RSA and direct it back to the source. Once this anger has been expressed, the survivor can permit feelings of sadness to emerge. It is critical that survivors are able to express both the surface emotions and the more deeply buried ones to fully work through grief and integrate the losses.

As survivors work through their grief they will become more aware of their negative beliefs about expressing anger or vulnerability or crying. In challenging these, survivors will be able to make more autonomous choices about how they wish to express their emotions without being controlled by their childhood conditioning and fears. This liberates them from the power and

control that the RSA and abuser still has over their lives. In taking back control through the grieving process, survivors can begin to take charge over their lives again.

Replacing losses

Once survivors have started the grieving process by identifying their losses they can begin to determine what was lost in childhood and is still absent in adulthood. While these losses cannot be replaced, survivors can compensate for the deficits by making sure that these no longer persist in their adult live. If survivors were deprived of play and fun in childhood then they need to ensure that they give themselves permission to play and have fun in adulthood.

Similarly, if survivors lacked nurturing and loving relationships in childhood they need to ensure that they build healthy, loving relationships in adulthood. Building a good support network in adulthood can make up for the neglect and abuse of the past. Survivors who felt psychologically orphaned as a child can create a new 'family' wherein they feel respected, loved and nurtured. While this will never make up for the abuse and loss in childhood it will improve the quality of life in the present.

Spiritual losses can also be replaced by exploring alternative ways of expressing spirituality. Grieving the loss of faith and beliefs, although painful, does present a unique opportunity to re-evaluate inherited or conditioned religious beliefs and explore alternative faiths. It also allows survivors to explore internal and more concrete forms of spirituality through connecting to the spirit within (see **Restoring spirituality and forgiveness** on page 164).

Readjusting to life

Recognising losses and mourning them will help survivors to place the RSA in the past where it belongs, and help them to readjust to the world as it is now. Through the grieving process survivors are able to relegate the RSA to the past rather than letting it dominate or control the present. More importantly, the RSA will no longer define the survivor in his or her entirety. This will help the survivor to move forward and embrace the future without being haunted by the memory of pain, terror and fear of abuse.

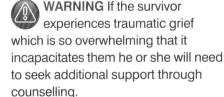 **WARNING** If the survivor experiences traumatic grief which is so overwhelming that it incapacitates them he or she will need to seek additional support through counselling.

15 Understanding the impact on spirituality and faith

A central feature of RSA is its impact on religious beliefs, faith and spirituality. This is true for both primary victims as well as secondary victims (see **Who is at risk and who has been affected?** on page 45). Many regular church goers and worshippers have lost trust and belief in church authorities, religious institutions and faith leaders and are dismayed at how allegations of sexual abuse have been handled. This has led many to question not just their faith in their church, and what it stands for, but also their belief in God.

Challenges to religious beliefs

A common challenge to religious beliefs for Christian survivors is the nature of God. Survivors of RSA begin to wonder who God is, what he stands for, and whether he is benign and forgiving. Moreover they question that if God is benign why did he not intervene and stop the sexual abuse? Was God a co-conspirator in the sexual abuse, and therefore partly responsible? If God is forgiving will he forgive them, as well as their abuser? Does this mean that if the abuser repents and is forgiven that the survivor is condemned to meet their abuser in the after-life? These are such terrifying thoughts for some survivors that they deliberately act and behave in ways that reduce their chances of meeting their abuser after death. As heaven is no longer seen as a safe place they would rather go to hell. This can lead to aggressive and destructive behaviours that ultimately compromise the survivor's integrity which further erodes their belief in themselves. In behaving against their true moral integrity, they descend into a spiral of shame, self-blame and guilt – not realising that this replicates precisely what the abuser made them feel.

The eternal conflict with God makes it hard to trust, or engage in any of the sacraments, including prayer and contemplation. When prayers have been left unanswered at a time of greatest need it is hard to continue to trust in the concept of prayer. In addition, being in the presence of religious rituals such as kneeling to pray, taking communion or ritual washing can revive memories of the abuse. These can give rise to trauma reactions especially when these are combined with other sensory cues associated with the RSA such as the smell of incense, lighting candles, religious robes or other religious iconography.

Avoidance of religious practices

The fear of triggering trauma reactions force survivors to avoid religious practices and rituals. Many survivors of RSA by RC priests also avoid the sacraments of confession and holy communion as they have lost all their meaning and they do not wish to collude in what they have come to see as hypocrisy. They also begin to question whether religious officials and clergy really are true representatives of God, and whether the hands that sexually molested them really were holy and sacred. In addition, accepting communion or absolution from someone associated with the abuser, no matter how loosely, can trigger conditioned responses and trauma reactions such as flashbacks and intrusive memories.

It is extremely hard for survivors to reconcile themselves to such stark contradictions, and to continue to trust those that abused them together with and the religious institutions that have prioritised the protection of the abuser over the victim. This secondary betrayal by faith leaders, church authorities and religious institutions makes it impossible for some survivors to ever reconcile such fundamental contradictions.

The way that church authorities and religious institutions have handled allegations of RSA has had a significant impact on victims and faithful worshippers. Many primary and secondary victims are disheartened and disillusioned by the lack of appropriate response from faith leaders to victims, and consequently feel deeply betrayed. This has been intensified by the lack of accountability and responsibility of religious institutions, the cover ups that exposed more children to risk as offenders were relocated, and the lack of effective apology.

The recent Cloyne report[12] exemplifies this in providing evidence that despite policies and procedures being in place to protect children, these are not being fully implemented. What has added further insult to injury is the implication that the hierarchy of the RC Church are not truly committed to implementing their own policies and procedures and are complicit in obstructing reporting and investigating allegations.

Loss of faith and belief

Loss of faith in church authorities, religious institutions and faith leaders means that many survivors no longer trust clergy or the church hierarchy to offer a safe place for truth telling. This has led many to turn away from the institution of the church or places of worship, with less people attending regularly. The betrayal felt by both primary and secondary victims have created doubts about whether they can trust that their children will be safe and protected within the church.

This has led some to question the safety of their children attending Sunday school, serving as altar boys or girls, joining the choir, and being confirmed. The view is often if '**I can't trust my priest, vicar or minister, who can I trust?**'. Given the number of sexual abuse allegations against religious schools, convents and faith schools, many parents are rightly concerned about the risks of enrolling their children. Knowing that offenders have been protected by church authorities, relocated to other parishes or ministries, without knowing that they have offended, demands the need to be more vigilant. Increasingly faith communities have become disillusioned with the integrity and duplicity of religious officials and institutions.

The loss of belief in God and the loss of faith feels like the loss of a part of the individual's sense of identity, as well as the loss of a spiritual family. As survivors come to feel lost in relation to God, the rest of the faith community and their spiritual identity, they face considerable theological conflict and spiritual dissonance. Some survivors feel ashamed for their loss of faith and yet may continue to attend church and their place of worship. While this feels hypocritical they nevertheless feel compelled to go through the motions and perform the necessary rituals

without being able to believe. Over time they begin to feel increasingly empty and hollow their integrity is compromised.

As they become more and more alienated from the church and from God, survivors begin to build a fortress around themselves to ward off the pain of loss. This allows them to disconnect from feeling the pain and injury of the loss of a central part of their belief system. As they become more alienated from – and invisible to – God, the church, and others, they begin to lose their own sense of self. This can lead to despair and a sense of hopelessness in which the purpose and meaning of life, and death are questioned. The subsequent existential anxiety can lead some survivors to question their very existence as they experience a psychological and spiritual death.

In the absence of a religious or spiritual belief system the survivor feels increasingly fragile and vulnerable, and lost in the world. Rather than be able to turn to God or the church for solace, sanctuary or spiritual guidance, they feel abandoned at a time of their greatest need. As they can no longer seek healing in their spiritual home, they seek to manage their loss and pain in other ways. While some may seek support from other survivors, or through justice, others may seek sanctuary in numbing their pain through self-medication or self-harming behaviours. All too many seek the cessation of pain through suicide.

Theological conflict

Survivors of RSA who lose their faith in the church, or belief in God, face considerable **theological conflict**.[18] If they lose their faith in their church, but not their belief in God or a higher power or deity, they can resolve this conflict by changing their denomination by turning to another religion or faith. This allows them to retain some belief in a higher power making them feel less abandoned by God. Some survivors however are not able to retain their belief and come to doubt the very existence of God, or higher power and adopt agnostic or atheistic beliefs

Existential vacuum and anxiety

The absence of religious beliefs can create an **existential vacuum** both in this world and the next. Many survivors become not only fearful of life which no longer has meaning, but also fearful of death and dying. Being robbed of an important belief and philosophy of life generates immense uncertainty around the very purpose of life which can leave the survivor directionless. This lack of

focus and structure of sustaining beliefs can lead spiritual emptiness. The fear of meeting their abuser in the afterlife is so terrifying that many survivors of RSA fear death and dying.[18]

Impact on spirituality

The sense of spiritual emptiness reinforces the many other losses and abandonments. This leads to an overwhelming sense of inner emptiness. The lack of a structured belief system can make some survivors fear losing control, as they no longer have a support system to contain or sustain them. This is reinforced if they have felt stigmatised by the faith community or their family and friends.

These multiple betrayals can be so overwhelming that the survivor becomes out of contact with the spirit within. The struggle to survive in the absence of acknowledgment of the harm caused can lead some survivors to give up all hope in a better future or better world. The spirit becomes so exhausted that it also threatens to abandon them. And yet it is possible to revive that spirit and restore spirituality.

Restoring spirituality

To prevent a total loss of faith and belief in God, it is important to be mindful that it is sometimes easier to feel angry with church authorities, religious institutions or God than with the actual abuser. This resembles the dynamics seen in incestuous families, wherein the anger towards the abuser is diluted and deflected onto the non-abusing parent for not protecting them from the sexual abuse. Many survivors of RSA often feel more angry with, and let down by church authorities, faith leaders and God than the actual abuser. While this is understandable, it is important to balance and evaluate the degree of responsibility for sexually abusive behaviour.

REMEMBER Survivors must not let their abuser or religious institution destroy their faith – it is possible to find their own personally meaningful spirituality.

Identifying who is responsible for committing the RSA, those who failed to protect the child from the sexual offender and who betrayed them through silencing can help survivors to focus their anger more specifically and directly at those responsible. This will allow some survivors to retain their faith in God, whilst rightly expressing their anger at the abuser and individual religious or church officials – rather than abandoning the whole of their faith and religious beliefs.

READ *The Warrior Within* has useful exercises to help focus anger at those responsible for abuse.

In this, survivors will be able to recognise and acknowledge that there are many good priests, ministers and pastors who do not abuse, and some bishops and faith leaders who do act appropriately. It is crucial not to let those that abuse colour and contaminate all aspects of religion or faith. This can lead to embitterment and destruction of what has been an important and sustaining belief system. Most importantly, being forced to abandon faith is testament to the fact the sexual abuser still wields enormous power over the survivor in destroying a once highly-valued belief system.

Those survivors that do lose all faith and belief in their religion or faith can still restore their spirituality by ensuring that they do not lose faith in themselves and reviving the spirit within. In connecting to the inner spirit, survivors can begin to find their own faith which is self-defined and personally meaningful to them (see **Restoring spirituality and forgiveness** on page 164). Survivors will need to begin the process of healing which is the focus of the following section.

Part three
Healing from religious sexual abuse

16 The process of healing

The process of recovery is unique to each survivor and varies from person to person. The process can be gruelling at times with stops and starts, obstacles and blockades, detours and diversions, as well as miraculous breakthroughs. Survivors will find that it is made up of a continuous chain of small achievements rather than big leaps. To restore control and take charge over their lives and their future survivors will need patience, stamina, hope and commitment. One way to help survivors to take ownership of their recovery is to find a metaphor or symbol that represents their healing process.

Starting the process of healing

To start the process of healing it helps to aid identify inner strengths and resources that have aided survival so far and ensure that there are safety structures in place. Ideally this needs to include a good support network of trusted people. This can include family, or friends as well as professionals such as a counsellor, or a survivor's support group.

Regaining control over trauma reactions and symptoms is the first step in recovery. This needs to must be accompanied by healthy sleeping and eating patterns, as well as physical exercise. As these become established,

survivors will discover an increase in energy and vitality which can be channelled to triumph over trauma and restore a sense of purpose and meaning to life (see **Understanding trauma reactions** on page 87).

READ *The Warrior Within* has useful exercises and activities to help create safety structures and regain control over trauma reactions.

REMEMBER The most positive factors in recovery from trauma are control and a sense of purpose

Pacing the process of healing

Pacing the process of healing is critical so as not to rush it. It helps to break down the process of recovery into small manageable steps and validate each accomplishment. It is important to savour achievements and take pleasure in them. This allows for monitoring of goals set and reached. It is important not to rush the process of recovery as this increases the likelihood of setbacks.

REMEMBER To maximise achievement, survivors must not rush recovery.

Survivors often rush through experiences to avoid fully experiencing the full range of emotions. This is conditioned during the RSA as the survivor wished for the sexual encounter to be over as quickly as possible and avoid feelings. Rushing recovery reduces the number of healing experiences, making it harder to value achievements. Slowing down also reduces trauma cues and gives the mind and body time to embed new ways of being. It is much better to start slowly and consolidate each step than to leap forward only to stumble backwards or relapse. While slowing down is frustrating at times it maximises the achievement and provides a better guarantee for future success. In addition making time to celebrate enables survivors to validate their courage and renewed self-confidence.

 REMEMBER It is important to reward the achievement of goals.

Coming out of survival mode

Regaining control, finding a sense of purpose and valuing achievements will facilitate coming out of survival mode. This restores energy, enabling the survivor to notice positive things in life and feel more alive. As they begin to embrace more positive aspects of life, they are to balance negative feelings and experiences with more positive ones. This balance opens up opportunities to make more personally meaningful choices rather than being dominated by negative thoughts and feelings associated with the RSA experiences. As they re-engage in more pleasurable activities, survivors will find new opportunities for growth.

 REMEMBER Coming out of survival mode restores energy and allows survivors to feel more alive.

Changing cues from the past

To counterbalance traumatic experiences, survivors need to replace sensory cues that were present during the RSA with alternative ones. For example, if the abuse took place in a place of worship with candles and incense burning, it is important to replace these cues with different lighting and smells. Changing sensory cues from the past means that there are fewer reminders of the RSA which reduces the likelihood of triggering flashbacks or intrusive memories. Replacing haunting cues from the past allows survivors to take more pleasure in activities which are personally meaningful.

 READ *The Warrior Within* has useful exercises and activities to help change sensory cues.

Engaging in more pleasurable activities will allow the survivor to live more in the present rather than be catapulted into the past, and begin to experience longer periods of peace and contentment. This will make it easier to manage difficult times with more vitality and renewed optimism. As the survivor becomes less haunted and controlled by the past, trapped energy will be discharged and released. This renewed energy helps survivors to wake up with enthusiasm and optimism for the day ahead rather than dreading it.

Reclaiming the spirit within

Recovery from RSA is not just about reclaiming one's self, it is also about building a more complete person through reviving the spirit within. As the spirit within is awakened and given a voice, survivors will discover aspects of the self that have been hidden and sealed away. Survivors often find that they are able to recover abilities and talents that have lain dormant for many years which give them a new direction in life. In reconnecting to these survivors feel more able to take charge of their life rather than it being dictated by the RSA, abuser or religious institution to which they belong.

REMEMBER Through healing, the past no longer dictates the present and the survivor becomes the author of his or her life and spirituality.

While survivors cannot undo what the abuser has done, they can reclaim their essence and spirit to determine the present and the future. This more positive focus will allow for post traumatic growth, and a return of vitality and spirituality. As survivors begin to appreciate life more they are able to focus more on what they do have rather than on what is missing. Becoming more consciously aware of the good things life has to offer also acts as reminder that the survivor is part of something bigger and enter a more spiritual dimension. This will allow for greater harmony and balance in life and help the survivor to bounce back more quickly from setbacks and feel thankful for the gift of life.

REMEMBER Every day before going to sleep recount three good things that have happened that day.

Obstacles to recovery

Although recovery is liberating and empowering it is also scary. Change can be very stressful and stir up powerful emotions, making it harder to manage any obstacles to recovery. It is important that survivors accept that obstacles are a normal part of the recovery process and are opportunities for growth.

REMEMBER The circle of life is characterised by change and rebirth in which growth becomes more vigorous and resplendent.

Change is always difficult as it is hard to give up habits and old patterns of thinking and behaviour. As these habits become more deeply ingrained it becomes harder to imagine alternative ways of being. As a result reactions become automatic and seem to occur outside of conscious awareness. This is because habitual reactions are frozen in time and will need to thaw. As the survivor acclimatises to change, and fear is reduced, obstacles to recovery can be more easily managed.

Many of the obstacles to recovery stem from the fear and stress of change. Each survivor will have specific anxieties and concerns that are unique to them. Some will welcome the opportunity for change, while others are terrified. It is normal to have mixed feelings about change and it is helpful to acknowledge these.

A common obstacle to change is that it will stir up overwhelming emotions which feel unmanageable. This will set off the emotional alarm system which demands attention. To manage these fears, survivors may resort to old patterns of avoidance or emotional numbing through the use of alcohol, drugs, food, work, sex or self-injury. A return to self-medication will inevitably create obstacles to emotional processing and hijack the recovery process.

REMEMBER Identifying fears is the first step to overcoming them

The fear of **re-traumatisation** can outweigh any gains of recovery, which could lead to an increased fear of failure and doubts about ever getting better. Fears and anxieties reduce the ability to make decisions, which can create further obstacles and interfere with recovery. These fears can lead to self-fulfilling prophecies by paralysing the survivor to such an extent that they are unable to function. Survivors often prepare themselves for the worst outcome, so that they prepare themselves for disappointment. Whilst this is designed to cushion the hurt and pain, it can become crippling. This spiral of fear is a good reason not to seek quick, radical changes but to savour and value each small step and achievement. Change which is more gradual and less noticeable will seem less terrifying and be a more solid foundation for recovery.

Another common stumbling block is the fear of **secondary traumas** linked to RSA. Survivors fear that they have sustained irreparable physical damage and therefore can't have children, or that their sexuality has been affected to such an extent that they will never find a partner. These genuine fears need to be addressed and objectively challenged. If the survivor has fears around physical damage it helps to have a full medical check-up to allay any fears.

Litigation – whilst empowering – can also generate obstacles to recovery as it can be a lengthy and gruelling process in which the RSA is frequently revisited in recounting the abuse experiences and having to provide statements. It is also fraught with delays, disappointments and decisions that provoke outrage and anger. Survivors need to make sure that they are robust enough and have sufficient resilience before embarking on such a course of action. They also need to ensure that they have a good support network, including access to professional support (see **Using the legal system for justice and healing** on page 176).

An increase in **trauma reactions**, such as flashbacks, nightmares or intrusive memories can lead to exhaustion and lack of energy which can present further obstacles to recovery. To minimise these, it important to build up both mental and physical strength through rest, work and play, as well as regular exercise. It also helps to eat healthily and regulate eating patterns. To increase energy levels it helps to reduce the intake of caffeine, alcohol and sugar. This will help to restore zest and vitality to life which helps to overcome any obstacles to change.

Feelings of anger can also become a stumbling block, especially if it they have been suppressed over many years. Survivors of RSA commonly feel angry – not only with the abuser but also the religious institution and the criminal justice system. Such powerful and unexpressed anger can become all-consuming and prevent recovery. While anger is an entirely natural and valid response, especially if the abuser has not been held accountable, it can become toxic and an obstacle to healing.

Shame and **guilt** are also obstacles to recovery, especially if accompanied with self-blame. Self- blame prevents survivors from legitimising RSA leaving them feeling responsible for the abuse. This is particularly the case when there has been a lack of recognition of RSA from others such as the abuser, family, friends, religious institution or the criminal justice system. A further source of shame is if the survivor experienced pleasurable sensations during the sexual abuse, or sought contact with the abuser. It is important to recognise that pleasurable sensations during sexual contact are normal and do not mean that the survivor wanted the sexual abuse. Similarly, seeking contact with the abuser is not evidence that the RSA was wanted or encouraged. Although obstacles that derive from self blame, shame and secrecy can seem insurmountable they can be worked through (see **Understanding shame, self-blame and self-forgiveness** on page 113).

Negative beliefs and critical self-talk can also present considerable obstacles to healing. For example, the belief that the survivor deserved the RSA can be crippling and lead to lack of self-worth. As the survivor feels worthless, he or she will not feel entitled to set boundaries, ask for needs to be met or be assertive. This can sabotage recovery as repeated critical self-talk or negative inner dialogue affects not only self-esteem but also mood. Such critical messages act as internal saboteurs which become major obstacles to change and recovery.

Current unhealthy relationships are often the most resistant obstacles. Such relationships commonly resemble the dynamics of the RSA in which fear prevents assertion and the open expression of thought or feelings. This

is made worse if the survivor feels he or she is not worthy of compassion or empathy. This is further complicated if partners or friends have a vested interest in preventing change, so that they can retain power over the survivor. Such unhealthy relationships act as a constant reminder of the RSA which will keep the survivor locked into a 'victim' role that can undermine recovery.

Gains and losses

Healing and recovery will produce gains and losses, and it is important to identify these so that the losses do not become major obstacles To prevent this it is helpful to be prepared for any losses so that they can be more accommodated (see **Understanding grief and loss** on page 135). Despondency and loss of hope are also obstacles to recovery. Taking time to accept and mourn losses rather than fighting them is a crucial element in healing. While losses are unavoidable this does not mean that survivors will necessarily lose all hope. It is important to remember that it is possible to recover from RSA and to maintain faith in the spirit within.

REMEMBER The willingness to believe that change can occur and that experiences, emotions and thoughts are not set in stone but are dynamic will help the healing process.

Setbacks and relapses

Setbacks and relapses are part of the recovery process and these provide opportunities for discovery and learning. It is important to keep faith and not lose hope. The process of healing and recovery is not linear and is made up of detours. Setbacks are inevitable and should be seen as opportunities to use all the new skills learnt during the recovery process. As some setbacks are predictable it is helpful to think about how you might manage these in advance.

REMEMBER Setbacks are part of the recovery process and provide opportunities for discovery and leaning and to use new skills.

Setbacks are essentially signals and reminders of areas of vulnerability and outstanding work that needs to be done. They also help in measuring recovery and reviewing goals. It may be necessary to revise goals as healing takes place. Focusing on potential setbacks in advance can help to prepare the survivor to manage these more easily before they become immobilising. When faced by setbacks survivors need to go back to the basic skills learnt. The most important thing is to remain realistic and be open to experimenting with various methods to reach goals, and be prepared to revise them.

 READ *The Warrior Within* has advice on dealing with setbacks.

REMEMBER Be realistic in setting goals and how they can be achieved. Setbacks may be due to unrealistic goals rather than failure.

In the case of **relapses** it is important to reduce any other pressures and commitments. This is often a time to be assertive, say 'no' and to make time to focus on your own needs. It may also be a time to ask for help from others without feeling a failure. It is important to access as much support as possible during such crises until things return back to a more manageable level. The focus has to be on reducing areas of stress and maximising stabilisation.

Bouncing back

It is unrealistic to expect to be free of any distress or trauma reactions, and survivors need to accept this. The most important factor in measuring recovery is not the number of setbacks, but how fast the survivor is able to 'bounce' back. The more skills the survivor has to manage stress and trauma reactions, the faster he or she will be able to restore stability and feel in control. The skills learnt during the process of recovery will enable the survivor to manage trauma reactions and to bounce back more quickly.

REMEMBER The most important factor in measuring recovery is not the number of setbacks, but how fast the survivor is able to 'bounce' back.

A fundamental aspect of healing and recovery is to restore reality and trust in the self. In connecting to the self, survivors will be able to be more in touch with their inner experiencing. This will restore intuition and allow the survivor to make choices that come from an inner knowledge rather than driven by outside forces.

Restoring the spirit within and inner wisdom

The more survivors listen to the spirit within, the more they will be able to access their own inner value system and inner wisdom. Accessing inner wisdom, or relying on an 'internal locus of evaluation', will restore trust in the self which allows survivors to rebuild self-esteem and make more positive choices.

As survivors start to listen to the spirit within they will become more in touch with their needs, especially spiritual

ones. This will lead to what is known as an '**internal locus of control**' in which survivors feel more in control of thoughts, feelings and actions.

Reviving the spirit within allows survivors to trust their internal value system more, which allows for greater self-reliance and a decrease in their dependency on others. Such self-reliance must not be confused with fierce self-sufficiency, which is protection from others. This self-reliance will enable survivors to express and meet their needs without being derailed by others or being coerced into adopting the beliefs imposed on them.

Self-reliance also allows survivors to challenge and re-evaluate inherited or conditioned beliefs, including religious ones. In listening to the spirit within survivors can begin to make their own choices in defining what faith means to them and how they wish to practice their faith. This allows them to find the source of their spirituality within rather than being dominated by external forces. This will not only be empowering and liberating, but will enable survivors to rebuild relationships, restore faith and spirituality and triumph over trauma – which will all be explored in the following chapters.

17 Rebuilding relationships

Rebuilding relationships is a crucial part of recovery and healing. It is an opportunity to improve turbulent relationships or to start communicating again after many years of silence. This could enhance the survivor's relationship with his or her family, friends, partners or children and increase access to a support network. This can reduce the sense of isolation, loneliness and emptiness. The fear of intimacy and closeness takes its toll on relationships which prevents intimacy and reinforces lack of relational worth.

Relational fears

The betrayal of trust in RSA gives rise to a number of relational fears such as fear of showing vulnerability, fear of revealing aspects of the self, fear of dependency, fear of reaching out and fear of saying 'no' or expressing needs. Many survivors also fear that they will be hurt or abused again, and therefore are reluctant to get too close. These fears can inhibit survivors in how they relate to others and result in excessive self-reliance and self-sufficiency, or overwhelming dependency needs. To manage these fears, survivors of RSA either avoid closeness and intimacy or seek refuge in relationships to make them better. This can result in turbulent, conflicted and confusing relationships that are stressful and damaging rather

than a secure base in which to heal and grow.

A central part of survivors' healing will be increasing access to protection and support which can only be achieved through being close to trusted others. To reduce fears around intimacy it is important to build up trust in self and others, set boundaries and be able express needs without feeling guilty. This will allow survivors to interact with others more openly in an atmosphere based on mutual respect and care Some relationships may not be possible to rebuild and will need to be mourned as a significant loss in order to readjust to the world (see **Understanding grief and loss** on page 135).

 READ *The Warrior Within* has exercises and activities to help build up trust.

Rebuilding relationships with God

For survivors to rebuild their relationship with God they will need to distinguish between their faith and their belief in God, and how much this was corrupted or tarnished by the abuser and the RSA. Although many abusers use distorted religious beliefs and the concept of God in order to manipulate and abuse the child, these can be challenged and re-evaluated. It is important for survivors to acknowledge that God did not abuse them, the abuser did. Many survivors are able to heal their relationship with God by re-focusing their anger, hurt and pain on the source of the harm done which is the abuser.

Some survivors feel so betrayed that they lose all faith in God and this cannot be restored. This needs to be grieved so that the survivor can explore alternative faiths or religious beliefs. This presents a unique opportunity to re-evaluate inherited or conditioned beliefs and to find alternative sources of spirituality, either external to themselves or though accessing the spirit within. **Restoring spirituality and forgiveness** on page 164 looks at how survivors can restore faith and spirituality.

While many survivors can – and do – manage to rebuild their faith in God, many are less able to restore their relationship with the religious institution or church. This is often because they feel they have not been listened to or understood. Until faith leaders or religious institutions acknowledge the harm done and extend effective apologies along with genuine assurances that children and vulnerable adults will be protected in the future, they will not be able restore trust or faith. As a result, some survivors will no longer engage in religious practices or attend their usual places of worship. Those that do may feel that their relationship with the church or religious institution is damaged but they continue to go through the motions of worship.

Rebuilding relationships with the faith community

To rebuild relationships within the faith community is often very difficult for survivors who were disbelieved, stigmatised or ostracised for making allegations of RSA. Some members of faith communities, who take their lead from their religious institutions, tend to reinforce denials of RSA and often rally around to protect the abuser while accusing victims and survivors of seduction. This feels like a secondary betrayal for survivors as they are excluded from their spiritual family. The pain and sorrow of such abandonment can make it hard for survivors to trust again.

To rebuild such relationships, survivors need to understand that the denial may be as a result of religious duress in which some members feel they have no choice but to believe faith leaders. This is most likely if the faith community has been kept naïve and uninformed. In many respects they too have been duped by the abuser and the religious institution and are therefore not able to make informed choices about who to believe. Acknowledging this can help some survivors to see the members of the faith community as secondary victims of RSA. This can allow them to find common ground on which to rebuild relationships with those that are willing to. If this is not possible survivors will need to grieve this loss and explore other sources of support, or a new spiritual family.

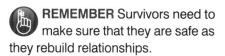 **REMEMBER** Survivors need to make sure that they are safe as they rebuild relationships.

Rebuilding relationships with family members

In order to rebuild relationships with family members, survivors will need to be clear about their feelings and needs and be able to state them in an assertive way. To gain confidence in expressing themselves, survivors may need to practice what they want to say with a trusted friend. The more survivors are able to rehearse what they want to say in the initial conversation the easier it will be. It is important, however, to only say as much as the survivor is comfortable with. If they are not ready to reveal they must not feel they have failed, as it takes time to rebuild trust and they must pace themselves accordingly.

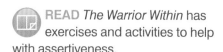 **READ** *The Warrior Within* has exercises and activities to help with assertiveness.

The '**ripple effect**' of RSA means that it will have affected family members too. Survivors need to be mindful that some family members may be overwhelmed with disbelief, or anger, guilt or shame for not listening to the survivor, or failing to protect him or her. This is not necessarily because they did not love or care about the survivor but because the abuser groomed them too. Abusers are highly skilled at manipulating not just victims but as their families and other adults. When this is combined with religious duress and the power and authority of the abuser it is easy to see how they avoid detection.

Survivors will need to explore to what extent the family was controlled and manipulated by the abuser. This will allow for some common ground in identifying how they were victims too. This will have prevented them from recognising the RSA or being able to stop it. While the survivor may still feel let down or betrayed, being able to listen to how family members feel without judgement can help to heal any deep rifts. In joining forces in placing full responsibility for the abuse onto the abuser, families will have a common focus for their pain and hurt rather than being divided by it. This will allow families to reconnect and rebuild.

REMEMBER Family members will also have been groomed, controlled and manipulated by the abuser.

In rebuilding family relationships survivors will have access to an extra valuable resource in their recovery. Not only can families provide an additional support network but they can also help the survivor if they decide to seek justice through the legal system. Litigation can be gruelling and survivors will need as much support as possible. Being able to rely on family members will enhance the survivor's resilience and reduce the stress associated with criminal or civil action. Most importantly the survivor and family members can begin to get to know each other again. Survivors who are gay, lesbian or bisexual may also want to take this opportunity to reveal their sexual orientation, although this must only be done if they feel safe enough.

If the manipulation by the abuser was too great, and some family members refuse to believe the survivor, then it is important to mourn this loss. Rather than be consumed with anger with the family member, survivors will need to

acknowledge the power the abuser had over the whole family. If possible, survivors will need to transform their anger and sense of betrayal into compassion both for themselves and the family members. This will allow survivors to respect the family member's decision and keep an open channel of communication in case they change their minds in the future.

Some survivors may feel the need to apologise for their past behaviours in their family relationships. In such instances, it is important to only apologise for what the survivor is actually responsible for. Survivors may want to want to apologise for withdrawing from the relationship, or for any anger or hostility. In doing this survivors must ensure that they fully explain why they needed to do this.

When reconnecting, survivors will need to contact the person they wish to reconnect with to discuss how the relationship can be rebuilt. Survivors will need to establish contact and request that they meet, preferably on neutral ground. If the prospect of a face-to-face meeting is too frightening then the survivor may feel safer to initially send a letter, or go to the first meeting with a trusted friend. It is important to ensure that the survivor is ready to talk, and is prepared with brief but full explanation of why they feel the relationship broke down and how they wish to repair it.

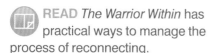
READ *The Warrior Within* has practical ways to manage the process of reconnecting.

Rebuilding relationships with partners and children

Relationships with partners may also need to be rebuilt – especially if they have been turbulent and conflicted. If the survivor has not disclosed the RSA to their partner they will need to do so, to enable the partner to make sense of what has happened and how this has impacted on the relationship. If survivors have been controlling, domineering or manipulative in their relationship they need to acknowledge this and apologise unreservedly. By being open and honest with their partner are more likely to be able to rebuild the relationship. Some survivors may also wish to rebuild relationships with ex-partners or friends who they feel they treated unfairly in the past. This will show respect for their ex-partner and allow them to make reparation.

Some survivors may also wish to rebuild or improve their relationship with their children, particularly if they feel they have let them down in the past with their behaviour. This is best done if the children have entered adulthood and are no longer dependent on the survivor. The survivor will need to explain how the RSA affected him and her and how this impacted on the relationship with the children. They will need to apologise for either being controlling and domineering or for being emotionally absent and neglectful and take responsibility for any damaging behaviour. It may take time for partners or children to come to terms with any harm done and survivors must be respectful of this and not expect immediate reparation.

In repairing their relationships with partners and adult children, survivors may find that once loved ones understand their behaviour they may become powerful allies in the healing process. Partners and adult children can be valuable assets in the process of recovery. They can also provide additional support through any legal proceedings or in becoming active in survivor organisations that increase awareness of RSA and how it affects families, partners and children.

Some relationships cannot be rebuilt

Survivors need to be aware that not everyone they approach will respond positively or wish to rebuild their relationship. Survivors must not impose too many expectations on loved ones, as these may not be achieved. It is important that survivors listen openly and empathically to their reasons for not wishing to rebuild the relationship and try to accept and respect their decision. Some family members will require time to digest the disclosure and come to grips with it. They need to accept their loss of trust in the abuser and grieve the loss of their relationship with the survivor.

It is important not to become too discouraged if families, partners or children respond negatively. It may be impossible for them to rebuild the relationship immediately. Survivors need to give them time and tell them that if something changes in the future they will be willing to discuss it then. What matters is that the survivor tried to rebuild the relationship. If the relationship cannot be repaired then it is essential that the survivor mourns its loss. This will need to be done without self-blame and an acknowledgement that the attempt was made and that the other person is not able to yet respond positively.

 WARNING Some relationships cannot be rebuilt – and survivors will need to accept and respect this and make sure they mourn the loss.

Disclosure

In rebuilding relationships, survivors will need to disclose the RSA – which can be very difficult and painful. The decision to disclose lies solely with the survivor and must never be dictated by others, including professionals. Only the survivor can decide when and to whom to disclose to. It is essential that it is survivors feel safe in making a disclosure. Many survivors hope that revealing the secret of RSA will bring the family closer together and allow relationships to be rebuilt. While this happens in many cases this is not a guaranteed outcome. There is always a risk that some family members will not believe the survivor and this can increase the survivor's sense of abandonment and isolation. There Is always a danger that the family becomes even more divided and that the survivor is permanently excluded. It is essential to think about all possible outcomes before disclosing the RSA.

It is for this reason that disclosure and attempts to rebuild relationships need to be carefully timed. Disclosure and rebuilding relationships is best left until the survivor is feeling stronger and more assertive. Survivors need to be able to cope with the reactions of family members, partners or children and any rejection or disbelief they may encounter. It is crucial that survivors pace themselves and do not attempt this prematurely. If the survivor is not ready, it is better to wait until they are further into the recovery process and are more resilient and have mastered more assertion skills.

 WARNING Be prepared for the disclosure to be disappointing.

Confronting the abuser

Some survivors will want to confront the abuser as part of their recovery. This can only ever be the survivor's decision and must not be imposed by someone else, including professionals. Confrontation must only ever be undertaken if the survivor believes that it will be beneficial to him or her and aid recovery. If survivors do confront they must ensure that they feel safe to do so. If they do not feel safe then it is imperative not to confront. Alternatively, if it is too dangerous to confront the abuser face to face, then it can be done by letter or a third party.

Survivors will need to be prepared for disappointment when confronting the abuser. Some abusers do acknowledge the RSA, but most deny it or blame the survivor for seducing them. It is important that survivors are strong enough to withstand the response and

not let it erode the reality of the RSA. If the abuser is no longer alive, then the survivor can confront them through a therapeutic letter in which they express their feelings about the abuser and the abuse, how it impacted on them.

WARNING Survivors must make sure they are safe, as confrontation can be dangerous. If possible, survivors need to have a trusted other with them for extra support.

It might be easier to confront indirectly by letter, or by making an audio or video tape which can sent to the abuser. This can help the survivor to rehearse what and how to say what needs to be said, and assess his or her feelings.

READ *The Warrior Within* has a section which discusses ways to manage sensations and feelings.

Being aware of the likely reactions can ease the anxiety around the confrontation. If the survivor chooses to meet the abuser face to face they may prefer to meet on neutral territory, or in a public place to limit the risk of harm. It is better not to confront alone and survivors will benefit by having a trusted other with them to provide support both during and after the confrontation. Confrontation can be extremely liberating even if the abuser denies the abuse, or blames the survivor. In taking the risk of confronting the abuser and giving voice to their thoughts and feelings, survivors are able to reclaim their power and take charge of their recovery and healing.

Relationship skills

In order to rebuild relationships, survivors will need to develop not only emotional worth, but also develop relationship skills. This is difficult when survivors avoid relationships. Survivors will need to develop more of an understanding of what it means to be in relationships and the range of relational dynamics. All relationships change in quality, and experience cycles of closeness and distance. The initial excitement usually develops into deep affection, while passion transform into compassion and an increased feeling of security and emotional intimacy. These changes sometimes feel like boredom or terror as the emotional intimacy intensifies.

Some survivors may experience boredom – not realising that this may be due to hidden anxiety and unfamiliar feelings of security and intimacy. In contrast, some survivors will experience fear and end relationships prematurely without examining what the fear

might represent. Survivors may also find that what initially attracted them to the person becomes a source of frustration or irritation. For example, if the survivor was attracted to a person's independence, serenity or attentiveness, this can, under stress, transmute into distant, unemotional or fussing.

Understanding how relationships fluctuate can help survivors to accept that even healthy relationships are messy sometimes and are punctuated by ruptures and closeness. What is important is to know is that, despite arguments and differences in opinion, these can be navigated and worked through, rather destroying the relationship. The emotional temperature of the relationship will vary for many reasons and does not mean that the relationship is dysfunctional. What is important is to have an open channel of communication to express feelings and thoughts with mutual respect.

Inexperience in relationships can lead to reduced confidence and social skills, making it difficult to get close to others. Survivors may need to develop more social skills such as awareness of body language and eye contact. Many survivors also lack confidence in their relationships which makes it harder to express their feelings or to be assertive.

When feelings and needs have been ignored or punished it will be terrifying to express them. To manage this, survivors will repress or deny their feelings and become out of touch with their needs. As they do not feel entitled to express or ask for their needs to be met they do not know how to do this in relationships. To give these feelings and needs a voice, survivors will first need to identify them before attempting to express them.

To make the expression of feelings and needs safer survivors will need to ensure that boundaries are in place. These must be based on mutual respect for each other's point of view and the ability to listen non-judgementally. Survivors must not confuse assertiveness with selfishness or hostility but see it as a sophisticated social skill which balances respect for the self and respect for others. Being assertive means respecting the rights of others while keeping one's own respect in mind. It means conversing in a non-manipulative, non-aggressive and proactive way. To maintain respect needs to be carefully balanced between one's own needs with what is fair and reasonable, and respectful of others.

READ *The Warrior Within* has advice and exercises to help improve social skills, the expressing of needs and being assertive.

Some people may refuse to acknowledge assertion, preferring instead to interpret this as opposition or even defiance – especially if it threatens the status quo or long-established ways of interacting. No matter how assertive survivors are, it helps to be prepared for potential opposition and manipulation. This may be direct and explicit, or more subtle in terms of emotional manipulation, disapproval or redirection of blame. To manage potential opposition, survivors will need to stand their ground and restate their case assertively – sometimes several times.

Survivors need to remember that even if others refuse to listen to their feelings or needs, this does not invalidate them or a valid reason to not express them. Others will sometimes be unreasonable, and if they remain negative in their responses, the survivor may need to accept this. Some people will continue to try to manipulate, or refuse to enter into a discussion. This does not mean that the survivor has failed – it merely shows that this person is not able to respect the survivor's needs. Survivors need to remember that they are entitled to express how they feel and this is a way of respecting themselves.

WARNING Those who have had power over the survivor may not respond well to assertion and may resort to punishment and manipulation to restore their power and control. It is important to proceed with caution and stay safe.

Setting boundaries and assertion will enable more open and honest communication and rebuild trust. Ultimately such relationship skills will help survivors to distinguish between honestly nurturing and nourishing relationships and those that are forceful and controlling. It will empower survivors to monitor their relationships and cope with any difficulties effectively instead of avoiding closeness or intimacy.

Forgiveness

Alongside confronting the abuser, survivors may also wonder whether they want to forgive the abuser. It is important that survivors explore what forgiveness means to them and whether this is necessary for healing. Forgiveness is a personal choice and must never be imposed by others, including faith-based beliefs. Only the survivor can choose to forgive or not. Many faiths insist that forgiveness is the only way to heal although there is little scientific evidence of this. This is another belief that may need to be challenged by the

survivor (see **Restoring spirituality and forgiveness** on page 164).

 READ *The Warrior Within* has help and advice to help with forgiveness.

Survivors who choose to forgive must ensure that they do not do this prematurely, or because of pressures from religious or social groups. Some survivors find that premature forgiveness does not bring peace or healing to them but intensifies self-blame and reinforces negative self-beliefs. Forgiveness does not have to be all or nothing, and survivors may find it easier to forgive some aspects associated with the abuse – such as forgiving family members or the religious institution for not having protected them.

There is no compelling evidence survivors need to forgive in order to heal. If anything, it is more healing for survivors to forgive themselves for submitting to the abuse or not being able to stop it. It is essential that survivors are aware that they can find peace and heal whether they choose to forgive or not and rebuild their relationships. The following chapter will consider the role of forgiveness in restoring faith and spirituality in more depth.

18 Restoring spirituality and forgiveness

The spiritual injury associated with RSA can be extremely damaging, leaving survivors riddled with doubt, despair, anger, guilt and a fear of death. Many survivors not only lose their faith in religious institutions, but also their belief and trust in God. This foreshortens spiritual growth, with survivors becoming blocked in their spiritual development. Their sense of betrayal and anger with God leads many survivor to reject God as a source of spiritual support.

The loss of God and faith leads to a deep sorrow and a resistance to life and growth. This fear and rejection of life and spiritual growth is a sign of how much control the RSA and the abuser still has over the survivor. It is evidence that the abuser's manipulation of religious beliefs and the role of God as co-conspirator is still distorting and colouring the survivor's belief system, and spirituality.

To heal from spiritual injury, survivors need to challenge these imposed distortions, and re-evaluate their religious belief and spirituality. Spiritual injury offers a unique opportunity for spiritual growth through self-chosen beliefs rather than ones that have been inherited, conditioned or imposed by others. Survivors can and do rediscover their spirituality and transform the spiritual vacuum left in the aftermath of RSA by entering into a spiritual dialogue in which they can define what is sacred and spiritual to them. This spiritual re-engagement can also be found through exploring alternative religions or faith traditions, or by reconnecting with the spirit within.

Spiritual needs and beliefs must not be minimised as they give identity, a sense of belongingness, and structure and meaning to life and experiences.[17] However these need not be confined to traditional religious beliefs or be defined by religious institutions or structures. The Oxford English Dictionary defines spirituality as '**the quality of being connected with religion or *the human spirit***' (author's highlight). This means that survivors can choose to what, and to whom, they want to feel connected to. For some this will be connection to a religious or faith-based community, while for others this will be to the human spirit through human connection and the spirit within.

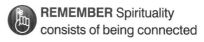 **WARNING** Spiritual needs and beliefs must not be minimised as they provide identity, a sense of belongingness, and a structure and meaning to life and experiences.

REMEMBER Spirituality consists of being connected

with religion or the human spirit. This gives survivors a unique opportunity to evaluate and choose what or to whom they wish to connect to.

Challenging distorted religious beliefs

In order to challenge distorted religious beliefs, survivors need to separate out religious teaching, and the distorted images and beliefs inserted by the abuser, who has manipulated religious beliefs and the concept of God to groom victims and justify the RSA. By making God a co-conspirator, abusers are able to hide behind their actions and avoid taking responsibility. In this respect God becomes a fellow victim, as do the rest of the congregation, the wider faith community and non-offending faith representatives.[v]

To help restore spirituality, survivors need to decouple the abuser from God, and the religious institution. RSA is the antithesis of what religious teaching represents, and has to be seen within the context of the abuser's manipulation of power and authority. If survivors can separate the betrayal of the abuser, and any subsequent betrayal by the church or religious institution, they are more able to focus on the harm done and the degree of spiritual injury.

If survivors feel they have been betrayed by religious institutions they are more likely to lose their faith in the institution, yet retain their belief in God. This may mean that they no longer choose to go to their church, mosque or temple but can continue to pray and engage in meaningful religious practices and rituals, albeit in other places of worship or of forms of spirituality.

Spiritual disillusionment can be overcome through questioning old religious beliefs, experimenting with new ways of thinking, and allowing for different spiritual experiences, This can allow survivors to re-evaluate and re-examine spirituality, explore different choices, and to redefine what spirituality means to them. It also enables them to find new aspects of the self that have lain dormant, by reconnecting to their inner experiencing and releasing the spirit within.

READ *The Warrior Within* has useful exercises and advice to help connect with the inner spirit.

Although loss and betrayal leaves confusion, emptiness, and uncertainty about life and death, it also opens up opportunities for growth. To compensate for loss and betrayal, survivors may seek different forms of recompense. Some may seek this through litigation (see **Using the legal system for justice and healing** on page 176) or restitution from the religious institution that failed to protect them. Others may reject religious institutions altogether, and refuse to accept what they see as hollow apologies, false assurances, or 'blood money'. Some survivors choose to seek healing by retaining their belief in God, but not attend official places of worship, while others take control by redefining their spirituality and embracing their own spirit within. Healing is a very individual thing and must not be prescribed, with survivors encouraged to make their own choices, without judgement.

Many survivors feel that while some religious institutions have provided financial compensation to some victims as a result of legal action, this does not necessarily mean that there is an acceptance of moral responsibility by the religious institution. Accountability and responsibility can only be achieved through structural and systemic changes which take time and effort. If such changes are resisted by religious institutions, then they must be driven by congregations and the laity.[14] The systemic changes needed will take time – something that many survivors may feel they no longer have as they continue to age. Rather than wait for these changes to occur, some survivors choose to take control over their own spirituality by rejecting the institution that has failed them, and which can no longer be trusted.

Re-evaluating religious beliefs

While it is not easy to replace spiritual ties, or to live without the sustenance of a spiritual family, it is possible to find alternative forms of connections. Some survivors choose to sever all ties with the religious institution, including adversarial ones, as they do not wish to get trapped in a struggle that can entrap them further into a victim identity.

The process of re-evaluation does not necessarily mean a total rejection of all previously-held beliefs. Survivors can choose to take what is and has been valuable, and discard what is not. It helps to be mindful of what has been sustaining, and what worked before it was polluted and contaminated by the RSA and the abuser. This allows the survivor to grow in new directions which are self-chosen rather than imposed by birth or family tradition.

Some survivors find this a unique opportunity to keep divine experiences while shedding structural aspects of religious institutions that no longer uphold the fundamental principles of their faith. While some survivors will be able to reconnect with God, some will look for the divine and sacred in other places. Some will want to find alternative and more meaningful metaphors, or names for God and their faith, while others find that they very act of living, and being present becomes a spiritual practice. A proportion of survivors will find their spirituality in more concrete forms such as nature and creativity – such as seeing the sunshine dappling on leaves, watching the setting sun or in the sound of birdsong. Alternatively, some survivors will find the divine in inner experiencing by connecting to the spirit within.

Alternative meaningful connections can be made, and although these do not necessarily have to be religious they can be just as powerful and sustaining. Many survivors find spiritual nourishment in new relationships, creativity, art, music, community service, conservation or political action. All of these can inspire, nurture and nourish in the way religion and faith once did. One liberating aspect of this is that these are self-chosen rather than imposed through birth, tradition, or heritage, or conditioned by family, community or the church. Connecting to other communities, religious traditions, or spiritual families can be equality divine and give purpose and meaning to life. Survivors need to be open to experimenting with new traditions and connections.

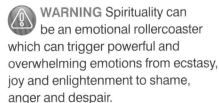 **REMEMBER** Alternative meaningful connections can be made – and although these do not necessarily have to be religious they can be just as powerful and sustaining.

Throughout this process of re-evaluation, survivors need to be mindful that spirituality can be an emotional rollercoaster which can trigger powerful and overwhelming emotions from ecstasy, joy and enlightenment to shame, anger, and despair. It is critical that survivors can accept the range of emotions and normalise them as part of spiritual healing. When exploring new religions or traditions, survivors also need to be aware that if any similar patterns of misuse of power and authority emerge that resemble their abuse experience that protective measures are in place.

WARNING Spirituality can be an emotional rollercoaster which can trigger powerful and overwhelming emotions from ecstasy, joy and enlightenment to shame, anger and despair.

Spiritual transformation requires finding a voice so that the survivor can reclaim some of the power taken from them. It is this voice which will help survivors tell their story and provide release from the spiritual injury. Release can also come through visualisations, ritual purification, contemplation and meditation. These allow survivors to envision alternative representations of the sacred and good. For instance, some survivors transform imposed beliefs about their deity as distant, intolerant or punitive to one that is more caring, compassionate and nurturing. To do this they need to grieve the loss of their old belief system before integrating newly chosen beliefs, and move from anger to peace.

Forgiveness and spirituality

Forgiveness is a fundamental principle in most faiths as the only way to move towards to healing. This can be very difficult for survivors who may not wish to forgive. Religious institutions, faith leaders, families, partners and therapists who believe in the power of forgiveness often try to persuade survivors to forgive. However, forcing forgiveness is never appropriate as it only increases survivor's anxiety, rage and further trauma. It is much more helpful to try to understand each individual survivor's needs and support their choices and decisions.

Forcing forgiveness diverts empathy away from the survivor and onto the abuser. Before the survivor can truly feel empathy for the abuser, they need to be able to feel empathy and compassion for themselves and the harm done. The danger of premature forgiveness is that the avoidance of anger and aggression may masquerade as empathy. The process of forgiveness involves experiencing the full range of emotions associated with the RSA, including anger and aggression as well as compassion. An important stage of mourning any loss is anger and if this is stage is avoided it can lead to prolonged and complicated grief [see **Understanding grief and loss** on page 135).

Survivors must be given permission to feel anger before they can feel compassion for their abuser and begin to forgive. Some survivors feel that the harm done is so extensive that compassion and forgiveness are not possible. This must remain their choice despite the religious or psychological agenda of others. In addition, before forgiveness can take place the abuser must admit responsibility and not hide behind their faith. Some religious sexual abusers know, and expect that they will be forgiven by God, their congregants, the religious institution and their peers, and use this to dilute the harm done. To expect survivors to forgive is a form of '**religious window dressing**' which can be a further form of abuse in which the survivor is made to feel ashamed for not being able to forgive and embrace such a fundamental religious principle.

All too often, religious institutions and faith leaders have asked survivors for forgiveness without fully admitting responsibility for their role in protecting abusers and minimising harm done. Expecting survivors to forgive in the absence of meaningful and effective apologies can add insult to injury, which only fuels the sense of betrayal. It also adds to their fear that forgiveness is being manipulated primarily to exonerate the abuser rather than restore spirituality and peace to the survivor. Many survivors feel that some abuses are beyond forgiveness and that doing so dilutes the harm done while increasing their sense of betrayal.

In contrast, some survivors feel compelled to forgive to compensate for their part in the abuse. In forgiving the abuser they hope to obtain grace, or forgiveness from God. This rarely has the desired effect as the survivor has not worked through the abuse sufficiently to develop self-compassion. Survivors need to shed their self-blame and need to forgive themselves, not for the abuse as that was not their fault, but for their reactions to it. Many of the trauma reactions, such as freezing, or physiological arousal are outside of conscious control and therefore not a source for self-blame. Similarly, the silencing strategies, both overt and subtle, used by the abuser prevented voluntary choices.

Focusing on self-forgiveness is a much stronger aid to recovery than premature forgiveness as it allows the survivor to let go of self-blame. This is what truly releases the power the abuser had – and still has – over the survivor. If the survivor then wishes to forgive the abuser, or others who have harmed him or her, they can then make a much more informed choice without compromising their spirituality.

Forgiveness, whether self-forgiveness, or forgiving others, is a very complex and demanding process and must always be a personal choice. There is no conclusive evidence that forgiveness is necessary for healing, or to restore spirituality. Some survivors find it extremely helpful, while others do not. The process of forgiveness is not just confined to the survivor but radiates out to others such as the victims, and perpetrators families, partners, non-offending religious representatives, as well as the wider faith community and religious institutions. Each of these will need to exercise their own personal choice around forgiveness..

While empathy for the abuser is important, especially if they were victims themselves, this should not be imposed on – or demanded of – survivors. It is up to religious institutions and mental health professionals who treat them to provide empathic understanding. This however needs to be balanced with clear acknowledgement that RSA is never acceptable under any circumstances. The responsibility for the abuse is that of the abuser and excuses must not be tolerated. Many people who were sexually abused in childhood do not go on to sexually abuse as adults. In addition, any expressed remorse on the part of the abuser must be genuine and not another form of manipulation or deception.

It must be remembered that some survivors have ambivalent feelings about their abuser ranging from love and compassion to anger and rage. These conflicted feelings may be hard to reconcile. Survivors need to find a way to tolerate both realities, rather than cancel them out. Forgiveness is one way for some survivors to achieve this. Survivors who choose to forgive must also choose how this can be achieved. Some survivors may wish to do this by letter, or meet the abuser face to face. Others may prefer to do this in their own mind, while others will not be able to forgive until the abuser is dead.

Whatever survivors choose to do they need to pace themselves so that they can be in control of the healing process to truly free themselves and to restore their spirituality.

Hope and spirituality

Spiritual injury and disillusionment can be transformative allowing for a renewed appreciation of life. Many survivors who have lived with darkness and despair often face a loss of hope. And yet it is hope that welcomes light in – even in the darkest moments. It is in the moments of despair that hope can really come alive and shine the light to guide the survivor towards healing and recovery. Hope is the belief that you will not always be numb, or broken or lost in the dark, but can be open to reconnect to life and spiritual experiencing. It is this hope that is testament to the recognition that the spirit within has not been obliterated and can be re-awakened.

In re-awakening the spirit within the survivor can find the sacred in the self and connect to an inner spirituality. This will allow for a greater sense of control over spiritual experiencing, and allow for greater balance and harmony. Restoring faith and spirituality can help survivors to truly triumph over trauma, which is explored in the following chapter.

19 Triumphing over trauma

As survivors begin the process of recovery and healing, they will move from being dominated by a tortured inner world to one of greater calmness and stability. This will release vital energy that allows for reconnection to the world. Survivors find that they are finally able to appreciate life more and enjoy being alive. Coming out of survival mode allows the survivor to be more present in the world and to notice and appreciate the natural world around them. In restoring faith and spirituality, and accessing the spirit within, they are able to live more authentically and triumph over trauma.

REMEMBER In restoring faith and spirituality, and accessing the spirit within, survivors are able to live more authentically and triumph over trauma.

As survivors become less preoccupied with managing trauma reactions, they can begin to connect to others and restore a sense of belongingness. This is vital as it reduces social isolation and helps the survivor to feel a part of the community and their newly-defined 'spiritual family'. The process of recovery and restored spirituality restores a new sense of purpose and meaning to life in which survivors want to reach out to others rather than hide away in shame.

Renewed vitality and purpose

As survivors experience a new sense of vitality and purpose they will seek to channel this renewed energy in ways they have never considered before. Many survivors find that in reviving the spirit within and restoring spirituality they discover aspects of themselves that have lain dormant for many years. As childhood RSA interrupts the natural emotional, psychological and cognitive development, many survivors are forced to abandon interests, passions and pursuits that gave them pleasure and enjoyment. As all their energies were hijacked to managing trauma reactions they lacked the energy and sense of safety to be spontaneous in pursuing their dreams.

Return to study

The healing process provides survivors with opportunities to revive hidden talents and abilities that enable them to connect to pursuits that seemed out of their reach. Some survivors rediscover an interest in learning more about a subject they were passionate about as a child – such as history, geography or science. As children, many survivors, especially those who were abused in religious or faith schools, were not able to concentrate on learning or were told that they were stupid or lazy. This meant that many were not able to realise their academic and intellectual potential. As learning became associated with fear of failure, shame and fear of punishment, many survivors were prevented from reaching the educational attainment they were capable of.

As survivors begin to triumph over trauma they may wish to return to education and study subjects they were passionate about as children. Some will do this purely for pleasure while others may go on to study at university and a get a degree. This is incredibly liberating, as it provides direct evidence that they are not stupid or lacking and is a potent way of disproving negative messages from childhood.

Enhanced employment opportunities

Survivors who return to study will find that their employment opportunities are enhanced. The renewed confidence that comes with educational attainment permits survivors to develop their careers beyond what they thought they were capable of and seek promotion. Some survivors find the confidence to retrain and enter a new career that they have always yearned for but felt excluded from, together with the sense of achievement associated with studying. Enhanced employment

opportunities and potential career changes are vital in empowering survivors to take charge of their lives. It is also provides direct evidence of their triumph over trauma.

REMEMBER The recovery process provides survivors with opportunities to revive hidden talents and abilities and enhance educational and employment possibilities.

Releasing creativity

For some survivors, the healing processes reveals a well of hidden creativity. Shame, fear of spontaneity and being too visible will have prevented some survivors from expressing themselves creatively, leading them to suppress creative talents and abilities. Many survivors will have a negative association to certain types of music, and singing – especially if they were a choirboy or choirgirl. This can lead to an avoidance of anything musical and repress their pleasure in singing.

As all of the survivor's energy was been diverted into survival there was nothing left to engage in painting, sculpting, dancing or any of the other creative arts. Even going to art galleries and looking at paintings which depict religious themes can trigger flashbacks and intrusive memories and prevent survivors of RSA from appreciating art ad painting. Accessing their creativity allows survivors to take up painting, sculpting, pottery, singing or dance.

When in survival mode, many survivors were not able to concentrate sufficiently to take pleasure in reading. The renewed vitality as a result of healing can free up energy that can now be devoted to reading for pleasure such as novels, poetry and plays. This can revive an interest in the theatre and other performing arts. Many survivors find that by exploring their creativity and engaging in creative activities gives the spirit within a new voice and a channel for its expression.

Helping others

Helping others is another powerful way to triumph over trauma.[5] Survivors find that in helping others they are able to find some positive meaning in their abuse experience. In addition, sharing the insights gained through the healing process and using these to help others is an essential part of healing. Many survivors will initially want help other survivors or victims, although some may find this too harrowing. It is critical that survivors have a choice whether to help or not and to pace the amount of support they can offer to others.

Helping others not only feels good but also provides a sense of purpose. Helping others, especially other victims or survivors, is a powerful way of restoring faith in fundamental religious teaching in which the strong help rather than exploit or prey on the weak or vulnerable. In this survivors become a living embodiment of compassion and what it means to be human. This is a powerful way to reverse the dehumanisation that occurs in RSA and provides direct evidence that the abuser has not destroyed the spirit within.

 REMEMBER Helping others not only feels good but also provides a sense of purpose.

In supporting those who have experienced RSA, the survivor becomes an inspiration to those who are only just beginning the healing process. It can give hope to others that, despite the damaging and traumatising effects of RSA, it is possible to recover and heal. It is also a direct reminder to the survivor who is helping of how far they have come in their own recovery and healing process. In addition, focusing on helping others becomes an outlet for compassion and empathy and facilitates connection to others.

Before survivors commit to helping others, it is crucial that they are ready to do so. Survivors need to be careful in what they choose to do and ensure that it is manageable and realistic. If a survivor is socially isolated, then becoming involved in the community and becoming part of a support group can reduce his or her isolation. However, if the survivor has still has fears around physically interacting with people then he or she may be better placed helping from their own home via the internet or telephone.

Survivors as wounded healers

Survivors need to make sure that they are ready to help, by ensuring that they have enough energy and confidence to manage whatever commitments they make. Helping others is best done if the survivor has learnt to manage trauma reactions and is able to regulate their emotions. It is also important that survivors choose something that will improve well-being rather than re-activate traumatic reactions. Helping people who have been abused can trigger flashbacks and intrusive memories which can undermine the recovery process.

If there is an increase in trauma reactions or re-emergence of overwhelming emotions then the survivor will need to reassess whether they are ready to help in this way. It may be that they are not

ready to help other survivors yet. This does not mean that they cannot help others, it just means that they need to revise what kind of help they can offer and to whom. Survivors make excellent 'wounded healers' provided they have worked through their own trauma first and do not over identify with those they are helping.

Some survivors find it easier to start by helping others in the community, such as an elderly person or someone who is infirm and needs help with shopping or gardening before supporting other survivors. Alternatively, some survivors gain enormous satisfaction in mentoring a child, or by providing a specific skill to help those in need.

Survivors who feel ready to help others who have been abused can offer their services to charities that help to protect children such as The NSPCC, ChildLine, Barnardos or the Nation Children's Homes (see **Resources** on page 208). They could also volunteer for mental health organisations such as Mind or Samaritans, or charities that specialise in working with survivors of CSA and RSA, such as One in Four.

Survivors as activists

Another potent way of triumphing over trauma is to join an action group that works on behalf of people who have been abused. This can be very empowering as it validates and acknowledges RSA and keeps it in public awareness, as well as helping to protect children from harm in the future (see **Using the legal system for justice and healing** on page 176). More importantly, it provides a sense of belonging and identity which can reduce shame and stigmatisation.

If survivors choose to help other survivors of RSA it is essential that they have access to a good support network to ensure that they do not get too overwhelmed or embedded in trauma. When helping others, in whatever capacity, survivors need to guard against ignoring their own needs and becoming immersed in the needs of others. To keep a healthy balance, survivors must make sure that they access other sources of pleasure and enjoyment outside of trauma and RSA. This is vital to minimise the risk of '**burn out**' or **secondary traumatic stress**. This is a risk that even professionals face when working with survivors of trauma. As result survivors, as well as professionals, must ensure that they look after themselves so that they can fully help others in their recovery.

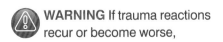 **WARNING** If trauma reactions recur or become worse,

survivors must take a break from helping others and focus on restoring their sense of well-being.

In helping others, survivors are able to shift their focus away from the negative effects of RSA – which not only restores a sense of purpose and meaning to life but also reinforces their recovery and healing. As survivors begin to feel more empowered through discovering dormant and hidden aspects of themselves, they will be able to embrace their future with renewed vitality. This energy can be channelled in a variety of ways to triumph over trauma and allow for post-traumatic growth. Some survivors will find this through taking legal action, which is explored in the following chapter.

20 Using the legal system for justice and healing

One in Four's advocacy service supports clients through the legal system. This is primarily through the criminal justice system, in reporting sexual crimes committed against them as children. That process is set out in the companion One in Four handbook entitled *The Warrior Within*. One in Four also offers support to enable clients to access appropriate professional advice to pursue civil claims which are the primary focus of this chapter.

Survivors coming to terms with their abuse seldom start by thinking of using the legal system. The issues raised by abuse are so deep and personal that talking with other survivors or therapists is usually the first step on the road to understanding and healing. The legal system seems remote, strange and fearsome. The whole idea of a prosecution or of seeking compensation from an abuser, or the institution that allowed the abuser to operate with impunity, is not necessarily the first or indeed the second thought of most survivors.

The legal process can be a powerful tool for a survivor. Bringing a case to court helps a survivor to experience healing and to reclaim their power after abuse. A legal action allows the survivor to gain strength by pursuing justice, exposing the truth and protecting others from harm.

Lawyers working in this field have found that there are three critical aspects of their representation that help their survivor clients to heal and recover their power. The first is **validation and acknowledgment** – that is, to be believed. Many survivors have spent years or decades not being believed, by parents, siblings, loved ones, people in authority – so much so that many have stopped believing in themselves. Robbing survivors of their own truth is one of the cruelest results of abuse. Survivors need to be respected. For many their first encounter with lawyers will be a continuation of the process which has already been started through appropriate therapy and support. The very real loneliness that commonly ensues from RSA – blaming it on themselves or believing they were the only victim of their abuser – can start to diminish through talking to experienced people who understand the dimensions of abuse, and who respect their account.

The second thing the legal process can do to empower survivors is to try to ensure that **no further harm is done** to the survivor or their family. A survivor will have experienced betrayal of their trust by authority figures upon whom they depended. Now the authority of the law is deployed instead in the service of the survivor. The legal process also provides a mechanism to show that the hold which the perpetrator or institution had over them has been broken.

The third way the legal process helps survivors to recover power is by allowing them to take part in **helping protect others from harm**, which for many is the most important goal. They yearn to do something positive to raise awareness of abuse, to help unmask those who have abused and those who have colluded, and to hold them accountable, all of which makes it less likely that other children will be abused in the future.

A case in court exposes the abuser publicly and may empower other survivors, who may be struggling in silence, secrecy and shame, to come forward also. By doing so, survivors make known to themselves and others that they are not alone. It is always supportive to learn of the experience of others and gaining knowledge of this shared experience can be a source of strength.

The only real justice would never to have been abused in the first place. But the legal system, though imperfect, provides a way to rebalance the scales. Punishment or money won in damages can never undo the pain abuse caused. But if abusers and their institutions are punished or have to pay damages, they may begin to understand the wrong they have done and the hurt they have caused.

Besides punishing individual abusers and keeping them from harming others, taking institutions to court that have allowed sexual abuse to take place unchecked and making them pay damages forces them to look at the cultural and systemic practices which have led to their appearance in court. The power of the law to compel documents to be produced, evidence to be given, and money to be paid to those who have been abused can not only help right wrongs that have already been committed, but also send a message to a wider audience that abuse will no longer stay hidden or be without cost to the abuser. In this sense, attaining justice for an individual helps to create the conditions for greater justice.

RSA has several characteristics that make accountability through the law a particularly important tool for survivors.

First, while there is always an imbalance of power between the adult abuser and the child preyed upon, many faiths have doctrines and organisational structures that amplify this. For example, a priest is God's representative on earth, with the capacity to forgive sins and perform other sacraments. He is normally trusted, respected, and revered by the community. Parents trust him to look after their children, and feel favoured if he pays their family attention. There have been many cases where religious leaders have deliberately groomed children by spending time with their families. In such cases even if a child has the courage to confide in a parent that the Faith leader abused them, the reaction is often horrified disbelief - which may undermine the relationship of trust with their parent. Many abused children are also told by their perpetrators, in a misuse of religious doctrine, that the fault lies with them for providing the source of temptation.

Abusers deserve all the sanctions the law can impose whatever their role or denomination. All too often religious officials have acted as if their faith was a law unto itself. They have claimed that faith law has supremacy over civil law and that their freedom to worship without interference should also prevent the state, or lawyers for survivors, from gaining access to records which would identify abusers, provide evidence of ineffective child protection policies or collusion with perpetrators. Lawmakers and the courts have rejected those arguments, but religious officials continue to make them. Similar

arguments have been made by other organisations, extending from care institutions to youth organisations, which have allowed a culture of abuse to flourish. The law, both criminal and civil, has been the only force strong enough to force faiths to examine the culture and systemic processes that consciously or unconsciously support RSA and protect abusers.

For clients, recovering their power through the law often goes hand in hand with meeting and working with other survivors who share their story and life experiences. When a survivor comes forward to seek justice through litigation, they stand not just for themselves, but for every other survivor, both those who have already come forward, and those who have yet to do so. Each case provides a building block for another.

Using the legal system for justice and healing will assist in ensuring that there will be no place in which perpetrators can find shelter or hide.

Jeff Anderson and Ann Olivarius
Partners of Jeff Anderson Ann Olivarius Law

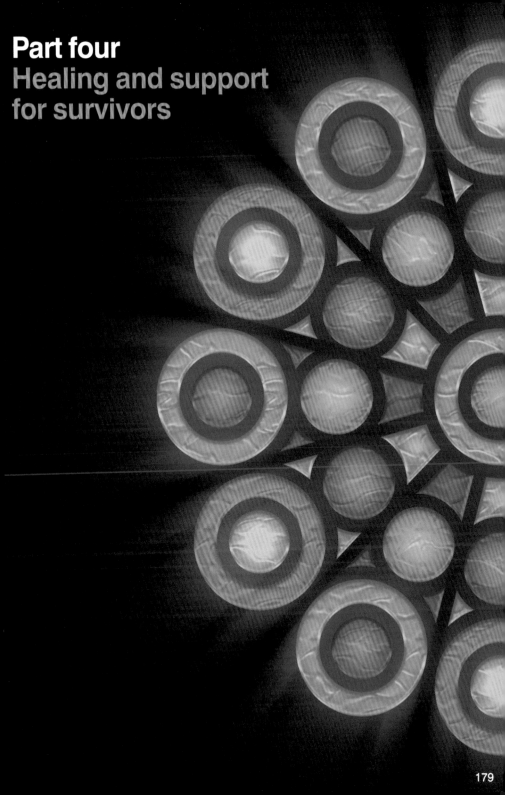

Part four
Healing and support for survivors

21 How faith leaders and religious institutions can help survivors to heal

This chapter aims to help faith leaders, clergy and members of religious institutions to have a better understanding of how to respond to victims and survivors. It will emphasise the importance of listening empathically and how to apologise more effectively. It will also consider how training and increased knowledge can aid understanding of the effects of RSA and how this can help in responding not just to victims and survivors but also all those who are concerned by the scale of RSA and how allegations have been managed.

In order to move towards healing survivors, religious institutions such as the church and faith leaders must firstly fully acknowledge the harm done by RSA and provide an effective apology that is genuine and meaningful to survivors. To date, the RC Church and its leader, the Pope, have made a number of public apologies, both written and verbal. However these have often been carefully crafted by lawyers and have felt insincere. The focus on forgiveness and prayer has offended many survivors who no longer trust hollow well-crafted words, or religious doctrine, but who seek action to support the apologies that are made.

REMEMBER To heal, religious institutions must fully acknowledge the harm done by RSA.

To truly support and respond to survivors, religious institutions and faith leaders need to listen empathically to survivors, and provide a full, effective apology for harm done by individual offenders and the institutions that have protected abusers. They also need to provide solid initiatives, supported by action, to ensure that children are no longer exposed to the risk of RSA. It is not sufficient to draft safeguarding policies and procedures, often driven by insurance companies, without a full and genuine commitment to them. Policies and procedures only protect if they are complied with and fully implemented. The non-compliance highlighted in the Cloyne report[12] has dismayed and angered not only survivors, but also non-offending clergy, faith communities and society as a whole.

The motivation behind implementing safeguarding policies must be a genuine concern for the protection of children and vulnerable adults. It should not be used as a form of compliance to insurers, or as a reaction to recommendations made by public inquiries and reports. It is critical that these policies and their implementation are robust – not just a way to tick the right boxes.

In addition, it is essential that safeguarding policies and procedures are supported with improved training in child protection and comprehensive understanding of the traumatising impact of RSA. Such training needs to be supported by regular independent auditing, supervision and psychological support. Religious institutions will also need to address systemic factors that consciously or unconsciously support RSA, and make appropriate structural changes.

Empathic listening

Listening is the most powerful instrument of healing. To listen empathically and non-defensively allows for genuine understanding of how RSA impacts on victims and how it continues to harm survivors. All too often, faith leaders have heard – but not listened to – survivors and been defensive in their responses. This has created blocks to listening and prevented a full understanding of the harm done. This lack of understanding makes it harder to respond empathically and provide genuine and effective apologies. Listening not only informs but has the capacity to transform and heal.

Many faiths argue that repentance, forgiveness and absolution are the most powerful instruments of healing. However, this cannot occur without empathic listening. Many survivors of RSA are no longer able to trust religious teaching in relation to healing when so much harm has been done and find

it hard to forgive. Forgiveness must always be a personal choice and not be imposed on survivors. Whether to forgive or not is part of the process of recovery and healing and takes time. Insisting on forgiveness before the survivor is ready or able can create a powerful block to recovery or healing (see **Restoring spirituality and forgiveness** on page 164).

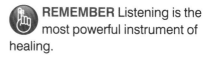 **REMEMBER** Listening is the most powerful instrument of healing.

Effective apologies

Listening to survivors, and being open to understanding how RSA has affected them, maximises the ability to provide an effective apology that can aid recovery and healing. For apologies to be effective, they need to include four fundamental components, each of which need to be fully addressed. These are **acknowledgement**, **explanation**, **expression of true remorse** and **reparation**.

Acknowledgement of harm caused

Before an effective apology can be made, there needs to be a genuine acknowledgement of offences and the harm caused. Many survivors of RSA feel that this has not happened.

This is especially true in the case of the RC Church where accountability and responsibility are consistently denied, sexual abuses are covered up, and victims and survivors are silenced or coerced into settling out of court. Such responses are disrespectful and wounding and frequently re-traumatise survivors. Protracted and prolonged court cases, and blocking the release of funds to pursue therapeutic help, fails to acknowledge the suffering of victims and survivors and merely serves to deny their experiences and hurt.

Religious institutions and faith leaders can help survivors to heal by showing real sorrow and remorse for what has happened, and by taking responsibility for failing in their spiritual duty of care to protect the most vulnerable children and adults. They also need to explicitly acknowledge the systemic failures of the church in: not reporting allegations of RSA; for relocating clergy and putting them into different situations where sexual abuse can continue; for covering up the scale of RSA; and silencing victims, survivors, their families and other clergy who have expressed concern.

Explanations for offences and harm caused

There is no justification for the sexual abuse of children or adults, yet religious institutions, and in particular the RC Church, have provided a number of erroneous explanations for RSA and reasons to defend their lack of action to deal with abusers appropriately. These explanations have varied over time and range from blaming it on a lack of knowledge about the sexual abuse of children, sexual orientation and homosexuality, the stress of being in ministry, to blaming victims for their abuse, and most recently what has been referred to as the '**Woodstock defence**'. This argues that RSA is due to society's loosening of morals during the 1960s and 1970s.[26]

For explanations to have any value, they must be based on an honest and authentic evaluation of the range of contributing factors – not least those of the individual abuser but also systemic factors related to the hierarchical structure of religious institutions. This involves examining the role of authority and power within church culture, the impact of religious duress (see **What is religious sexual abuse** on page 14), the role of silence and clericalism which tolerates duplicity and allows clergy to lead double lives with impunity. Institutional factors that prioritise the protection of abusers above the protection of children and vulnerable adults need to be challenged and reviewed, with a commitment to ensuring that requisite changes are made.

The role of religious doctrine that denies sexuality and promotes sexual shame also needs to be examined, and how this contributes to RSA and the management of sexual expression. It is only with critical evaluation and the commitment for genuine change that apologies and assurances can be believed and trusted.

Expression of remorse

The expression of true remorse, shame and humility is also central for effective apology. Such expression must be genuine in showing real empathy and compassion for the suffering endured. Many survivors of RSA do not feel that there has been any genuine expression of remorse from faith leaders or religious institutions. This is especially the case while they continue to deflect accountability by hiding behind fallacious explanations, rather than admit that they should have known better. Irrespective of historical time, psychological knowledge, lack of procedures or prevailing social mores, the protection of children is always of paramount importance. Sexual abuse is never acceptable whatever era or context it occurs in. The fact that this has not been fully acknowledged in canon law as it is in criminal and civil law is indefensible.

Reparation

Reparation is a further necessary requirement for an effective apology. Real or symbolic reparation can be achieved through a genuine commitment to change, or effective punishment for guilty parties – including those who covered up or failed to report RSA. This needs to be supported through appropriate action, such as instigating criminal investigation into individual abusers and mandatory resignations of those who were complicit in the abuse or who protected the abuser. Alongside this, reparation can be made by providing appropriate funds to victims, so that they can afford specialist long term psychotherapy to restore mental and physical well-being, and to pursue missed academic or professional opportunities. Financial claims against the religious institutions should not be viewed as questionable but as an opportunity for real reparation to enable survivors to move towards healing.

How apologies heal

In order to move towards healing, a number of basic psychological needs have to be satisfied. Firstly there needs to be a **restoration of dignity** through a clear admission that the harm committed was wrong. This needs to be accompanied by **validation** that the victims were not responsible for the abuse and an **assurance** that all children are safe from a repetition of offences. This needs to be followed by **reparative justice** in which offenders are appropriately punished. This must take the form of criminal investigations, and the charging and sentencing of abusers. In addition abusers must be stripped of the power and authority associated with being a religious figure either through laicisation, or 'defrocking' and removal from the religious institution. In faiths where religious officials wear clothing that identifies their status, such as a collar or robes, the right to wear such items must be removed so that abusers can no longer hide behind the power authority associated with such clothing. Removing this assigned power and status means it will be harder to control and dominate vulnerable others by exercising authority over them.

Alongside reparation to compensate for the pain and suffering incurred, it is also necessary to enter into a **dialogue** that allows victims and survivors to express their feelings towards the offender in a safe and secure setting. It is critical that faith leaders and religious institutions are able to hear the pain and to respond to it in a caring and compassionate way. Until this is done victims cannot grieve and move forward. The need for honesty and truth can facilitate not only healing but also allow for reconciliation and the potential for restoration of trust and faith.

REMEMBER Honesty and truth can facilitate not only healing, but also allow for reconciliation and the potential for restoration of trust and faith.

Accountability must be embraced and accepted for the delays in taking action in the past and not implementing standardised protocols in a timely and effective manner. Most religious institutions and faiths have responded to allegations of RSA by developing safeguarding policies and procedures for current disclosures of sexual abuse. However procedures for historic allegations often vary across –and even within – faiths and take considerable time to fully investigate. What is needed is a clearly-defined set of safeguarding procedures for all faiths worldwide. The guidelines for reporting to allegations need to be transparent and easily available to victims and survivors, with clear guidance on how allegations will be dealt with. More importantly, they must be properly and promptly implemented.

To facilitate true reconciliation the trauma of RSA must be heard and responded to with an honest acknowledgement of the failure of responsibility before healing can occur. It is crucial that responses are genuine and not purely offered as a form of damage limitation. Survivors will know whether they are genuine or not, and reject any attempts at superficial window dressing. It is imperative that religious institutions and faith leaders stop compounding the harm already done through responses, attitudes and practices that not only alienate survivors, but continue to traumatise them.

The way forward

To move forward, religious institutions and faith leaders need to incorporate good practice safeguarding procedures in place which are built upon zero tolerance of any form of sexual abuse. These need to be implemented properly with clear guidelines that are easily available and transparent. Following the Cloyne report[12] it is critical that the implementation of procedures is done in an honest and accurate way, with mandatory reporting. To date, the implementation of procedures and appropriate reporting has been self-regulatory. This has permitted some church authorities such as the RC Church and Anglican Church to avoid proper investigation of reported cases.[12]

Clear, explicit guidelines and standardised procedures need to be publicly available to all members of the church and congregation. This needs to be accompanied by an explicit code of conduct for all those in ministry. In addition, all allegations and complaints need to be independently audited to ensure that they are appropriately dealt with.

Leaflets on how to report RSA need to be placed in all churches and places of worship. As some survivors avoid going to places of worship for fear of triggering trauma reactions, such leaflets should also be made available through GP surgeries, hospitals and mental health organisations such as Mind, as well as libraries, community centres and relevant internet sites. These need to include information on pastoral care as well as a list of organisations that provide professional psychological help or counselling, and local survivor groups that can offer support.

All allegations must be subject to criminal investigation not just canon law as has been the case in the RC Church

– including immediate suspension of the offender pending investigation. During the investigation it is crucial that victims and families are offered support, including the choice of pastoral care or secular professional counselling, and funding to support this.

Training

To maintain good practice and ensure that effective responses are sustained, it is critical to provide continuous training and professional development to those entering religious life and those who are already in ministry. There are a number of training needs that must be addressed to fully support current and historic victims of RSA. These training programmes need to be delivered to all those in religious ministry, clergy, safeguarding officers, lay ministers and parish workers – as well as those entering religious life.

Safeguarding training must be undertaken by all – not just designated officers – to include policy, procedures, reporting, record keeping and how to respond to concerns and allegations to ensure a good practice model. Ideally this training needs to include basic counselling skills to facilitate non-defensive listening, sensitive and empathic responses to victims, survivors and their families. It is critical that all ministers know the safeguarding procedures so if they believe that procedures and guidelines are not being adhered to they can raise concerns.

A good practice model of pastoral care that contains fundamental secular and pastoral counselling skills is essential and must be delivered by psychologists and trained psychotherapist with clinical experience of working with survivors of sexual abuse to ensure appropriate responses to victims and survivors. This must include: increased awareness of good ethical practice; the importance of professional standards; the responsibility that comes with having a duty of care to others; and the importance of boundaries to protect all those involved. Boundaries protect both the survivor and the member of the clergy or faith by reducing the risk of misunderstanding and misinterpretation of actions and behaviour.

All clergy, lay ministers and pastoral workers need access to knowledge and increased awareness of the nature and dynamics of RSA, and its impact and long term effects on survivors. This must include a clinical and secular – not just pastoral – understanding of the effects of trauma and spiritual injury on survivors, and how to provide genuine and effective apologies. Attention must also be paid to individual and institutional risk factors that can lead to RSA and the requisite prevention strategies needed to maintain religious and spiritual integrity.

Mandatory continuing ministerial development (CMD) is essential to maintain competence and good practice. This must consist of up to date psychological research and knowledge about sexuality and sexual abuse, and the long term effects of RSA on survivors. In addition CMD needs to support a professional code of ethics and conduct and provide regular supervision and reflection on practice.

Training for all those entering religious life or seminaries needs to include a comprehensive psychosocial understanding of sexuality, based on current research not just on religious beliefs. Such training must focus on the management and expression of sexual feelings in a healthy, safe and non-harmful way. This is especially the case in those faiths that are predicated on celibacy. In addition, emphasis needs to be placed on how to manage relationships, loneliness, stress and the effects of social isolation. Alongside this, there needs to be open discussion and exploration of the nature, dynamics, and impact of sexual abuse within religious institution, and its impact on victims, families and wider society.

Such training will be a direct demonstration of commitment by religious institutions and faith leaders to prevent future RSA and provide some assurance of zero tolerance of sexual abuse. If this is accompanied by significant structural and systemic changes, victims and survivors will feel that their experiences are finally taken seriously which allow them to move forward towards healing.

Systemic and structural changes

Systemic and structural changes within religious institutions and church authorities will also need to be considered. It is critical that guidelines and procedures are adhered by all those in ministry, throughout the hierarchy. The Cloyne report[x] has highlighted that some within the RC Church senior church officials, such as bishops and cardinals, are not complying with their own safeguarding guidelines and procedures. This reinforces the sense of betrayal of victims and survivors and undermines any apologies made to date. It also fuels the lack of trust and confidence in the commitment of faith leaders to the protection of victims.

Until religious institutions and faith leaders actively demonstrate that abused children and adults are prioritised over the reputation of the abuser or the institution, reparation and reconciliation cannot occur. Faith leaders must also understand that until their responses to allegations of RSA are properly managed and appropriately responded too, that church authorities and religious institution will continue to lose credibility.

Healing and growth

There is considerable evidence that trauma provides opportunities for healing and growth.[6] This is true for individual survivors as well as institutions. To move towards healing, faith leaders must listen with heart and soul to the harm done and use this as an opportunity to transform the trauma. In listening more attentively to survivors, their families, the laity and non-offending clergy they will be able to learn much about compassion, humility and humanity.

The spiritual injury in RSA affects not just survivors but also affects whole faith communities and religious institutions. Rather than taking an adversarial and defensive stance, the emphasis needs to be on how they heal each other and return to the fundamental principles of religious teaching. This will allow for the compassion and humanity needed to undo the dehumanising effects of RSA and heal all those affected by it.

The following chapter will examine how families, friends, partners and professionals can help support survivors of RSA and how post-traumatic growth can revive the spirit within.

22 How families and partners can help survivors to heal

This section is for families and long-term partners of survivors. Its aim is to look at how they can best support someone who is recovering from RSA. While the main focus is on families and long-term partners it will also be helpful for friends, colleagues and fellow survivors.

Learning about the effects of sexual abuse through reading books (see **Resources** on page 208) will help families to understand the impact of RSA. From this they will recognise the tremendous amount of energy it takes to manage trauma reactions. In learning about RSA, they will also send a clear message to the survivor about how committed they are to supporting them. Learning about the impact of RSA is not easy and can raise strong feelings, so it is really important that families and partners have support too. It helps to have a number of people that can lend support and are available to listen. If partners or family feel they cannot cope then it is worth considering seeking professional help, or joining a survivor support group.

 READ *The Warrior Within* has a list of useful reading material.

REMEMBER Families and partners can aid survivors' recovery through listening to them and learning about RSA.

Family members and partners are often secondary victims in RSA as they are also impacted by the abuse. Family members may have been abused too, or failed to see that their loved one was suffering. The guilt associated with this may make it hard to have an open dialogue about the abuse. In addition, family members may be split in terms of believing the survivor which can lead to deep rifts in families. Such rifts must be explored and healed. If this cannot be done within the family it may be necessary to seek some family therapy to process what has happened to the whole family. Some family members may lose their own faith and belief in God and they will need to grieve this loss.

 WARNING Family members and partners are often secondary victims in RSA as they are also impacted by the abuse and will need support.

Prioritising the survivor's recovery

Prioritise the survivor's recovery by putting his or her healing first. This is not always easy, especially if family members, or partners or you yourself are suffering. Survivors rarely permit themselves self-compassion or self-empathy, so by giving them permission to do so they may be able to embrace their recovery more easily. It is also a way of showing them how serious the intention is to support them, and that they have no need to feel guilty or selfish. This requires containment of own needs for a period of time, which may need to be supported by trusted others.

Providing support

To support survivors of RSA it is critical families and partners help them identify their needs. This has to be explicit and cannot be done through mind reading as each survivor will have different needs. Some survivors find it helpful to talk, while others do not. Some need affection and reassurance, whereas others prefer physical and emotional space. Some survivors will be unsure about what they want or need, in which case it is important to reassure them that is okay, and that the support is there for them nevertheless.

Support networks are a powerful source for healing and can help survivors. Identifying these and making the initial contact if the survivor is too scared to can be helpful. There are number of survivor networks worldwide that provide support through raising awareness and connecting to other survivors. This does not always have to be face to face but can be done through the internet, websites and user forums. It is also helpful to encourage him or her to access professional support such as counselling (see **Resources** on page 208).

For **professional support** to be most effective, it is critical that it is someone who specialises in working with sexual abuse, and who has a thorough understanding of the abuse of power and authority and the dynamics of institutional abuse. It is not advisable to encourage pastoral counselling at the beginning of the healing process as this can trigger traumatic reactions and re-traumatise the survivor. It is important to check how involved the survivor wants family members to be in the healing process, with some wanting a lot of support while others prefer to pursue avenues of healing independently as this restores autonomy and control. This needs to also be balanced with what can be realistically managed.

Disclosure requires additional support, especially if the survivor intends to make a formal allegation or disclosure, wants to confront the abuser or pursue litigation. Such decisions must never be taken lightly and must be carefully considered. To aid such a decision it is worth seeking expert advice from survivor groups or a firm of solicitors who have experience of representing survivors of RSA. Reporting RSA can be extremely stressful and requires a lot of energy and support. The survivor must make sure that he or she has come out of survival mode and has the energy and resilience to take on such a mammoth task. During this time he or she will need considerable support and it is critical that families or partners also have the energy and robustness to proceed.

It is important to not pressurise survivors to report RSA or confront their abuser. This decision can only be made by the survivor. Similarly, families must not pressure him or her to forgive and forget. Forgiveness is a very personal thing and must never be imposed on the survivor. It is better to support the survivor to make their own choice whether to forgive or not, and make sure that the necessary support is available irrespective of his or her decision. Whatever the survivor chooses to do, it must be his or her own decision and not contaminated by your other people's feelings, beliefs or agenda. If family members cannot support the survivor's decision then they must seek professional help, making sure that their loved one's privacy is respected and confidentiality is maintained. Family members or partners must never discuss the survivor's abuse experiences without their permission.

Litigation and compensation can be an effectual way for some survivors to restore power, and obtain validation and acknowledgement while helping to protect others from harm (see **Using the legal system for justice and healing** on page 176). The decision to recover power through the law has to be the survivor's and must never be forced. The legal process can be lengthy and extremely gruelling, with no guarantee of the outcome. During this process the survivor will need a lot of extra support. It is critical family members or partners are realistic in how much support they can provide, rather than making assurances that they cannot fulfil. If the support can be distributed among family members, partners and friends it will make it easier for all – including the survivor. Pooling resources and sharing the load will also strengthen the connection to others and help the survivor to feel more bonded.

⚠ **WARNING** The legal process, while empowering is often lengthy and gruelling. During this process, survivors will need a lot of extra support from family and friends. It is critical that families are realistic in how much support can be provided.

The legal process can be exhausting as well as rewarding, and it is necessary to ensure that the survivor and his or her supporters are ready to take on such a mammoth task. It is best done when the survivor feels more able to regulate their emotions and is able to control trauma reactions (see **Understanding trauma reactions** on page 87). Revisiting the RSA through statements to the police and solicitors can trigger trauma reactions which will need to be managed. It is crucial that survivors, and those who support them, have access to psychological support or therapy throughout the legal process. This can be through counselling from professionals who specialise in CSA, RSA or trauma, or through survivor organisations that have access to advocacy workers and other professionals who can help. In the absence of such support, survivors and those who support them, are at risk of re-traumatisation.

Whatever decisions the survivor makes with regard to disclosure, confrontation, litigation or reporting the RSA, it must be self-chosen and not imposed. All those who support the survivor need to ensure that they have the physical, psychological and emotional resources to do so. They will have to be realistic about what they can offer and seek support if necessary .

Respect is essential to the healing process as it makes up for the lack of respect during the RSA and helps the survivor feel more comfortable about expressing their needs. A fundamental form of respect is respecting the survivor's needs even if these are not always compatible the needs of families or partners. Knowing that he or she is respected can help the survivor to feel more comfortable in expressing the full range of feelings, thoughts and needs.

Listening is another powerful way of supporting survivors, especially as they were not listened to during the abuse, or when they tried to disclose. Survivors of RSA were not only silenced during the abuse, but this often persisted into adulthood. Such silencing makes it very difficult to share thoughts and feelings as it increases a sense of vulnerability and terror.

When listening it is important to listen empathically and to understand what is being said from the survivor's point of view rather than one's perspective. It is also critical to show the survivor that they have been heard and understood. This will give him or her confidence to express feelings and thoughts more fully. It is important not to ask too many questions and let the survivor go at his or her own pace. Too many questions can distract the survivor from expressing him or herself making them feels as though they have not been heard.

It is also important to be non-judgemental and not minimise their experiences, even if they do so. It takes monumental courage to talk about RSA especially when they have been terrorised into silence and secrecy. It is even more difficult when the abuser is a respected member of the community who has unchecked power and authority over them.

Listening to the sexual abuse can trigger powerful feelings, and can bring up disturbing or negative childhood memories. If this is the case, it may be necessary to limit the amount of time spent discussing the RSA with the survivor. It is critical if, while supporting the survivor, overwhelming feelings emerge, these are processed not with the survivor but with friends, other family members or a counsellor.

Survivors of RSA will feel ashamed about their abuse and how they reacted to it. Supporters must reassure him or her that they have nothing to feel ashamed of and that he or she is not bad, wicked or sinful. It also important to reassure them that they are lovable in the family's – and God's – eyes. They will need reassurance that they have not committed a sin and remind them they were exploited by someone who used God and religion to manipulate and coerce them into sexual activities that their faith deems sinful. Such reassurance must be regularly repeated as well as reflected in actions that clearly show how much the survivor is respected and valued.

Survivors must never be blamed for their abuse and must be applauded for their strength and courage and what they have achieved in surviving RSA. It is important to reassure them that the family or partner will be there for them throughout the recovery process and for as long as it takes. Such assurance must always be tempered with a realistic appraisal of what is possible, as it is important not to make promises that cannot be kept.

Given the silence, secrecy and deception in RSA it is critical to be **open and honest** in all communication. Family and partners need to be honest and explicit in expressing their own hopes, fears and vulnerabilities. Sharing these demonstrates the ability for open and honest dialogue which enhances closeness and intimacy. It also reduces the survivor's tendency to '**mind read**' and become preoccupied with how others feel rather than focusing on their own feelings. Survivors must be given permission to prioritise their feelings and balance this with the need for others to express theirs.

Feelings about the abuser can be a source of difficulty especially if he played a significant role in the family's life or is known to the partner. Survivors of RSA often have ambivalent feelings about the abuser, ranging from love, reverence and adoration through to fear, rage and sadness. Family members and partners may also experience a similar range of emotions. It is important to acknowledge that such ambivalent feelings are normal in CSA and RSA and that these must not be judged.

If the abuser was the family priest, or minister there may still be reverence for him or her as a representative of the church and it will be hard to acknowledge, or believe that he could commit sexual abuse. Partners may know the abuser through the faith community, or because he officiated at weddings, baptisms or confirmations, or at a family member's funeral. Alternatively, the abuser may have been the partner's priest or minister at the same time as he sexually abused the survivor. The range of feelings will vary enormously depending on the relationship the supporter has to the abuser. Whatever the range of feelings it is crucial that family members and partners express these in a non-judgemental way.

It is important for all family members, friends or partners to discuss how they feel about the abuser without fear of judgement or shame. While this can highlight strong divisions between the survivor and those who support him or her, it is also an opportunity to heal. Each individual is entitled to their feelings and these must not be manipulated to cancel one another out. Healing is in balancing and tolerating ambivalent feelings and coming to terms with these. It only through such healing that the power of the abuser can be reduced and opportunities for support can be maximised. Remember that abusers triumph when they are able to divide and conquer and sever family ties and bonds. Uniting and strengthening bonds is one of the most potent antidotes that families and partners have to dilute the abusers power.

If feelings become too overpowering to express safely or appropriately, supporters will need to consider seeking **psychological support or counselling**. It is important that supporters are able to discharge any overwhelming feelings and do not get preoccupied by their feelings about the abuser. Those that support survivors of CSA and

RSA sometimes find that their anger can become misplaced and directed at the survivor for not stopping the abuse or disclosing at the time. While understandable, this is inappropriate and adds to the survivor's self-blame and shame. It is critical that the feelings of family members and partners do not contaminate the survivors feelings. Commonly, if the supporter expresses negative feelings towards the abuser, the survivor feels compelled to counter these with positive feeling to restore balance. This can block recovery, leading them to defend or protect the abuser.

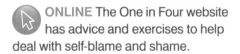 **READ** *The Warrior Within* has advice and exercises to help deal with self-blame and shame.

ONLINE The One in Four website has advice and exercises to help deal with self-blame and shame.

Meeting spiritual needs

The survivor may have lost his or her faith in God or the religious institution to which they belonged. As a result he or she may no longer wish to continue to worship. This can become a problem if family members or partners still have their faith, or wish to bring up their children, or grandchildren within the faith. Alternatively, the survivor may still have faith and wish to continue to worship whereas family members and partners have lost theirs. It is important that any differences are openly discussed and agreement sought on how to manage individual spiritual needs, and those of the children or family. Supporters may need to consider alternative sources to meet their spiritual needs (see **Resources** on page 208).

It is important not to impose religious or faith-based beliefs on to the survivor. If he or she decides to explore alternative sources of worship or spirituality it is helpful to support this, even if it is in stark contrast to one's own beliefs. Restoring spirituality is a unique opportunity to examine previously held beliefs, and explore alternative faiths or spirituality which are self-chosen rather than inherited, imposed or conditioned (see **Triumphing over trauma** on page 171). This can lead to renewed faith, albeit in a different form, which can restore a sense of meaning and purpose to life.

Looking after yourself

In supporting a survivor through the process of recovery it is crucial to ensure that supporters look after themselves. It is inevitable that family members and partners will feel overwhelmed, beleaguered, neglected, drained, angry and resentful at times. This is absolutely normal, and should not become a source of guilt. To avoid becoming too drained it is important to balance the support for the survivor with one's own support and self-care. The more supporters are able to take care of themselves, the more they will be able to support the survivor. It is for this reason that it is necessary to take regular breaks by engaging in activities that are not abuse related to restore energy and vitality.

REMEMBER Families, friends and partners will need support too. It will help if they have a good support network and access to professional advice.

Safety concerns

If family members or partners have concerns about the survivor's safety, it is crucial that you seek professional advice. If there is an increase in self-destructive behaviours such as self-harm, suicidal thoughts or behaviours or wanting to harm others, it will be necessary to seek professional help for him or her. This is best done by consulting the survivor and getting his or her permission to contact the GP, or counsellor. Remember that nobody can stop someone attempting suicide, but seeking professional help before suicidal thoughts take hold can help that person.

WARNING If there are concerns about the survivor's safety it will be necessary to seek professional advice.

23 How counsellors and professionals can help survivors to heal

Counsellors and professionals are a valuable support to survivors. Given the nature of RSA, counsellors and professionals working with victims and survivors will require additional skills and expertise. They will need to have considerable knowledge of CSA and the impact of trauma, as well as an understanding of the spiritual injury that accompanies RSA. It is critical that professionals do not contaminate the therapeutic space with their own faith agenda, so that the survivor can make their own choices and decisions in restoring spirituality.

Working with people who have been traumatised can have a significant impact on professionals and they need to be aware how the work affects them so that they can fully support survivors and all those affected by RSA. Those survivors who support other survivors through survivor organisations need also to be aware that, despite the valuable and inspirational work that they do, listening to the stories of others can retrigger their own experiences which can be overwhelming.

To minimise **vicarious traumatisation**, it is critical that all those who support survivors in whatever capacity, have access to support and ensure that they look after themselves too.

This chapter is for all professionals who work with survivors – in particular, pastoral and secular counsellors and therapists, and safeguarding officers and members of religious institutions to whom historic allegations of RSA are made. It also includes advocacy workers, lawyers and police officers, as well as insurers and faith leaders. The importance of self-care will also be of interest to survivors and survivor organisations that support victims and other survivors. Those helping professionals who are not familiar with *The Warrior Within* may wish to consult this companion volume for a range of useful exercises and activities that can aid recovery and healing.

⚠ **WARNING** To minimise vicarious traumatisation, it is critical that all those who support survivors in whatever capacity, have access to support and ensure that they look after themselves too.

Pastoral or secular counselling

Survivors who wish to enter counselling may be unsure whether this should be pastoral or secular. While it is important that survivors have the choice whether to enter pastoral or secular counselling, it is generally thought to be better if this is initially within a secular setting. Many survivors are fearful of pastoral counselling as this is too reminiscent of the abuse experience. In addition they will be reluctant to trust someone who has the same power and authority as their abuser.

REMEMBER Survivors of RSA need to know that they have a choice in whether to enter pastoral or secular counselling.

Survivors need to know that they have a choice in which type of counselling they deem most helpful. To minimise re-traumatisation, pastoral counsellors need to be aware that religious settings, clothing and artefacts can trigger trauma reactions and flashbacks. It will also take significantly longer to build trust and engage in the therapeutic relationship.

Whatever setting the counsellor works in, when working with the dehumanising effects of RSA, it is critical that survivors are offered a secure base where they can explore the psychological, emotional, physical and spiritual impact of RSA.

Safe trauma therapy

To work with survivors requires a good practice model for safe trauma therapy to protect both the survivor and the counsellor. Some counsellors may already have experience of working with survivors of CSA and RSA, or may be entering new territory. Counsellors who are new to working with survivors of CSA or RSA will need to develop their knowledge and understanding through additional training. It is also useful to assemble a list of specialist organisations, or counsellors to form links with and to have access to further information.

Working with RSA

A central component of working with survivors of RSA is not judging whether or not the abuse experience is true or false. It is impossible for counsellors to know this. What is critical is that the survivor is supported in their belief and feelings about their experience rather than a search for factual evidence. The therapeutic space is not a court of law to judge truth or facts. Rather, it is a respectful and safe space to explore their experiences from which to draw their own conclusions and work through any challenges and concerns.

To do this, counsellors need to listen empathically rather than focusing on confirming or disconfirming the RSA. Counsellors need to validate and honour the survivor's willingness to trust again despite past betrayals. To invest trust in someone who has power and authority through their professional status is a huge risk and a testament to hope. It also represents an opportunity to transform the traumatising and dehumanising effects of RSA through a human relationship.

REMEMBER To invest trust in someone who has power and authority through their professional status is a huge risk for a survivor.

Counsellors need to be prepared and informed when working with RSA survivors. They need to expand their knowledge and understanding, not only around trauma and RSA, but also around sex and sexuality to manage the sexual elements of RSA. Counsellors must be able to feel comfortable talking about sexual elements of RSA without embarrassment or shame to minimise shaming the survivor. It is also useful to have a deeper understanding of trauma and the need to self-medicate through alcohol, drugs or food, or self-harming behaviour.

To minimise contaminating survivor experiences, counsellors need to develop self-awareness of their own experiences of power and control, abuse experiences ,and sexuality and gender issues. Most importantly they need to examine their own faith-based beliefs, and the role spirituality plays in their life. If the counsellor does not have faith-based or spiritual beliefs, it is still necessary to develop an understanding of the importance of religious beliefs and faith, and how this these impact on self-identity and sense of belongingness to a spiritual family. Counsellors who do not have a faith may nevertheless need to familiarise themselves with religious concepts, rituals and practices and terminology to fully understand the survivors experiences.

WARNING To minimise contaminating survivor experiences, counsellors need to develop self-awareness of their own experiences of power and control, abuse experiences, sexuality and gender issues as well as spirituality.

To be fully equipped, counsellors need to commit to extra training and Continuing Professional Development (CPD) and ensure regular supervision. As an addition to supervision, it can help to consultant someone who specialises in CSA and/or RSA to ensure good practice is maintained. If working with survivors of RSA triggers past experiences for the counsellor, or raises concerns around their own faith and spirituality it is important that counsellors return to personal therapy, or seek spiritual guidance. Some counsellors find it helpful to set up their own peer support group to share their experiences and support each other to ensure ethical practice. All of these help to prevent perpetuating myths, and to avoid projection or contamination of the client's material.

Creating a secure base

In order to work most effectively with survivors it is critical to establish safety first. This can only be done in a secure setting in which the survivor can pace their recovery.[5,6] It is critical that the recovery process is not rushed, as this is reminiscent of the abuse. It is essential to encourage the survivor to take small manageable steps to restore control and maximise recovery. The therapeutic process needs to be a collaborative one, in which there is mutual respect for the survivor's knowledge and survival so far. The therapeutic relationship must be an essentially human one, which is based on honesty and openness as well as warmth and sensitive attunement.

To avoid disempowering the survivor, it is crucial to avoid becoming the dominant force in the recovery process by assuming that the counsellor is the only source of healing. Counsellors, while a significant part of the recovery and support process, are not the only resource. It is helpful to encourage other sources of support such as survivor groups, as well as a good peer and social support network. This will encourage autonomy and help the survivor to value and develop the coping skills and resources he or she already has. In addition handbooks like the this one, and the warrior within are an excellent source of support in between sessions for survivors to feel more in control of their healing.

The importance of choice

Counsellors must never pressurise survivors to adopt the course that they think is best, especially in terms of forgiveness and their religious or fait-based beliefs. Counsellors must also avoid projecting their own views on to the survivor. While the counsellor's knowledge and experience are a rich source for ideas they may not be the best form of healing for the survivor. It is important to acknowledge that this is the survivor's process, and that counsellors are companions on his or her journey towards healing. Counsellors need to be honest and explicit and avoid ambiguity, minimise the risk of confusion, distortion of reality and prevent mind reading. In addition, they must not make promises that cannot be fulfilled and acknowledge their limitations to avoid disappointment.

Counsellors must remain patient as recovery from RSA is not a linear process. Survivors of RSA often become distracted, or diverted or become stuck. This is a part of the healing process, and does not always indicate resistance. Survivors find it extremely difficult to trust and they will need to test how much they can trust any professional. Counsellors need to remember that trust is not dichotomous, or 'all or nothing' but is built slowly over time and tested throughout the process.[5] Insisting on trust too early can put unnecessary pressure on the survivor and impede the therapeutic relationship.

REMEMBER Trust is not dichotomous or 'all or nothing', but is built slowly over time. People who have been sexually abused by those in authority will find it hard to trust and this must not be rushed.

If the survivor is going through a legal process of litigation, they are likely to fluctuate in their recovery. While litigation is a powerful way of healing the hurt, it is also a gruelling process. Progress is often accompanied with disappointments and loss of hope which can impede the therapeutic process. Counsellors need to have an understanding of the difficulties survivors face (see **Using the legal system for justice and healing** on page 176) and ensure that the survivor has sufficient resilience and robustness to sustain any legal action. It may be necessary at times to shift the focus of therapy and provide the necessary psychological and emotional support required during the legal process.

The therapeutic relationship

The therapeutic relationship is important to aid recovery and rebuild relationships with others. To facilitate this, counsellors need to provide an essentially human relationship in which the survivor is respected and valued. It is that which ultimately helps the survivor to reconnect to others. The therapeutic relationship has to be a collaborative one, where both survivor and counsellor work together towards recovery. Counsellors need to reflect on their reactions to the work, as it is a rich source of information that can hint at what the survivor has not been able to express.

Counsellors need to be mindful of not making assumptions and to check perceptions, feelings and thoughts with the survivor. To keep counsellors safe and on track, it is critical to have regular supervision. To maximise supervision, it is beneficial to find additional supervision from a supervisor who is experienced in this area.

Pitfalls and difficulties

There are a number of pitfalls and difficulties associated with working with survivors of RSA. It is essential that counsellors feel confident in managing these. The essential thing is that there is a good match between counsellor and survivor. If this is not the case, counsellors will need to help the survivor to find a more suitable match and refer them on. By helping the survivor to find a better match the counsellor is serving his or her needs rather than satisfy their own.

A common pitfall is not believing the survivor. In such instances it is imperative that this is explored in supervision so that appropriate action can be taken. One confusing difficulty that some counsellors encounter is becoming aroused when listening to the survivor's experiences. While this is natural, if it becomes too frequent or intense then this must be addressed in supervision. Counsellors must remember that such arousal may not necessarily be sexual but have its origins in fear which has been eroticised. This usually represents and mirrors the survivor's experience during the abuse. It is crucial that if counsellors are preoccupied with sexually arousing feelings that these are discussed either with a supervisor, or trusted colleague.

Sexual feelings should never be acted upon, even with former clients.

Counsellors must avoid being intrusive in order to avoid making the survivor feel as though they are being abused again. They must also curb their curiosity, and desire to ask too many questions, especially sexual ones as these can feel voyeuristic. In addition, counsellors must guard against becoming too involved, or becoming lost in the survivor's despair and hopelessness. This can result in excessive identification with client and lead to projection and negative counter-transference reactions. Counsellors must avoid imposing their own world view and spiritual beliefs on survivors. This is especially true in relation to forgiveness and how to restore spirituality, which only the survivor can choose to do. Counsellors must guard against trying to influence the survivor as this recreates the abuse of power and authority seen in RSA. To undo the psychological and spiritual control associated with RSA, counsellors must ensure they facilitate, rather than impose choices. When professionals impose their own faith-based beliefs or spiritual views on the client they are replicating the survivor's abuse experience. This is at best unethical and at worst abusive, as it is a reminder of the abuser imposing his or her beliefs onto the survivor. To truly respect survivors of RSA, counsellors help them to restore their own reality and reach their own conclusions about their faith and spirituality.

Given the nature of RSA it is important to be explicit around boundaries, including touch. Generally it is not a good idea to touch clients, no matter how well intentioned. Some therapists do believe in the healing power of touch as long as it is used judiciously and well bounded. If counsellors do believe in the benefits of therapeutic touch they must always seek the survivor's permission first. Boundaries around touch must always be explicitly stated at the beginning of the contract, and sexual touch is never permitted.

Counsellors must also be mindful of sensory cues that have the potential to trigger traumatic reactions or flashbacks. They will need to pay attention to what they are wearing including clothes or jewellery that have religious connotations such as a Christian cross. It is also important not to have lighted candles or incense burning in case these act as a trigger. Alongside this they need to be aware that if the consulting room contains any religious iconography or paintings or books with religious themes that this might impact negatively on the survivor. Counsellors will also need to monitor

their use of language and make sure they have some understanding of faith-based terminology so that they are able to understand what survivors are trying to communicate.

Working with spiritual injury

Healing the spiritual injury is critical to recovery from RSA. Religious neutrality of the counsellor is critical, so that personal or faith-based beliefs do not contaminate the therapeutic process. It is also critical that counsellors provide secular psycho-education on sexuality, shame and forgiveness. This will help the survivor to make autonomous decisions rather than be coerced. Counsellors need to have a good understanding of the importance of faith and religious beliefs and how this impacts on self-identity, sense of belongingness and meaning of life and death – regardless of the counsellor's own personal or faith-based beliefs. It is essential to explore the survivor's faith and beliefs in a non-judgemental way, and that ensure that he or she is not influenced consciously or unconsciously in their future beliefs.

Survivor support groups

Some survivors find comfort and solace in support groups and group therapy. This can be an important aspect of healing and needs to be supported. In addition, it may helpful at times to facilitate a therapeutic meeting with family members, or partners so that they can have a better understanding of how RSA has affected the survivor and how this has impacted on the family, or partner. The internet can be a good way of being in touch with other survivors and to share information with each other.

Professional self-care

Working with survivors can be emotionally and physically draining, so it is essential that professionals take care of themselves. To avoid **vicarious traumatisation** – or '**burn out**' – it is critical that professionals have access to regular supervision, and professional and personal support. Such support is necessary, not just for counsellors but all professionals that support survivors in some capacity. This includes members of the clergy involved in processing and investigating allegations, safeguarding officers, solicitors and legal professionals, advocacy workers and police officers, as well other survivors.

To minimise the negative impact of exposure to RSA it is important to ensure that practitioners and the range of professionals have a healthy balance between work, and their personal life. If possible it helps to balance the work with survivors with other clients, or other types of work. Taking regular physical as well as mental breaks can minimise the development of secondary traumatic stress. It also helps to take regular exercise, to keep up physical energy levels and to remain embodied.

Professional self-care is imperative to restore vitality, enthusiasm, and energy. Working with survivors has the potential to shatter assumptions about the world, human nature and the meaning of life and death. It is vital that professionals do not allow this to destroy their own belief system by engaging in activities that help them to sustain their faith in human nature, and maintain their zest for life. All in all, like survivors, professionals must make sure they remain connected to their spirit within. Through self-care and preservation of their own spirituality professionals can ensure that they remain compassionate and are truly able to accompany the survivor on his or her journey to recovery and allow the spirit within to heal.

24 Post-traumatic growth

As survivors and all those affected by RSA begin to recover and heal they will experience what is known as **post-traumatic growth**. As individuals and institutions recover, they find that they begin to open up to further potential growth. This growth is predominantly a result of what has been learnt through the process of healing and recovery in the aftermath of RSA.

Areas of post-traumatic growth

Post-traumatic growth can usually be seen in six significant areas of life. The first is in a renewed sense of **personal strength**. This is because when vulnerability coexists with an increased capacity to survive, the individual or institution becomes stronger in its faith and beliefs. Although vulnerability is often perceived as dangerous, leading to defensive and self-protective survival strategies, it is also an opportunity for growth.

The second is a **greater appreciation of life**, especially the more ordinary, everyday things. This appreciation is seen in refocusing priorities, implementing changes that are more meaningful and restore connection to others. This is true for survivors, faith communities and religious institutions as they strengthen their sense of belongingness to the human and spiritual family. As the trauma recedes, there will be more time and energy available to appreciate and notice the miracle and wonder of life. Survivors can take more time to appreciate nature and marvel at the mystery of creation. Noticing such details is a reminder that individuals are a part of something bigger and feel more connected to the natural and spiritual world. Being more present also allows survivors to be more in touch with the full range of their experiencing and take more pleasure in life.

The third area is when post-traumatic growth involves **getting closer to other people** – especially friends, family and community. Survivors often find that, as they begin to trust again, they find renewed value in their relationships and feel more comfortable with intimacy. As they reconnect to others they feel isolated and a greater sense of belongingness. Equally faith communities and religious institutions will experience a deeper communion which will allow for more spiritual connection.

The fourth area of post-traumatic growth is that of **greater self-understanding**. Healing is process of self-awareness and self-discovery which allows the survivor to reconnect with the spirit within and strengthen self-identity.

As religious institutions begin to heal there will be greater awareness and understanding of how they are perceived by the faithful, and how some religious customs and practices which distance them from worshippers. Such awareness will promote positive systemic and structural changes and strengthen the bonds within the spiritual family. This will also allow the hurt and pain to heal and provide meaning where once there was only confusion.

The fifth area is a fundamental area of post-traumatic growth involving **spiritual development**. When people, and institutions experience trauma, they are faced with fundamental questions about the meaning of life and death, and that which is sacred. While trauma challenges all previous assumptions and beliefs it also raises deep questions about the value and purpose of life, and the divine. This is especially the case in RSA which is characterised by spiritual injury and a loss of faith or belief. Some survivors find that this deepens their faith, while others experience a spiritual death. Reviving the spirit within allows for a renewal of spiritually that is self-defined and, as it springs from within, can feel more empowering.

Faith communities and religious institutions also benefit from spiritual development and a renewal of faith.

Open and honest communication, greater empathic listening, and a return to the fundamental principles of religious teaching will not only revive the spiritual family but also create the resilience for healing and future growth. Ultimately, recovery from RSA is spirituality transformative which allows individuals and institutions to experience life and the sacred at a much deeper level of awareness.

The sixth and final area of post-traumatic growth can involve **an opening up of new possibilities** which can be life-changing. A new and changed perspective on life and the divine can be the beginning of changing the meaning and direction of your life. For survivors this is often a career change, moving to a new environment, or country, starting a new relationship, going back to college, or a change in priorities.

It also opens up new possibilities for religious institutions and faith leaders to examine institutional and systemic factors that consciously or unconsciously support RSA. Acknowledging the harm done, understanding and listening empathically to survivors, the faithful and the disillusioned, will allow change and healing to occur. Openness to change and working more collaboratively with all those who have been harmed will not only ensure greater protection for children and vulnerable adults in the future, but also allow for a renewal of faith and strengthening of bonds.

In essence, post-traumatic growth can lead to a greater sense of meaning and purpose in life and renewal of spirituality for all those who have been affected by RSA. The process of healing and recovery will revive the spirit within.

Resources

Sources of help

As a GP, health visitor, social worker or other professional can assist you in getting help from a clinical psychologist or other therapist. Do not be afraid to ask to see a woman if you feel uncomfortable talking to a man (or vice versa).

The national addresses or phone numbers for various organisations are listed below. For information on local sources of help contact the national office or try your local telephone directory. Please include a stamped self-addressed envelope for written replies.

Telephone helplines

The organisations listed below offer someone to talk to, advice and sometimes face-to-face counselling.

One in Four
One in Four offers a voice to and support for people who have experienced sexual abuse and sexual violence, including RSA, offering low-cost, long-term one-to-one therapy.
219 Bromley Road, Bellingham, Catford SE6 2PG
Email admin@oneinfour.org.uk
www.oneinfour.org.uk

Also see **One in Four Ireland** on page 217.

Childline
Children can phone 0800 1111 (free) or write to Freepost NATN1111, London E1 6BR if they are in trouble or are being abused. Also for parents, children, abusers and professionals 0808 800 500 (24-hour helpline)

Family Matters
Counselling service for children and adult survivors of sexual abuse and rape.
13 Wrotham Road, Gravesend, Kent DA11 0PA
Telephone 01474 536 661
Monday to Friday 9am to 5pm
Helpline 01474 537 392

Rape and Sexual Abuse Support Centre
For women and men, staffed by trained female volunteers.
Helpline 01483 546400 (women)
Helpline 01483 568000 (men)
Sunday to Friday 7.30pm to 9.30pm

The Lantern Project
Supports victims of child sexual abuse and RSA.
Telephone 0151 638 7015
www.lanternproject.org.uk

Rights of Women
Informs, educates and empowers women on their legal rights.
52-54 Featherstone Street, London EC1Y 8RT

Administration 020 7251 6575
Email info@row.org.uk
Advice line 020 7251 6577
Tuesday to Thursday 2pm to 4pm and
7pm to 9pm, Friday 12pm to 2pm
Sexual violence legal advice line
020 7251 8887
Monday 11am to 1pm and
Tuesday 10am to 12pm

Solace Women's Aid
*Charity providing a range of services
for women and children affected by
domestic and sexual violence.*
www.solacewomensaid.org

The Survivors Trust
*A national umbrella agency for 130
specialist voluntary sector agencies
providing a range of counselling,
therapeutic and support.*
Telephone 01788 551 150
www.thesurvivorstrust.org

NAPAC (National Association of People Abused in Childhood)
*NAPAC is a registered charity based
in the UK, providing support and
information for people abused in
childhood.*
PO Box 63632, London SW9 1BF
Support line 0800 085 3330
www.napac.org.uk

SAFE: Supporting Survivors of Satanic Abuse
*Helpline for survivors of ritual and satanic
abuse. Offers counselling, listening,
advice and referrals.*
PO Box 1557, Salisbury SP1 2TP
Telephone 01722 410889
Wednesday 6.30pm to 8.30pm
Thursday 7.00pm to 9.00pm

Samaritans
*24-hour listening and befriending service
for the lonely, suicidal or depressed.*
Telephone 08457 90 90 90

Victim Supportline
Telephone 0845 30 30 900
Monday to Friday 9am to 9pm
Weekends 9am to 7pm
Bank Holidays 9am to 5pm

Organisations supporting survivors of RSA

The London Irish Centre
*Offers advice and a range of services for
Irish people throughout Britain.*
50-52 Camden Square, London NW1 9XB
Telephone 020 7916 2222
Email info@londonirishcentre.org
www.londonirishcentre.org

MACSACS (Ministry and Clergy Sexual Abuse Survivors)
www.macsacs.org.uk

Christian Survivors of Sexual Abuse

CSSA offers advice and support to Christian adults who were sexually abused in childhood. Contact by letter only.
CSSA c/o 38 Sydenham Villas Road, Cheltenham, Gloucestershire
GL5 26DZ

The Churches Child Protection Advisory Service (CCPAS)

This is part of Pennington County Child Care Association (PCCA). CCPAS offers training and advice to churches and individuals on all aspects of child protection. They have recently published a video and training pack for churches called Facing the Unthinkable: Protecting Children from Abuse. *The video, 'A duty to care', can be ordered separately for £25.*
PO Box 133, Swanley, Kent BR8 7UQ
Telephone 01322 667207/ 660011
Fax 01322 614788
Email ccpas@aol.com
www.ccpas.co.uk

Vashti Scottish Christian Women Against Abuse
Telephone 01738 850 995

S:vox
An organisation for survivors of any sort of abuse as a child or an adult. Offers support, education and advocacy.
www.svox.org.uk

CIS'ters
Support service for childhood incest survivors.
PO Box 119, Eastleigh SO50 9ZF
Telephone 023 8033 8080

MOSAC
Supports non-abusing parents and carers of sexually abused children.
141 Greenwich High Road, Greenwich, London SE10 8JA
Telephone 0800 980 1958
www.mosac.org.uk

Counselling Directory
Counselling Directory provides the UK with a huge counselling support network, enabling those in distress to find a counsellor close to them and appropriate for their needs. This is a free, confidential service that will hopefully encourage those in distress to seek help.
www.counselling-directory.org.uk

Innocent Voices UK
www.innocentvoicesuk.com

Help for male survivors

Survivors UK
For male survivors of rape and sexual abuse.
www.survivorsuk.org

National Register of Male Sexual Assault Counsellors (males only)
2 Leathermarket Street, London SE1 3HN
Telephone 0845 122 1201

AMSOSA (Adult Male Survivors of Sexual Abuse)
Offers two support groups to male survivors of sexual abuse either as a child or adult.
Telephone 0845 430 9371
www.amsosa.com

Mankind UK
Provides counselling and support for victims of male rape, male sexual assault and violence, as well as sex abuse support (males only).
PO Box 124, Newhaven,
East Sussex
BN9 9TQ
Telephone 01273 510447
Email admin@
mankindcounselling.org.uk

Children at risk

NSPCC Helpline
A 24-hour helpline to ring if you are concerned about a child at risk or wish to discuss child protection. The helpline will take children at risk referrals and pass them on to the relevant social services department.
Telephone 0800 800 500

Kidscape
Helps parents to keep their children safe.
2 Grosvenor Gardens, London
SW1W 0DH.
Telephone 020 7730 3300
www.kidscape.org.uk

Childline (part of the NSPCC)
See **Telephone helplines** on page 209.

Help for those at risk of abusing children

Stop It Now
A public information and awareness-raising campaign regarding child sexual abuse.
Telephone 0808 1000 900
www.stopitnow.org.uk

For disabled children

Respond

A therapeutic service supporting people with learning difficulties, their families, carers and professionals affected by trauma and abuse.
3rd Floor, 24-32 Stephenson Way,
London NW1 2HD
Telephone 020 7383 0700
Helpline 0808 808 0700
www.respond.org.uk

National Deaf Children's Society

Agency catering for deaf children and their families. Can offer books and information to professionals.
15 Dufferin Street, London EC1Y 8UR
Telephone 020 7490 8656
Helpline 0808 800 8880
Monday to Friday 9.30am to 5pm
Email ndcs@ndcs.org.uk
www.ndcs.org.uk

Church child protection agencies/ head offices

It is important to make yourself aware of your local child protection contact in your church. The following are head offices where you might obtain information about your local region. You should also be able to find policies and procedures concerning abuse in respective churches on their websites. If you cannot access the website or documents you need, contact MACSAS.

CSAS – The Catholic Safeguarding Advisory Service
CSAS is the national agency for driving and supporting improvements in safeguarding practice within the Catholic Church in England and Wales.
Queensway House, 57 Livery Street,
Birmingham B3 1HA
Telephone 0121 237 3740
www.csas.uk.net

National Catholic Safeguarding Commission (NCSC)
www.catholicsafeguarding.org.uk

Baptist Union
Has all the documentation on child protection to download and advice on obtaining 'Safe To Grow'
PO Box 44, 129 Broadway, Didcot.
Oxfordshire, OX11 8RT
Telephone 01235 517700
www.baptist.org.uk

United Reformed Church
Church House, 86 Tavistock Place,
London WC1H 9RT
Telephone 027916 2020
www.urc.org.uk

Society of Friends (Quakers)

Friends House, 173-177 Euston Road,
London NW1 2BJ
Telephone 020 7663 1000
www.quaker.org.uk/meeting-safety

Evangelical Alliance

*Has a resource page on organisations
and relevant books.*
186 Kennington Park Road,
London SE11 4BT
Telephone 020 7207 2100
www.eauk.org

Congregational Federation

Has information for youth workers.
8 Castle Gate, Nottingham NG1 7AS
Telephone 0115 911 1460
Email admin@congregational.org.uk
www.congregational.org.uk

Anglican and Methodist

*Rev. Pearl Luxon is the Safeguarding
Advisor (Children and Adult Protection)
responsible for advising on child
protection in both churches.*
c/o Methodist Church House, 25
Marylebone Rd, London NW1 5JR
Telephone 020 7467 5189
Email luxon@methodistchurch.org.uk

CRB (Criminal Records Bureau)

www.homeoffice.gov.uk/agencies-
public-bodies/crb/

Preventing abuse

*Phone one of the helplines listed or
contact the following agencies if you
suspect a child is being abused or is at
risk of abuse, or you know of an abuser
who has any contact with children.*

Police

Many districts now have a special
police unit that works with sexual abuse.
Phone your local police station and ask
to speak to the officer who deals with
sexual abuse.

Social services

Phone your local office and ask for the
Child Protection Officer or Duty Officer.

If you are abusing children or have
urges to abuse children contact the
NSPCC, social services or the police.

Therapy/counselling and support

Action for Children
Provides a national network of child sexual abuse treatment centres-providing support and counselling for children and their families. Adult survivors also.
Chesham House, Church Lane, Berkhamstead, Herts HP4 2AX
Telephone 0300 123 2112
www.actionfor children.org.uk

British Association for Counselling and Psychotherapy
BACP House, 15 St John's Business Park, Lutterworth LE17 4HB
Telephone 0870 443 5252
or 01455 883300
Monday to Friday 8.45am to 5pm
Email bacp@bacp.couk
www.bacp.co.uk

Children 1st
83 Whitehouse Loan, Edinburgh EH9 1AT
Headquarters 0131 446 2300
ParentLine Scotland 0808 800 2222
www.children1st.org.uk

Citizens Advice Bureau (part of the overall grouping Citizens Advice)
Can direct you to local groups who can help. Find the number of your nearest office in the phone book.
www.citizensadvice.org.uk

Clinical psychologists

Your GP can refer you to a clinical psychologists or you can ask another professional for advice on how to get to see a psychologist, or visit the website of the British Psychological Society at www.bps.org.uk

Child And Woman Abuse Studies Unit (CWASU)
Specialist research unit with a wealth of experience in researching child and woman abuse.
Email cwasu@londonmet.ac.uk
www.cwasu.org

DABS Directory & Book Services

DABS collate information and produce a national directory for resources for survivors. They also provide an excellent mail order service for books.
4 New Hill, Conisbrough, Doncaster DN12 3HA
Telephone/fax 01709 860023
Monday and Friday 10am to 6pm
www.dabsbooks.co.uk

EMDR (Eye Movement Desensitisation and Reprocessing)
For information about EMDR and help to find an accredited therapist in the UK.
www.emdrassociation.org.uk

MIND

Offers individual counselling and group work.
Information helpline 0845 7660163
Monday to Friday 9am to 5pm
Email info@mind.org.uk
www.mind.org.uk

Relate

Can help with relationship difficulties and sexual problems. Provides couple counselling, face-to-face or by phone.
Premier House, Carolina Court, Lakeside, Doncaster, South Yorkshire DN4 5RA
Telephone 0300 100 1234
Email enquiries@relate.org.uk
www.relate.co.uk

SEREN

SEREN is a specialised counselling service in Wales for adults who have been sexually abused as children.
2nd Floor, Natwest Chambers, Sycamore Street, Newcastle Emlyn SA38 9AJ
Telephone 01239 711772
www.seren-wales.org.uk

Victim Support

Co-ordinates nationwide victim support schemes. Trained volunteers offer a practical and motional help to victims of crime including rape and sexual assault.
Hallam House, 56-60 Hallam Street, London N1W 6JL
Telephone 020 7268 0200
www.victimsupport.org.uk

Women's Therapy Centre

Offers group and individual therapy by women for women.
10 Manor Gardens, London N7 6JS
Psychotherapy enquiries 020 7263 8200
Monday to Thursday 2pm to 4pm
Email appointments@
womenstherapycentre.co.uk
www.womenstherapycentre.co.uk

ACT (Ann Craft Trust)

Provides an information and networking service to adult and child survivors with learning disabilities and workers involved in this area.
Monday to Thursday 8.30am to 5pm
Friday 8.30am to 2pm
Centre for Social Work, University Park Nottingham NG7 2RD
Telephone 0225 951 5400
Email ann-craft-trust@notiingham.ac.uk
www.anncrafttrust.org

Accuracy About Abuse

Information service providing a background to media controversies.
www.accuracyaboutabuse.org

Beacon Foundation

Services for survivors of satanic/ritualistic abuse and their carers, and support for the professionals.
3 Grosvenor Avenue, Rhyl,
Clwyd LL18 4HA
Helpline 01745 343600
Weekdays 10am to 4pm

Legal services

AO Advocates
Thames Wharf Studios, Rainville Road,
London W6 9HA
Telephone 020 3080 3911
www.aoadvocates.com

CICA (Criminal Injuries Compensation Authority)
Telephone 0800 358 3601
www.cica.gov.uk

Gay, lesbian, bisexual and transgender

London Lesbian and Gay Switchboard
Telephone 020 7837 7324
Daily 10am to 11pm
www.llgs.org.uk

Irish organisations

The Rape Crisis Network
24-hour helpline for victims of rape and sexual abuse.
Telephone 1800 778888.

The National Counselling Service (NCS)
Telephone 1800 477477

One in Four (Ireland)
2 Holles St, Dublin 2
Telephone 01 6624070
Monday to Friday 9.30 to 5.30pm
Email info@oneinfour.org
www.oneinfour.ie/

Towards Healing
A new counselling and support service for survivors of institutional, clerical and religious abuse, funded by the Catholic Church (replaced the Faoiseamh Counselling Service).
Helpline
Freephone Ireland 1800-303-416
Freephone UK 0800-0963315
Email info@towardshealing.ie

The Shame of Ireland website
For survivors of the Irish Industrial School System, their family members and friends
shameofireland.co.uk

Dublin Rape Crisis Centre

Provides a comprehensive therapy programme for victims of rape and sexual abuse. It also provides education and training to professionals together with literature and leaflets to increase public awareness on sexual violence within our society.

Monday to Friday 8am to 7pm and Saturday 9am to 4pm
70 Lower Leeson Street, Dublin 2
Helpline 1 800 778 888
Email rcc@indigo.ie
www.drcc.ie

The CARI (Children at Risk in Ireland) Foundation

Charity providing a professional child centred therapy and counselling service to children, families, and groups who have been affected by child sexual abuse. This is available around the country and they also provide a telephone helpline service.

110 Lower Drumcondra Road, Dublin 9
UK and Northern Ireland helpline
00353 18308523
Monday to Friday 9:30am to 5:30pm
Email info@cari.ie
www.cari.ie

The Irish Society for the Protection of Cruelty to Children (ISPCC)

A child protection and child advocacy agency providing services to children and parents in Ireland.

29 Lower Baggot Street, Dublin 2
Telephone 01 6767 960
www.ispcc.ie

MASC (Male Abuse Survivors Centre)

Confidential support service for adult male survivors of sexual abuse, sexual assault, incest and rape.

3 Ruxton Court, Dominick Street, Galway
Telephone 091 534594

The National Counselling Service (NCS)

A Health Board Service providing counseling to adults who have experienced sexual abuse. It was established initially to provide counselling to adults abused in institutions but also offers support to adults abused in other settings.

www.hse-ncs.ie

USA

SNAP (Survivors Network for those Abused by Priests)
Survivors network that has groups throughout the United States and members throughout the world
www.snapnetwork.org

Walk-In Counseling Center
Gary Schoener's Walk-In Counseling Center in Minneapolis has offered free, easily accessible counseling for people with urgent needs and few options since 1969.
www.walkin.org

Richard Sipe
This renowned author and commentator on the RC Church has a wesite ful of useful articles and links including to Fr Tom Doyle's Clergy Sexual Abuse Bibliography
www.richardsipe.com

Abuse Tracker
A blog documenting the abuse crisis in the RC Church
www.bishop-accountability.org/abusetracker/

Films and documentaries

Films

La mala educación (Bad Education) (2004) by Pedro Almodovar

Beyond the Fire (2009) by Maeve Murphy

The Boys of St. Vincent (1992) TV film by John N. Smith

Doubt (2008), based on the eponymous play

Hand of God (2006), documentary filmed for Frontline

The Magdalene Sisters (2002) by Peter Mullan

Our Fathers (2005), based on the book by David France

Song for a Raggy Boy (2003) by Aisling Walsh

Twist of Faith (2004), HBO

Vows of Silence (2008) by Jason Berry

Documentaries

Abused: Breaking the Silence (2011) A BBC documentary about the survivors of Rosminian

Deliver Us From Evil (2006) Made about the sex abuse cases and one priest's confession of abuse.

Sex Crimes and the Vatican (2006), A documentary filmed for the BBC Panorama documentary series that purported to show how the Vatican has used *crimen sollicitationis* to silence allegations of sexual abuse by priests.

Publications and references
Some of these publications have been referenced in this book

Self-help books for survivors

1 Ainscough C and Toon K. *Breaking Free: Help for Survivors of Child Sexual Abuse*. Sheldon Press, 1993. New edition 2000

2 Davis, L. *The Courage to Heal: A Guide for Women Survivors of Child Sexual Abuse.* Bass, Ellen and Cedar, 1990

3 Sanderson, C. *The Warrior Within: A One in Four Handbook to aid recovery of childhood sexual abuse and violence.* London, One In Four, 2010

Books for therapists

4 Courtois, CA. *Healing the Incest Wound.* 2nd Edition. NY, WW Norton, 2010

5 Sanderson, C. *Introduction to Counselling Survivors of Interpersonal Trauma.* London, Jessica Kingsley Publishers, 2010

6 Sanderson, C. *Counselling Adult Survivors of Child Sexual Abuse.* 3rd Edition. London, Jessica Kingsley Publishers, 2006

7 Sanderson, C. *The Seduction Of Children: Empowering Parents And Teachers to Protect Children From Child Sexual Abuse.* London, Jessica Kingsley Publishers, 2004

Books, articles and reports on RSA

8 Benkert, M and Doyle, TP. Clericalism, Religious Duress and its Impact on Victims of Clergy Sexual Abuse. *Pastoral Psychology* Volume 58, Number 3, 223-238, 2008

9 Berry, J. *Lead Us Not into Temptation: Catholic Priests and the Sexual Abuse of Children*. University of Illinois Press, 2000

10 Berry, J and Renner, G. *Vows of Silence: The Abuse of Power in the Papacy of John Paul II*. Central Free Press, 2010

11 Churches Together in Britain and Ireland. *Time for Action*. London, Churches Together in Britain and Ireland, 2002

12 *Cloyne Report: Report by Commission of Investigation into Catholic Diocese of Cloyne*, 2011

13 Cozzens, D. *Faith That Dares to Speak*. MN, The Liturgical Press, 2004

14 Cozzens, D. *Sacred Silence*. Collegeville, MN, The Liturgical Press, 2002

15 Cozzens, D. *The Changing Face of the Priesthood: A Reflection on the Priest's Crisis of Soul*. MN, The Liturgical Press, 2000

16 Doyle, TP, Sipe, AWR and Wall, P.J. *Sex, Priests, and Secret Codes: The Catholic Church's 2000 Year Paper Trail of Sexual Abuse.* LA, CA, Volt Press, 2006

17 Farrell, D. Sexual Abuse Perpetrated by Roman Catholic Priests. *Mental Health Religion & Culture.* 12;1:39-53, 2009

18 Farrell, Derek P and Taylor, M. Silenced by God – an examination of unique characteristics within sexual abuse by clergy. *Counselling Psychology Review.* 15;1:22-31, 2000

19 Fortune, MM and Longwood, WM. *Sexual Abuse in the Catholic Church: Trusting the Clergy.* Binghamton NY, The Haworth Pastoral Press, 2003

20 Frawley-O'Dea, MG. *Perversion of Power: Sexual Abuse in The Catholic Church.* Naashville, Vanderbilt University Press, 2007

21 Frawley-O'Dea, MG and Goldner, V (eds). *Predatory Priests, Silenced Victims: The Sexual Abuse Crisis and the Catholic Church*. Mahwah NJ, The Analytic Press, 2004

22 Geary, B and Greer, JM. *The Dark Night of the Catholic Church: Examining the Child Sexual Abuse Scandal.* Stowmarket Suffolk, Kevin Mayhew, 2011

23 Hildago, ML. *Sexual Abuse and the Culture of Catholicism: How Priests and Nuns Become Perpetrators.* Binghamton NY, The Haworth Press, 2007

24 Hill, A. *Habits of Sin: An expose of nuns who sexually abuse children and each other.* Philadelphia, Xlibris Corp, 1995

25 John Jay College of Criminal Justice. *The nature and scope of the problem of sexual abuse of minors by Catholic priests and deacons in the United States.* Washington DC United States, Conference of Catholic Bishops, 2004

26 John Jay College of Criminal Justice. *The Causes and Context of Sexual Abuse of Minors by Catholic Priests in the United States, 1950-2010.* Washington DC United States, Conference of Catholic Bishops, 2011

27 Kennedy, E. *The Unhealed Wound: The Church and Sexuality.* NY, St Martin's Press, 2001

28 Leedom, TC and Churchville, M. *The Book No Pope Would Want You to Read.* Eworld Inc, 2010

29 McMackin, RA, Keane, TM and Kline, PM(eds). *Understanding the Impact* *of Clergy Sexual Abuse: Betrayal and Recovery.* Abingdon, Oxon, Routledge, 2009.

30 Ministry and Clergy Sexual Abuse Survivors (MACSAS). *The Stones Cry Out: Report on the MACSAS Survey 2010.* London, MACSAS, 2011

31 Rauch, M. *Healing the Soul after Religious Abuse: The Dark Heaven of Recovery.* Westport CT, Praeger, 2009

32 Sipe, AWR. *Sex, Priests and Power: Anatomy of a Crisis.* New York, Brunner/Mazel, 1995

33 Sipe, AWR. *Celibacy in Crisis: A Secret World Revisited.* NY, Bruner-Routledge, 2003

34 Willmer, G. *Picking up the Pieces: A Survival Guide for victims of childhood sexual abuse.* The Lantern Project, 2008

RSA survivor accounts

35 Devane, J. *Nobody Heard Me Cry.* London, Hodder & Stoughton, 2008

36 Doyle, P. *The God Squad.* London, Corgi Books, 1989

37 Madden, A. *Altar Boy: A Story of Life after Abuse.* Dublin, Penguin Ireland, 2003

38 O'Beirne, K. *Kathy's Story.* Edinburgh, Mainstream Publishing, 2005

39 O'Doherty, I. *Stolen Childhood: Testimonies of the Survivors of Child Sexual Abuse.* Dublin, Poolbeg Press, 1998

40 O'Gorman, C. *Beyond Belief: The Story of the Boy who Sued the Pope.* London, Hodder Paperback, 2010

41 Touher, P. *Fear of the Collar.* London, Ebury Press, 2007

42 Touher, P. *Scars That Run Deep.* London, Ebury Press, 2008

43 Willmer, G. *Conspiracy of Faith: Fighting for Justice after Child Abuse.* Cambridge, Lutterworh Press, 2007

Other books of interest

44 Mooney, T. *All the Bishop's Men : Clerical Abuse in an Irish Diocese.* Cork Ireland, The Collins Press, 2011

45 Ridge, M. *Breaking the Silence: One Garda's Quest to Find the Truth.* Dublin, Gill & Macmillan, 2008

46 Robertson, G. *The Case of the Pope: Vatican Accountability for Human Rights Abuse.* London, Penguin Books, 2010

Appendix

Historic cases in England and Wales

As there has been no national inquiry in England or Wales into historic allegations of religious sexual abuse there is limited data available. The Nolan Commission (2000) stated that between 1995 and 1999 some 21 priests had been convicted, and six more had received a caution. A further 75 priests had been reported but were not convicted or cautioned. It is important to note that these only represent those cases which were reported and not the actual number of cases. Often religious institutions and church authorities claim that as the allegations are false they are not recorded, or they settle them out of court to avoid civil or criminal proceedings.

It is clear that there are still many victims and cases that have not come forward. A recent example of this is the allegations made against several priests at the Rosminian School in Leicestershire, and in Tanzania which came to light in 2010 and were the subject of a BBC documentary in 2011 entitled **Betrayed as Boys**. It reported that 22 victims are currently pursuing legal proceedings. This is just one example of investigations into many such cases which involve RC institutions with multiple perpetrators and victims. These include the **De La Salle Brothers** at St William's Children Home; the Benedictines at **Ampleforth, Douai Abbey, Worth Abbey, Buckfast Abbey** and **Ealing Abbey Schools**; **Stonyhurst School** run by the Society of Jesus in Lancashire; **the Christian Brothers at St Mary's College** in Liverpool, and **Priory Park** in Hexham & Newcastle, **Fr Hudson Children's Home** in Birmingham, **St John's School for the Deaf** in Leeds, and **Tingwell Hall School** for those with Learning Difficulties in Liverpool run by the **Brothers of Charity**. This by no means an exhaustive list and is merely an illustration of the type of cases currently being investigated.

One outcome from the **Nolan Commission** was a range of recommendations, which were subsequently adopted by the Church. While these recommendations go some way to stop future abuse taking place through improved safeguarding policies and procedures, they do not address how to repair the damage to those abused in the past. The work of the Commission was followed in 2001 by a book entitled *Time for Action*, produced by the Churches Together in Britain and Ireland (CTBI). It was set up by Church of England, the Roman Catholic Church, and the Methodist and Congregational Churches and contained recommendations for supporting victims. Although this was accepted by the Bishops Conference, they later rejected the proposed procedures for responding to victims put forward by the Catholic Office for the Protection of Children and Vulnerable Adults (COPCA) in the 2006 document *Healing the Wound*.

This was followed in 2007 by recommendations from the **Cumberlege Commission** in its report *Safeguarding With Confidence* which urged bishops and leaders of the religious congregations to reaffirm their commitment to a 'one church' approach and to ensure that there is one set of policies adopted by all denominations with a National Safeguarding Commission and better safeguarding procedures in place.

In May 2011 the survivor organisation **MACSAS** (Ministers and Clergy Sexual Abuse Survivors) published its survey *The Stones Cry Out* which identified 25 Roman Catholic priests and religious not previously convicted of any sexual offences against children and 10 other priests who had not been named. This survey provided further evidence that the number of abusers and victims is significantly higher than those reported by church authorities, religious institutions or court records. It is crucial to bear in mind that many cases of

RSA are never reported or are reported decades later, sometimes after the perpetrator has died, or after the victim has taken his or her own life.

While many of these investigations have focused on priests in the RC Church, the **Church of England** has not been immune from allegations of RSA. While the Church of England has appeared to be more responsive in developing and implementing safeguarding policies and procedures, the degree to which these are appropriately implemented is also dependent on individual dioceses.

In May 2011 **Baroness Butler-Sloss'** report on The Diocese of Chichester was published which investigated the handling of sexual abuse allegations against two vicars. The report highlighted the lack of understanding by the church authorities and the police of the seriousness of historic CSA allegations, and found evidence of lack of communication between bishops, safeguarding advisers and the police, alongside poor and chaotic record keeping. The report made several recommendations, including that allegations of RSA should be taken seriously whether historic or current, and that all victims should be treated with compassion and respect when they report cases. In addition, it stated that they need to be offered support throughout the investigation and assessment process, and that this should include funding for counselling over an open-ended period of time in acknowledgement of the harm they have suffered.

Recent and current cases in England and Wales

Cases since 2000 set out in the reports of the **RC Church Commission**, **COPCA** and the **National Catholic Safeguarding Commission (NCSC)** show that between 2002 and 2009 there were 435 sexual abuse allegations with 535 victims yet only five per cent of those accused of CSA were convicted and a further two per cent were cautioned.

It is clear from these reports and data that much RSA continues to remain hidden in England and Wales. This has given rise to a call from survivors organisations such as **One in Four**, **MACSAS**, **The Lantern Project**, and those who liaise with the **Catholic Safeguarding Advisory Service** to press for the Government to establish a commission to investigate the sexual abuse of children and adults within religious organisations, and to provide better support for victims to help them deal with the impact and consequences of such abuse.

Ireland

In contrast to England and Wales, Ireland has established a commission to investigate RSA in a number of dioceses and set up a number of inquiries. This has resulted in four reports: *The Ferns Report* (2005) which detailed extensive child abuse and the cover-up of paedophile activity in the south-east of Ireland; the *Murphy Report* (2005) on a commission which investigated clerical child abuse in the Dublin diocese; the *Ryan Report* (2009) detailing abuse at orphanages and industrial schools run by RC religious orders across Ireland; and, most recently, the *Cloyne Report* (2011) which investigated how church authorities responded to allegations of clergy-perpetrated sexual abuse within the Diocese of Cloyne between 1996 and 2009.

The Cloyne Report found that despite safeguarding guidelines and procedures which were drawn up for, and accepted by the church, these were not adhered to or properly implemented. This suggests that allegations are not being accurately or honestly reported. In response to the Cloyne Report critics of the RC Church, including Taoiseach Edna Lenny, have suggested that the obstruction of implementing its own procedures is supported throughout the church hierarchy including the Vatican. If this is the case, it is direct evidence of the deep systemic failures within the RC Church which still seems to prioritise the protection of the abuser and the image of the Church over the needs of victims. The Vatican's response to these criticisms of the Holy Sec's role in covering up cases of the abuse of children by clerics, has been to recall its envoy to Ireland.

Safeguarding policies and procedures

The Cloyne Report has highlighted that self-regulation and voluntary compliance is not working. This has led to calls for changes in the law to make reporting a mandatory statutory requirement, with failure to comply resulting in criminal prosecution and custodial sentencing. Currently the **National Board for Safeguarding Children** is auditing child protection investigations in all of Ireland's 26 dioceses, and a further 162 Catholic institutions run mainly by religious orders. Although these audits will not be completed until mid-2012, it will be interesting to see to what degree guidelines and procedures are in fact being implemented.

The findings of the Cloyne Report highlight a fundamental and crucial issue in RSA, namely that safeguarding policies and procedures are only as good as their implementation. It is essential that church authorities and religious institutions follow through on their policies. If they do not, they risk allegations of only developing safeguarding policies in response to pressure from victims and insurance companies, rather than out of a genuine concern to protect children or to respond sensitively to victims. Church authorities and faith leaders need to recognise that safeguarding children must be their priority. Otherwise their continued denial will only undermine their credibility and reinforce the belief that their promises and policies mean nothing. Most importantly, unless it is redressed this failure on the part of the church in Ireland will continue to traumatise victims and survivors and add to their anger and sense of betrayal.

REMEMBER Safeguarding policies and procedures are only as good as their implementation.

Ireland's Magadalene Laundries

One further investigation of note was carried out by the **United Nations Committee Against Torture** (2011) which found evidence of torture having been used against women in Magdalene Laundries. The recommendations of the Committee were that the Irish government must follow through with a statutory investigation, that perpetrators must be prosecuted and that victims must be given the right to claim compensation.

International inquiries

Although national inquiries have only been conducted in the **United States** and **Ireland**, there have been reports and prosecutions of RSA in many other countries, not least **Canada**, **Australia**, **New Zealand**, **Argentina**, **Austria**, **Germany**, **Belgium** and **Norway**.[28] Allegations are increasingly being made in **Latin America**, **Africa** and the **Far East**.[30] To some extent this is because priests who have had allegations made against them have been moved to other geographical locations as a way of covering up their abuse. Increasingly such abusers are sent to other countries, or to missions where there is less public awareness of RSA, and less pressure from the media and their lay congregations.

In early 2002 the **Boston Globe** drew attention to the sexual abuse of children within the RC Church in the United States. This enabled victims to come forward, and bring lawsuits and criminal cases which have generated considerable media interest. They have led to the formation of a number of US survivor organisations such as **Survivors Network of those Abused by Priests** (SNAP) who have worked tirelessly for acknowledgment and recognition of the harm done to victims and the fight for justice.

One outcome of the large scale of allegations against priests and clergy in America were two research studies published in 2004 and 2011. Both were commissioned by the U S Conference of Roman Catholic Bishops and conducted by the John Jay College of Criminal Justice. These two reports go some way to track both abusers and victims. However, the data is only on reported cases in the RC Church and is not generalisable to all abusers across all faiths.

The 2011 report also presents some unconvincing explanations as to the causes and context of the sexual abuse of children, not least what has become known as the 'Woodstock defence' which links RSA to the sexual liberalisation and permissiveness of society during the 1960s. In addition, its accuracy concerning the number of allegations and reported cases is in doubt, as they do not appear to tally with those made to criminal authorities.

The John Jay study has also been criticised for underestimating the proportion of sexually abusive priests at 6% whereas other authorities suggest this figure may be as high as 9%.[19] It is also likely that the number of victims has also been underestimated, as it can be assumed that many have still not come forward due either to shame, to advanced age or because they have died. The report also concludes, somewhat prematurely, that the sexual abuse of children by priests is likely to decrease as the result of better seminary training, more support and improved reporting procedures and safeguarding policies. However this suggestion is not supported by the findings of the Cloyne Report which found that allegations made as recently as 2009 were not reported, and policies and procedures were not being adhered to.

It remains to be seen to what degree RSA will abate, as we know that in the past most of it remained hidden especially in other faiths. In addition, most victims do not disclose for an average of 18-30 years so there may be a new wave of allegations in the future. It is clear that the risk of RSA cannot be minimised and that society needs to remain vigilant.

Reports referenced in this appendix

Cumberlege Commission. (Cumberlege Report) *Safeguarding with Confidence: Keeping Children and Vulnerable Adults safe in the Catholic Church.* 2007

Commission to Inquire into Child Abuse. *Ryan Report.* 2009

Commission of Investigation. (Murphy Report) *Commission of Investigation report into the Catholic Archdiocese of Dublin.* 2009

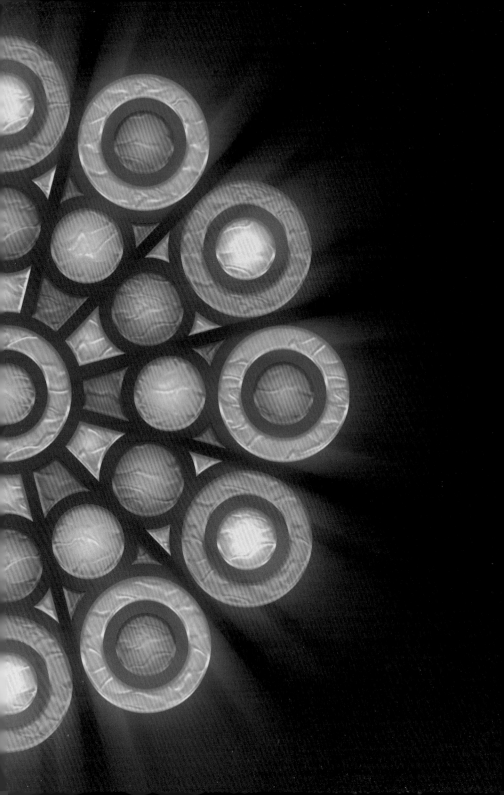